STRANGE HIGHWAYS

Borgo Press Books by DAMIEN BRODERICK

Adrift in the Noösphere: Science Fiction Stories
Building New Worlds, *1946-1957* (with John Boston)
Chained to the Alien: The Best of ASFR: Australian SF Review
(Second Series) [Editor]
Climbing Mount Implausible: The Evolution of a Science
Fiction Writer
Embarrass My Dog: The Way We Were, the Things We Thought
Ferocious Minds: Polymathy and the New Enlightenment
Human's Burden: A Science Fiction Novel (with Rory Barnes)
I'm Dying Here: A Comedy of Bad Manners (with Rory Barnes)
New Worlds: Before the New Wave, 1958-1964 (with John
Boston)
Post Mortal Syndrome: A Science Fiction Novel (with Barbara
Lamar)
Skiffy and Mimesis: More Best of ASFR: Australian SF Review
(Second Series) [Editor]
Strange Highways: Reading Science Fantasy, *1950-1967* (with
John Boston)
Unleashing the Strange: Twenty-First Century Science Fiction
Literature
Warriors of the Tao: The Best of Science Fiction: A Review of
Speculative Literature [Editor with Van Ikin]
x, y, z, t: Dimensions of Science Fiction
Zones: A Science Fiction Novel (with Rory Barnes)

Borgo Press Books by JOHN BOSTON

Building New Worlds, *1946-1957* (with Damien Broderick)
New Worlds: Before the New Wave, 1958-1964 (with Damien
Broderick)
Strange Highways: Reading Science Fantasy, *1950-1967* (with
Damien Broderick)

STRANGE HIGHWAYS

READING *SCIENCE FANTASY*, 1950-1967

JOHN BOSTON &

DAMIEN BRODERICK

THE BORGO PRESS

MMXII

Borgo Literary Guides
ISSN 0891-9623
Number Fourteen

STRANGE HIGHWAYS

Published by Wildside Press LLC

www.wildsidebooks.com

DEDICATION

As always, for Dori and the Guys

J.B.

ACKNOWLEDGMENTS

These books were first aired in more rudimentary form on the Fictionmags Internet discussion group, and benefited greatly from the robust and erudite commentary and correction customary among its members. In particular we thank Fictionmags members Ned Brooks, William G. Contento, Ian Covell, Steve Holland, Frank Hollander, Rich Horton, David Langford, Dennis Lien, Barry Malzberg, Todd Mason, David Pringle, Robert Silverberg, and Phil Stephensen-Payne, as well as David Ketterer, for the encouragement, insight, and information that they respectively provided.

—J.B. and D.B.

CONTENTS

INTRODUCTION

BY DAMIEN BRODERICK

Science fantasy is a blend, as you'd expect, of *science fiction* (the literature of drastic change precipitated by new phenomena and knowledge) and *fantasy* (the literature of unchecked imagination). So it tends to be bolder, more highly colored, than pure SF (as we'll abbreviate "science fiction" or "speculative fiction") but more disciplined than the exotic vapors or psychological uncanniness of pure fantasy.

As a commercial form, science fantasy got its clearest start with the American magazine *Unknown*, edited (rather surprisingly) by the classic nuts-and-bolts SF editor John W. Campbell, Jr., whose *Astounding Science Fiction*, later *Analog*, was the seed around which Golden Age SF crystallized in the late 1930s and early 1940s. Much of *Unknown*'s appeal lay in the imposition of the logic, or semblance of logic, of SF on the familiar matter of fantasy. Thus, in L. Sprague de Camp and Fletcher Pratt's famous *The Incomplete Enchanter* (1941), the characters are translated into worlds of myth by capturing and internalizing their laws and assumptions—building a syllogismobile, as one character puts it.[1] But while Campbell's SF stormed toward a kind of hegemonic success in the new literatures of imagination, his *Unknown* (retitled *Unknown Worlds* for its last two years) never really caught on except among aficionados. It lasted from March 1939 to October 1943, and was killed by wartime

---

1. One of the magazine stories combined into *The Incomplete Enchanter* was titled "The Mathematics of Magic" (*Unknown*, August 1940).

paper rationing, which disrupted many magazines.

It can come as some surprise, then, that a parallel universe of science fantasy developed in Britain around the middle of last century, sometimes borrowing stories from the established US writers and magazines but also developing its own distinctive strains of fantasy narrative, most famously by new or accomplished writers such as Brian W. Aldiss, J. G. Ballard, John Brunner, Michael Moorcock and Thomas Burnett Swann. This book looks closely at the classic British science fiction magazine, *Science Fantasy,* that played a key role in this parallel-but-entwined history. From 1950 through mid-1964 it captured the sub-genre in its title, and often if not always in its contents, while for its last three years it appeared in rather different form, as *Impulse* and then *SF Impulse,* before shutting down in February, 1967 when its distributor was bankrupted.

The voice *Science Fantasy* aimed for, at its best, is caught well by Kenneth Bulmer and John Newman, writing as "Kenneth Johns" on the magazine's tenth anniversary:

> The added element of fantasy...gave a lightness and freshness, a whole new dimension to the contents that a magazine devoted solely to science fiction must, perforce, lack.... Certainly the magazine set out to bring before its readers material with that delicate touch of literary and imaginative magic, that slender but electric spark of wonder, that was rapidly dying out of much magazine science fiction.[2]

§

Two companion volumes to this one examine *Science Fantasy*'s fellow British magazines, *New Worlds* and the younger sibling of both, *Science Fiction Adventures.* As noted in the other books, *Building New Worlds: The Carnell Era,* Volume One, and

---

2. Kenneth Johns, "The First Decade," *Science Fantasy,* 43 (1960), p. 108.

New Worlds: Before the New Wave: The Carnell Era, Volume Two, John Boston is an occasional amateur science fiction critic of long standing, and attorney (Director of the Prisoners' Rights Project of the New York City Legal Aid Society and co-author of the *Prisoners' Self-Help Litigation Manual*).[3] Several years ago, Boston read through every issue of Carnell's *New Worlds, Science Fantasy* and *Science Fiction Adventures*—sometimes with grim disbelief, sometimes with unexpected pleasure, often with gusts of laughter, always with intent interest. All three magazines were edited during their important early years by Edward John (Ted, or John) Carnell (1912-1972). Ted Carnell was a pillar of the old-style UK SF establishment, but gamely supportive of innovators—most famously, of the brilliant J. G. Ballard, whose first work he nurtured.

John Boston, for his own amusement, found himself writing an extensive commentary on those early, foundational years of *New Worlds, Science Fantasy*, and *Science Fiction Adventures.* He posted his ongoing analysis in a long semi-critical series to a closed listserv devoted to enthusiasts of popular fiction magazines. The present extensive study, published in three parts due to the length of its exacting but entertaining coverage of these fifteen years of publication, is an edited and reorganized version of those electronic posts. This volume covers not only Carnell's years with *Science Fantasy,* from the point at which it had become solidly established as a leading UK magazine of *fantastika,* but also its transformation and finally extinction under other hands.

I found Boston's issue-by-issue forensic probing of this history enthralling and amusing, and read it sometimes with shudders and grimaces breaking through, and often with a delighted grin at a neatly turned *bon mot.* Don't expect a dry, modishly theorized academic analysis. This is a candid and astute reader's response to a magazine that, by today's standards, was often not very good—but one that was important in its time. The story of

3. See "The Long Road Toward Reform," http://www.wahmee.com/pln_john_boston.pdf.

how *Science Fantasy* got better, achieving and consolidating its position, is an essential piece of the history of the genres of the fantastic in the UK, and indeed the world.

I had the good fortune, as an SF theorist and writer, to read these chapters as they arrived via email. Greatly entertained, often flushed by nostalgia (for this was the literature of my remembered youth), I insisted to John Boston that his work deserved to be read by as many interested people as possible. He was busy on important legal work in defense of those lost in an overburdened US criminal justice (or "justice") system, and had no time for such laborious scutwork. I rapped on his internet door from time to time, insisting that it would be a shame—a crime, even—not to allow this material to be read by the world at large.

At last he buckled, passed me his large files covering all the issues of Carnell's *New Worlds* and the short-lived *Science Fiction Adventures* (some quarter million words), plus the current book's worth of equivalent reading into *Science Fantasy* (my favorite as an adolescent, in colonial Australia). All three volumes of reading and commentary really comprise one large book of some 350,000 words. This third volume carries the saga through to the brief flowering of the New Wave in SF and fantasy both—a trend to which *Science Fantasy* stood in ambiguous and sometimes arm's length relationship.

§

Science Fantasy's forerunner *New Worlds* had a long and difficult gestation, and finally struggled into existence in 1946, although it managed only three issues before bankruptcy of its initial publisher, and only five more by the end of 1950 under the newly organized Nova Publications. It did not become a successful monthly until well into 1954, but in the meantime one of Nova's founders, Walter Gillings, became the first editor of the new companion magazine, *Science Fantasy,* in 1950. Gillings had already launched his own magazine, *Fantasy,* which failed after only three issues and was followed by a semi-professional critical magazine, *Fantasy Review* (later *Science-Fantasy Review*). Gillings attempted to continue his earlier interests in commentary as well as fiction in the new magazine, but it was buffeted by post-war printing strikes and paper rationing, and by the third issue the board of Nova decided to oust Gillings and save costs by bringing in Ted Carnell as editor of both their magazines—to Gillings' dismay and outrage.

Technical trade publisher Maclaren & Sons took over both magazines, later adding a reprint edition of the US *Science Fiction Adventures*, with the latter and *Science Fantasy* appearing bimonthly to *New Worlds'* monthly. By 1963, all were in trouble—perhaps due to competition with cheap imported paperbacks from the US—and both *New Worlds* and *Science Fantasy* were rescued the following year by a somewhat disreputable publisher, Roberts & Vinter, Carnell departing to create his own quarterly series of original SF anthologies, *New Writings in SF*, with *New Worlds'* editorship going to Michael Moorcock, although his notable work to that date had been the darkly brooding Elric fantasy stories published in *Science Fantasy*. Oxford art dealer Kyril Bonfiglioli (1928-1985) took on *Science Fantasy*, whose title he disliked and later changed to *Impulse*. When that title apparently confused the genre audience while failing to attract new readers of more refined tastes, it was switched, too late, to *SF Impulse*.

By general assessment, Bonfiglioli was a lazy and offhand helmsman, whose work was largely left to his assistants, James Parkhill-Rathbone and Keith Roberts (no relation to the magazine's publishing house Roberts & Vinter), especially after Bonfiglioli famously bought a Tintoretto at a country auction for forty pounds and sold it for a thousand times (or perhaps 10,000 times) as much.[4] Indeed, Roberts became, in effect, the

---

4. Different versions of this tale exist. Kevin Jackson, in *The Independent*, reports: "In 1964, Bon heard rumours that a Resurrection by a certain well-known 16th-century Venetian master was up for sale at an absurdly low reserve price. He went to the auction...and bought it, as if on an absent-minded whim, for 40 quid. It

editor, as well as providing some of the most remarkable fiction (especially the tales that would be compiled as *Pavane*) and many of the rather effective impressionistic covers.

For a brief moment it seemed that J. G. Ballard would become editor, and it is clear that he would have changed the magazine very drastically away from its science-fantasy roots—perhaps even more than Mike Moorcock was in the process of changing *New Worlds* into the battleship of the New Wave. In the event, Ballard was furious, and gone, when he learned that two issues (or at least the covers and tables of contents) had been put in process by Keith Roberts, and US writer Harry Harrison was brought in briefly to take the editor's chair. As before, Roberts did most of the grunt work and more besides, and Harrison soon decamped to Europe. The publishers' distributor went broke, and in February 1967, with its ninety-third issue under its third title, *Science Fantasy* was closed by Roberts & Vinter. It was a disheartening end to a magazine that in its various incarnations had provided a new kind of fiction not only to British readers but to the rest of the world as well, in the many stories drawn from its pages that appeared in US Year's Best and other anthologies, or were listed as Honorable Mentions by the premier SF anthologist of the day, Judith Merril.

For some of us, *Science Fantasy* still sings a sirens' song of magical memory, and its passing is a sting of frustration and rebuke. I am reminded of the opening of John Brunner's long novella "Earth Is But a Star," one of the great stories from the magazine:

"It's a very *small* star," said the man in gold doubtfully.

---

was, as he had immediately seen, a genuine Tintoretto. He immediately sold it for £4,000—a not inconsiderable sum...back in the Sixties" (19 July, 1999: http://www. independent.co.uk/arts-entertainment/celebrations-for-a-right-charlie-1107408. html) (visited 10/19/11). Brian Aldiss, who gets the painter wrong—he says it was "a Giorgione"—claims Bonfiglioli knew it was "worth a half million": http://www.solaris-books.co.uk/aldiss/html/glass_forest_4.html.

"Big enough," said Creohan, and thought how tiny Earth was in comparison. The man in gold eyed him, and then gave another glance at the image in the field of the great telescope.

"This, then, is your device for seeing into the years to come?" he asked. "And is that all it will show?" [...]

"I have given you the chance to see into the future," Creohan snapped. "Is it to be blamed on me that you have neither the wit nor the will to use that chance?"[5]

---

5. *Science Fantasy*, 29 (1958), pp. 2-3.

1: *SCIENCE FANTASY,* VOLUME 1 (ISSUES 1-3)

By the time of its demise in 1967, the British magazine *Science Fantasy* had an international reputation as one of the better magazines in the field. (Under new editorship begun in 1964, it was also known briefly, from March 1966, as *Impulse* and then *SF Impulse.*) Its specialty is captured in its title: neither traditional science fiction nor routine fantasy, but a blend of both—even if many stories wavered from this hybrid goal and fell back into one of the more familiar categories. I read through the file of *Science Fantasy* and successors for the first time during the early twenty-first century, and this book records the journey.[6] Executive summary: Pretty bad start. But the

---

6. Bibliographic and historical information not from the magazine itself, and not otherwise attributed, is from the *Science Fiction, Fantasy, & Weird Fiction Index* by Stephen T. Miller and William G. Contento ("Miller/Contento") and Contento's *Index to Science Fiction Anthologies and Collections* ("Contento") (both on CD-ROM from Locus Publications); from Mike Ashley's article on *Science Fantasy* in *Science Fiction, Fantasy and Weird Fiction Magazines,* edited by Marshall B. Tymn and Ashley (Greenwood Press 1985) ("Tymn/Ashley"); and from Ashley's recent histories of the SF magazines, *The Time Machines and Transformations* (Liverpool University Press, 2000 and 2005). Occasional references to the *Encyclopedia of Science Fiction* are to the Second Edition by John Clute and Peter Nicholls (St. Martins, 1995), the latest available at time of writing. Also notable is Philip Harbottle's *Vultures of the Void: The Legacy* (Cosmos Books, 2011). This book, very much expanded from an earlier, long out of print version, is a survey of UK SF publishing which emphasizes book publishing (especially paperbacks), but also includes useful information on

magazine improved, and eventually did live up to its reputation, and published much excellent work that might never have existed without *Science Fantasy*.

The magazine was published by Nova Publications, which by the time of *Science-Fantasy* issue **1** (dated Summer 1950) was, according to the back cover ad, about to publish *New Worlds* issue **8**. The first two issues were edited by Walter Gillings (1912-79), who had previously edited *Tales of Wonder* and *Fantasy* (the UK 1946-47 magazine); the now better-known E.J. (John or Ted) Carnell (1912-72), already editor of Nova's *New Worlds*, took over with the third issue.

The first two issues contain 96 pages plus covers, digest size (5½ x 7⅜ inches, to be precise), price one and sixpence. The cover stock has more of a matte finish than most of the digest magazines of its day.

The cover pictures are both quite well done in their modest way. The cover of issue **1**, by Powell, is a pleasant view of Earth from the remains of the Moon in muted colors. The cover of **2**, by Turner, is more striking and colorful, portraying a crowd of people with stylized angular faces, and several with stylized draped cloaks and/or hoods, who seem to be fleeing up a beach away from a craft of some sort at the shoreline, with an equally stylized raging sea behind it. It's pretty explicitly derived from Japanese painting, and offhand I don't remember seeing anything quite like it on an SF magazine. For that matter, I don't remember seeing anything like the cover of **1** on an SF magazine before—space scenes are almost always more colorful and dramatic.[7]

The interior illustrations—including those by Turner and Powell—are thoroughly undistinguished, though they are also

---

the Nova magazines, some of which we have referred to.

7. See these covers at http://www.sfcovers.net/mainnav.htm . That URL takes you to the main page and you'll have to navigate from there, but how to do so is self-explanatory. Among this site's virtues is an artist index. Another handy source—and probably easier to use—is http://www.philsp. com/mags/sciencefantasy.html.

poorly displayed. They are small and do not seem to be well reproduced, though one can't tell by looking what problems result from reproduction and sizing and what from the deficiencies of the original.

§

At first, *Science-Fantasy* probably gave more of its total wordage to reviews and criticism than any SF magazine before or since except possibly the much later British *Interzone*. Indeed, on the contents page colophon (though not on the cover) it identifies itself as "*Science-Fantasy*, incorporating *Science-Fantasy Review*," the latter title being Gillings' fanzine or critical journal.[8] The two issues feature respectively five and four "Articles and Reviews" whose nominal authors were mostly pseudonyms of Gillings (Geoffrey Giles, Valentine Parker, Thomas Sheridan, Herbert Hughes), though John K. Aiken (1913-90), who has a review article in each issue, was a genuine person, poet Conrad Aiken's son, in fact.

Most of these are review articles, running around two pages, of several books that are related thematically or otherwise. For example, Aiken's article "A History of the Future" in **1** reviews three books by Robert Heinlein, and his "The Charms of Space Opera" in **2** covers Nelson Bond's *Lancelot Biggs, Spaceman*; L. Ron Hubbard's *The Kingslayer*; George O. Smith's *Nomad* and *A Pattern For Conquest*; and Otis Adelbert Kline's *The Port of Peril*. (Bond—"approximately, the P.G. Wodehouse of science fiction"—comes out much better than Smith—"His dialogue is flat with a terrible flatness, despite the fact that no character ever says anything which cannot possibly be snapped, hissed, grinned, thundered, grimaced, chorused, laughed, exploded, wisecracked or snarled.") These reviews are all perfectly capable and literate, but not very interesting at this late date given the

---

8. These publications have been scanned and made available on the web at http://efanzines.com/FR/index.htm (visited 10/19/11).

familiarity or deserved obscurity of the subjects and the solemn tones and middle of the road opinions of most of the reviewers.

The other nonfiction items in **1** are Thomas Sheridan's "The Battle of the Canals," about the controversy over the existence of the Martian canals, and Herbert Hughes' "The Djinn in the Test-Tube," reacting to an article about SF by the celebrated scientist and humanist Jacob Bronowski (misspelled Brunowski) in the *Continental Daily Mail.* **2** features an article bylined Sheridan about the risks of Earth's colliding with a comet, plus Valentine Parker's "The Dawn of Space-Travel," which rambles from a Hayden Planetarium show to the films *Destination Moon* and *Rocket Ship X-M* to the book *The Conquest of Space.*

Advertisements on the inside front cover of **1** are from Arkham House and the bookseller Postal Preview; on the inside back cover, from the Fantasy Book Centre; and on the back cover for *New Worlds* and *Astounding Science Fiction* ("Famed throughout the world!"—no doubt the British Reprint Edition or BRE). The headline of the Postal Preview ad reads "Now is the TIME to obtain some of the absorbing books reviewed in this magazine," and the four time-travel books from one of the review articles are listed. This coordination between advertisement and the contents of the issue in which it appeared gives a hint of what a small world SF must have been in the UK at the time. The ads in **2** are similar to those in **1**.

§

The fiction...there's the rub. The fiction contents of **1** include one novelette, "The Belt" by J. M. Walsh, and four short stories: "Time's Arrow" by Arthur C. Clarke, "Monster" by Christopher Youd, "The Cycle" by P. E. Cleator, and "Advent of the Entities" by E. R. James. **2** similarly contains one novelette, F. G. Rayer's "The Ark," and four short stories: John Russell Fearn's "Black-Out," Arthur C. Clarke's "Silence, Please!" (under the pseudonym Charles Willis) and "History Lesson," and Norman C. Pallant's "Martian Mandate."

SF scholar Mike Ashley notes that some of this material was left over from the demise of *Fantasy*, Gillings' previous magazine, a few years before.[9] Frankly, much of it reads more like leftovers from the earlier *Tales of Wonder* or from Hugo Gernsback's inventory. The lead novelette in **1**, Walsh's "The Belt," posits that a planetoid sails by, causing the Moon to approach the earth and break up, its fragments becoming a Saturn-like ring, which, when the characters visit, seems to have resolved itself into a more or less solid object rather than a collection of fragments. The characters fly to it, walk around on it, and defend themselves from ravening moon worms with their electronic guns, and by spraying them with oxygen. This one seems straight out of the middle range of the 1930s *Wonder Stories*.

The lead novelette in **2**, Rayer's "The Ark," smacks of a later but not necessarily better vintage (*Thrilling Wonder Stories* circa 1940?). The world has been done in by nuclear power which first causes "radioactive infection" and then, after the atomic piles are shut down, a volcanic period that mostly wrecks civilization. Humanity has become divided into the governing Intellectuals and the beaten-down and brutish Workers. Now a comet is on the way to shut down the whole show. What to do but build an Ark to ride out the cataclysm and start a new civilization with a few carefully selected survivors? The obligatory beautiful stowaway is very much present and chewing the scenery, as are all the other stereotyped characters, and the plot is ponderously melodramatic.

Neither story fits the Fantasy part of the magazine's title. Both are examples of science fiction, although of a rather primitive kind more common decades earlier.

Most of the other stories are similarly old-fashioned—

---

9. Gillings confirms that the "main contents" of the first two issues of *Science-Fantasy* came from the *Fantasy* inventory, specifically referring to the stories by J. M. Walsh, John Russell Fearn, and Christopher Youd. Walter Gillings, "The Impatient Dreamers," *Vision of Tomorrow*, August 1970, p. 31.

smoothly so, in the case of John Russell Fearn, or clumsily in the case of "Advent of the Entities," a story as awkward and clichéd as its title, or "Martian Mandate," which puts forth the exciting proposition that Atlantis was colonized by Mars. In this company the three stories by Arthur C. Clarke leap out as deft, urbane, and clever, especially "Time's Arrow" ("History Lesson" being an extended gimmick, though a good one). "Silence, Please!" is bibliographically interesting. It is listed in Miller/Contento and probably elsewhere as one of the Tales from the White Hart,[10] but Miller/Contento does not note that the story was very thoroughly rewritten after this magazine publication, preserving nothing but the basic idea and sequence of events. There is no spoor of the White Hart itself in this version.

So what exactly did Gillings think he was doing? It's hard to say—apparently as hard for him as for anybody else. The first issue starts off with an editorial manifesto of considerable length but little discernible content. A sample:

> If few had faith in an inner world [referring to the Hollow Earth], there were thousands who believed in 1835 that there was a world of green mountains and blue lakes in the moon...and of flying men! Richard Adams Locke's science-fantasy, better known as *The Moon Hoax*, was presented in the New York *Sun* in such clever style that it seemed gospel truth—at least for a week or so. More recently, New Yorkers exhibited no less belief in Mr. Wells' invading Martians, as dispensed by radio by Mr. Welles. And the flying saucers? Space-ships, and little men from Venus...? Truly, science-fantasy has a potency which does not always depend on its plausibility; for its dreams very often come true.
>
> SCIENCE-FANTASY which is—intentionally— fiction. Science-fantasy which is—or might well

10. This series of related stories, purportedly told in a tavern by one Harry Purvis, was collected as *Tales from the White Hart* (Ballantine 1957).

be—fact. In this new magazine we shall be concerned with it in all its forms: with its significant ideas, its surprising prophecies, its sheer fictions, its evolution as a fascinating literature. We shall present both facts and fancies. Hence—SCIENCE-*FANTASY*.

Matters are not much clarified in the second issue, in which Gillings' editorial, titled "Going Your Way," starts with apologies for the irregular schedule, occasioned by a printing strike. **1** was Summer 1950 but there was no Autumn issue, and **2** is Winter 1950-51. He solicits the readers' views, not to mention their stories, especially those of 3,000 to 6,000 words. As to his plans, he intends to enlarge the non-fiction content, to present the best fiction he can get but to have no "fixed policy," and to "keep a careful eye to what [he] considers the proper development of this medium for an audience more concerned with literary quality than with the familiarity of authors' names or mere extravagance of conception."

Well, that's an idea, and not a bad one as far as it goes. What is conspicuously missing is any explanation of how *Science-Fantasy* was intended to differ from its companion magazine *New Worlds*, and what the point was of publishing a second quarterly magazine rather than increasing the size and/or frequency of the established magazine.[11] However, what if anything Gillings had in mind, other than his desire to be editor of an SF magazine, quickly became academic, since he was gone by the next issue, which did not appear for a year.

§

The editorial in **2** announces an intention to "enlarge on"

---

11. Those more sophisticated in publishing matters than I have explained that publishing two magazines at longer intervals can be economically preferable to publishing a single magazine at shorter intervals, since in the former case the issues will remain on sale longer. But Gillings says nothing of this concern, if indeed it was a concern.

the non-fiction content. The "In the Next Issue" squib promises "Nemesis" by Arthur C. Clarke. A box in one of the reviews says "it is hoped" to continue "Fantasy Forum," a letter column, and invites readers who have "any comments to make on the contents of this magazine or on any matters arising," to send them on.

None of these things came to pass. The third issue of *Science-Fantasy*—Winter 1951-52, a year after **2**—features no Clarke, no letter column, and no non-fiction except for a rather stiff "Guest Editorial" by Gillings titled "The Time Is Not Yet" noting with much verbiage and little explanation that he is out and John Carnell is now the editor. Gillings says, with customary vagueness: "[I]t has become evident that the plan of development I had in mind for *Science-Fantasy* can hardly be carried through successfully at this stage—for a variety of reasons, which it is hoped may not obtain once the magazine gets properly into its stride and the special features I envisaged can be introduced with the full effect of topical interest and critical value."

So what actually happened here? Mike Ashley's Tymn/ Ashley essay refers to "internal disagreements" within Nova Publications and the fact that the board of directors decided it was "uneconomical to keep two editors." Gillings lost the vote. What the internal disagreements were about is not recorded. But Ashley's SF magazine history *The Time Machines* adds that the decision was "swayed to some extent by the fact that the design and make-up of *Science-Fantasy* were more expensive than those of *New Worlds*." Why that should have been the case is not clear. A *New Worlds* issue (**10**) from midway between the two Gillings issues of *Science-Fantasy* has the same number of pages, the cover stock is slicker, page size and illustrations are larger and seem to be better reproduced. There's even a photograph. I suspect that the main "internal disagreement" may simply have been that Gillings' view of the field was hopelessly mired in 1939 or thereabouts, and Carnell was more forward-looking. Carnell maintained a tasteful silence in the magazine, and his later comments (in an interview reproduced in Philip

Harbottle's revised *Vultures of the Void)* pointed in two directions in consecutive sentences, first citing Gillings' "finding it more and more difficult to devote as much time editorially to the magazine as he wished," and then observing that Gillings' above-quoted editorial "reads obscurely, and does little to emphasize the fundamental differences of opinion that were then contributory causes for his relinquishing the editorship."

One of the minor mysteries of the transition is what happened to the promised Clarke story "Nemesis," but it's easily solved: *The Collected Stories of Arthur C. Clarke* (2000) says that it is the same story as "Exile of the Eons," which first appeared in *Super Science Stories*, March 1950, and then in Clarke's first collection *Expedition to Earth*. Why was it dropped from *Science Fantasy?* Maybe because by the time it would have been published (even on schedule, sometime in 1951) it would already have appeared in the US magazine—though later on, Carnell published plenty of stories that had appeared in the US.

I suspect, however, that it was a casualty of regime change. "Nemesis" is a *very* old-fashioned story for Clarke, about a militarist dictator referred to only as "the Master" who flees defeat in war through suspended animation, and millennia hence encounters Trevindor, who was banished from the inhabited Galaxy for philosophical nonconformity ("in the whitely gleaming Hall of Justice," no less, where he "stood proudly facing the men who had proved stronger than he.") Trevindor kills the Master. This story is full of the posturing and sonorous diction of 1930s SF—though rendered with Clarke's vastly greater skill—and is probably just the kind of thing the Carnelloids wanted to get rid of, however well done in this instance. ("The Master's dreamless sleep was more than half ended when Trevindor the Philosopher was born, between the fall of the Ninety-seventh Dynasty and the rise of the Fifth Galactic Empire. He was born on a world very far from Earth, for few were the men who ever set foot on the ancient home of their race, now so distant from the throbbing heart of the Universe.")

Other changes were made before the appearance of issue **3**.

New Worlds **10** has a list of authors to appear in that issue, and they include A. Bertram Chandler and "Robert Wright" (Robert Lowndes and Forrest J Ackerman), neither of whom actually appear. So here's the new *Science Fantasy*: 96 pages, 8 ½ x 5 ½ inches, glossy but flimsy cover stock, paper that looks higher-quality to my untutored eye than in the first two issues, price two shillings.

§

The most immediately striking feature of **3** is the cover by Reina Bull, which sounds pretty ordinary by genre standards in its elements but is rather bizarre in execution. It depicts a voluptuous, scantily clad woman being carried off into the sky by a caped humanoid cyborgesque monster, with futuristic cityscape in the background. It sounds like a typical Earle Bergey cover for *Thrilling Wonder Stories*, but it looks like what Bergey might have painted after a long night in an opium den with Hannes Bok or maybe Margaret Brundage. It has a sort of busy and overheated decadent quality to it that I don't recall seeing on SF magazines elsewhere.

The cover of **4**, the next issue, is of similar ilk though the use of color is less striking. Here a man is struggling in the tentacles of a mechanical monster, with more voluptuous, scantily clad women making stylized and futile gestures of distress. Bull did these two covers plus two more on *New Worlds* around the same time (*New Worlds* **11** and **18**). The style of the latter is similar to the *Science Fantasy* covers but the presentation is altogether more wholesome, without the Weird Menace overtones. The *Science Fantasy* covers are well worth looking at.[12]

---

12. See these covers at http://www.sfcovers.net/mainnav.htm or http://www.philsp.com/mags/sciencefantasy.html. Bull was the cover artist for a number of UK paperbacks and illustrated several books, and the "saucy" magazines published by Utopian Press, in the late 1940s, but little seems to be known about her career—if any—after the Nova covers. See http://bearalley.blogspot.com/2010/01/reina-bull.html and http://www.artslant.com/ny/

§

That issue **3** cover, though, has nothing to do with any of the fiction contents, from which skynapped voluptuous women are conspicuously absent. All the stories are short items, with none flagged as a lead story except by their order on the contents page.

In John Wyndham's "Pawley's Peepholes," gaggles of futuristic tourists suddenly start intangibly but visibly appearing in a small town. Solution: turn the town into a tourist attraction for people who want to gawk at the time travelers. It's an American town, probably reflecting an earlier sale in the U.S. (a different version of the story appeared in *Suspense*, Summer 1951). Later the story was Anglicized (or re-Anglicized) for reprinting in the UK *Argosy*, as "A New Kind of Pink Elephant," and retained the English setting in yet another revision in Wyndham's collection *The Seeds of Time*. This plot is essentially the same as in Bob Tucker's "The Tourist Trade," though the stories were published close enough together (*Worlds Beyond*, January 1951, for the Tucker) that given the publication delays involved, it's unlikely that one influenced the other.

F. G. Rayer's "The Undying Enemy" is old-fashioned but not too bad if one makes the necessary allowances: the protagonist grows up underground under the tutelage of an old man. He has custody of the remnants of humanity who are in suspended animation, figures out how to disable the war machines that make the surface uninhabitable, and wakes everybody up to start the new world.

William F. Temple's "Double Trouble" is a ponderous stab at whimsical fantasy about a man vexed by an entity whose job it is to give him bad luck, and his efforts to change his fortunes.

J. T. McIntosh's "Then There Were Two" is a silly story about a man who gets himself duplicated by hanky-panky with a matter transmitter so he can commit murder and have an alibi.

---

articles/show/19524 (both visited 12/4/11) for what is known about her.

It does not threaten the primacy of *Rogue Moon*[13] for use of this device (despite getting there much earlier) but is redeemed by its brevity and tightness.

E. R. James' "The Moving Hills" combines a comic device (a man's buddy is always talking him into things and getting him into trouble) with a complicated space exploration/alien contact plot, to completely self-defeating effect (but Colin and Brocky will be back, never fear). It collapses of its own uninteresting weight.

Characteristically slickly done, E. C. Tubb's "Grounded" displays a man who wants to go to the Moon, but is always thwarted. It is revealed that the government can't let anybody have the military advantages of getting there. Australian N. (for Norma) K. Hemmings' "Loser Take All" features those staples of an earlier SF day, a Professor with no discernible academic responsibilities and his beautiful daughter, whom the protagonist would like to get next to, in a style that obviates the need for parody: "From the centre globe, the pilot's compartment, a girl emerged, and his eyes strayed from Liza's metal curves in favour of softer ones. [Liza is the spaceship.] Jane Lawrence was a brilliant mathematician and research chemist and, with a name and profession like that should have been a very studious and unattractive girl blinking owlishly through horn-rimmed glasses. However, she was not, and her construction and general lines left nothing to be desired." The plot is an alien invasion, the denouement is we lose in the short run, but the aliens didn't bring their women so they will have to intermarry with us, promising—wait for it—"the new Earth."

None of these stories is particularly memorable by contemporary standards, though the best of them, Wyndham's, is a characteristically well turned trifle. But there is nothing so archaic as in the first two issues. Even the Hemmings story is redeemed by its unconventional conclusion.

---

13. Algis Budrys, *Rogue Moon* (1961).

§

There is a new and better lot of interior illustrators (Quinn, Clothier, and Hunter), though how much of the improvement is in quality and how much in presentation, I'm not sure (the illustrations are given more space on the page and the pages are larger, and the reproduction seems clearer). In any case, they are at best competent.

2: *SCIENCE FANTASY,*
VOLUME 2 (ISSUES 4-6)

In issue **4** (Spring 1952), the inside front cover is occupied by another small-worldy artifact. The headline is "At the Pub of the Universe," and it's an ad for the White Horse Tavern, complete with photo captioned "Resident Manager Lew Mordecai in a familiar pose"—drawing a cold one, or I guess in the UK a lukewarm one. The other ads are generally similar to previous issues, with the addition of one for the Second International Science-Fiction Convention at the Royal Hotel. G. Ken Chapman joined the masthead as Assistant with issue **4**.

Non-fiction this issue includes another Guest Editorial (these would go on for some time), this one by H. J. Campbell, editor of Carnell's competition *Authentic Science Fiction.* Maybe he didn't consider *Authentic* the competition at that point, since *Authentic* started out presenting nothing but complete novels— or, more likely, he didn't care. As Campbell says, his presence is "a tribute to the camaraderie that exists among members of the science-fiction fraternity." Just so. Summarizing or selecting cogent excerpts from his editorial is almost impossible because it is virtually content-free. I guess the best I can do is *SF is good, and it's good that we're all here, and that we have this good SF, and it's good that it's getting better.* It's exasperating to read now, but back in the small and beleaguered world of UK SF circa 1952, this sort of after-dinner speech reassurance probably served an important purpose, on the order of keeping the wolves on the other side of the campfire.

The other non-fiction item is "Forecasts and Ratings," equivalent to "The Literary Line-Up" in *New Worlds*, which appears in this issue but is not seen again in future issues. It contains ratings for the previous issue, which comfortingly put the more competent writers (McIntosh, Wyndham, Tubb, Temple) ahead of the less competent ones (Rayer, Hemming, James), and contains this interesting observation: "Readers had no doubts about the type of stories they preferred in *Science-Fantasy*, as the story ratings for the Winter issue show. The three *fantasy* stories in the issue were well ahead of the rest of the field." In fact, the three most highly rated stories are about matter transmission to Mars (McIntosh), time travel (Wyndham), and rockets to the Moon (Tubb)—not much more fantastic, to my mind, than the alien invasion, interstellar exploration, and war by machines of the three stories at the bottom of the heap. The only outright fantasy was Temple's farce about supernatural visitation, which came in squarely in the middle. Perhaps this reflects an extremely rigorous view of the line between SF and fantasy, or maybe Carnell was just confused. In any case, the notion that *Science-Fantasy* was for fantasy and *New Worlds* was for SF (if that was the idea) isn't really borne out by *Science Fantasy*'s contents, at this point or well into the future.

§

Issue **4**'s fiction line-up begins with John Christopher's lead novelette "Resurrection," about a future in which the world has been taken over by alien machines, and people live under their domination. Sound familiar? This does indeed seem to be the prototype for the his later Tripods stories. The machines have three legs, though as yet they aren't called Tripods. The mind-control caps do not appear. And the story ends with the central brain of the aliens killed by a human smuggling a bomb. It's an unpretentious intelligent pulp story of the sort one would have been pleased to find in one of the better US pulp magazines of its time, though in fact it did not appear in the US until the

March 1959 *Satellite* under the title "A World of Slaves."

The short fiction includes "Next in Line," a competent piece of yard goods by A. Bertram Chandler, in which the characters are shipwrecked on an island which proves to be dominated by mutant rats. "The Treasure of Tagor," by the veteran Sydney J. Bounds, is an overripe epic that reads like a *Planet Stories* outtake. E.g.:

> "You are an Earthman, an adventurer, a man hunted by the police of three planets," Yagho said. "A bold man, without fear—and such a one is needed to steal the Tagor treasure. I am offering you the chance of great wealth, a chance such as no man has had before. With my knowledge and your daring, the jewel of Tagor will be ours!"

F. G. Rayer's "Plimsoll Line" is a labored and gimmicky comedy about the rivalry between the canny space trader MacTavish, who of course travels with his beautiful daughter, and his obnoxious and humorless competitor Kennedy. Peter Hawkins' "Outworlder" is about interstellar colonists menaced by infiltration from an expanding extraterrestrial empire, but the inexperienced author isn't able to keep all the balls of the van Vogtian plot in the air. It also nicely illustrates the degree of amateurishness of a number of the stories Carnell published during this period, and apparently did not much editorially to help. It starts out with the viewpoint character having some last conversations before he leaves for his home world and retirement, then continues as he closes up his shop and packs his bags and heads off on foot towards the spaceport. As he approaches it, his steps falter, and he begins to have second thoughts, which prevail after several paragraphs, so he changes his mind, walks back and dumps his suitcase on his bed. *Then* the story begins, on the sixth page of 22. This story might have been rendered competent by throwing out the extraneous material, or telling the author to do so.

The interior illustrations look better this time, both those done by the previous suspects (Quinn, Clothier, and Hunter) and the illustrations for the Christopher story, by the praiseworthy Reina Bull. In this case Bull's cover too is actually an illustration for the story. Bull's interiors are not as impressive as her covers—a lot of what's captivating about her work is her use of color—but they are certainly more interesting than the others.

§

The fifth issue of *Science-Fantasy*, still in the large digest size, is dated Autumn 1952. No publication frequency is stated, appropriately for a magazine that has managed only four issues in two years.

The small-world theme continues on the inside front cover with another "At the Pub of the Universe" ad for the White Horse Tavern: "Science fiction personalities meet every Thursday throughout the year." This time the photo caption reads "Editors H. J. Campbell (left) of *Authentic Science Fiction*, and John Carnell of *New Worlds* discuss contemporary artwork." Carnell is showing Campbell a proof of one of Reina Bull's *New Worlds* covers.

The cover of this issue is another striking one—nice composition and use of color, and refreshing in that the shapely woman in the center of things looks to be pushing forty.[14] This one is by Quinn, who also does the best of the interior art (he seems to have been going to school on Virgil Finlay and Lawrence Stevens). The others are Hunter and Clothier, who remain nondescript.

This issue's Guest Editorial, "The Last Fifty Years and the Next," is by J. M. Walsh, veteran of *Wonder Stories Quarterly*, *Tales of Wonder*, and the first issue of *Science-Fantasy*, and currently, it says, serving as an Adjudicator of the International Fantasy Award. It's almost as insubstantial as H. J. Campbell's.

14. See these covers at http://www.sfcovers.net/mainnav.htm or http://www.philsp.com/mags/sciencefantasy.html.

Synopsis: I've been around for a while, and there was a lot of SF from Wells and the likes of George Griffith, then it faded out, then it came back. "Then like a thief in the night came the great recrudescence. The war of 1939-45, the coming of the atomic bomb, the vast strides made under the sheer pressure of necessity in almost all scientific achievements stimulated interest again." A bit loud for a thief in the night, wasn't it? "Anyway, the next fifty years are going to be a pretty interesting time. Human beings should still remain human beings, no matter in what situation they are cast." Walsh died the same year; his obituary was the first of the *"New Worlds* Profiles" in *Science-Fantasy*'s companion magazine, issue 18 (November 1952).

§

We are entering a period in *Science-Fantasy* in which J. T. McIntosh Rules, though Not Necessarily OK. In the next seven issues (**5-11**) he has five entries, four of them lead stories, and a Guest Editorial. The lead story in **5** (they're all short stories in that issue) is McIntosh's "Stitch in Time," a time travel story of surpassing murkiness. If I understand it at all, it says that time travel to the past wouldn't matter, because whatever changes would result have already resulted, similar to R. A. Lafferty's much more lucid "Thus We Refute Charlemagne." This is followed by E. E. Evans' "Was Not Spoken," involving telepathic contact with an inhabitant of Atlantis, her soul resident in a particularly sturdy coffin; Peter Hawkins' "Circus," a rather anti-climactic sequel to his earlier "Outworlder"; "Not As We Are," another tone-deaf "Colin and Brocky" story by E. R. James, discursively mixing comic and solemn elements without apparently being able to tell the difference. The best of the lot is probably "Enemy in Their Midst" by Alan Barclay (pseudonym of George B. Tait), a reasonably competent suspense story about a Martian ambassador extorting Earth with a smuggled bomb.

Next issue, **6**, dated Spring 1953 (another quarter skipped in the non-existent schedule) is fronted by the first serious turkey among this magazine's covers; Quinn again.[15] To figure out what's going on, you have to read the lead novelette, J. T. McIntosh's "The Volunteers," in which there's a galactic war on, but they only take volunteers. If you volunteer, you get the next five years to live like royalty with no one to say you nay. Then you show up for your service, and only 5% ever come back, and they won't talk about what's happened. The protagonist is a volunteer who falls in love with another volunteer. They try to contrive to avoid their service, but after an interval of hugger-mugger are caught.

Now the story proper starts, after three-quarters of its length has been consumed by prologue. Sent to the Moon, the volunteers learn that the war, and presumably the world, are really being run by a big computer called Solomon which can only work properly by having a series of human brains hooked up to it. Most people can't tolerate this, hence the 5% survival rate. And the reason none of the survivors ever talk about it is they can't remember it. He lives, she dies. And *that* is why the cover portrays, against a Lunar landscape, a man the top of whose head is bleeding into something vaguely mechanical-looking and who has a wire running from it into his high forehead— jacked-in, no less, long before cyberpunk.

The best of the rest are John Christopher's "Mr. Kowtshook," slight but characteristically professional, about a fugitive from interstellar justice, or vengeance, who takes up with a travelling circus until he gets caught, and Lan Wright's "Insurance Policy," an agreeably Clifford Simakesque story about a shipwrecked alien given sanctuary in a good-hearted farmer's henhouse, illustrated in an agreeably Edd Cartieresque fashion by Hunter.

It's downhill from there: E. C. Tubb's "Confessional," an uncharacteristically solemn and turgid alien culture story; Francis G. Rayer's "Traders' Planet," another one about the insufferable Mactavish and Kennedy; "One in Every Port" by Richard Lawrence (pseudonym of Lawrence Edward Bartle)

---

15. This is a case where Broderick disagrees with Boston, finding the image moderately okay, given the sort of thing it is.

about the domestic travails of a space captain with families at both ends of the journey. And J(onathan) F. Burke's "Time To Go Home," about Earth types on a far planet, too uninteresting to finish.

In this issue, there is no Guest Editorial but an actual Host Editorial by Carnell himself—his first, called "Evolutionary Expansion," which explains that *New Worlds* is about to shrink vertically, expand front to back, add 10,000 words, cost less, and stay bi-monthly. *Science-Fantasy* will go to the same format, but nothing is said about schedule. Carnell confesses some resentment and says he'd rather pay the authors more, but maybe this way their circulation will increase and they'll be able to do that later. The Nova SF Novels, a brief and troubled series of paperback reprints, are announced.

One interesting thing about this issue is that advertising has fallen to almost nothing. The *only* outside ad (as opposed to house ads for *New Worlds* and the Nova Novels) is half the back cover for the BRE *Astounding* and *Thrilling Wonder*. By contrast, the second issue has a half back cover for the BRE *Astounding*, the full inside back cover for the Fantasy Book Centre, half a page of small ads, and half the inside front cover for another bookseller, Postal Preview. How much this loss of revenue amounted to and what if any impact it had for the magazine's operations is lost to history.

3: *SCIENCE FANTASY,* VOLUME 3 (ISSUES 7-9)

Big news: the hyphen is gone from the magazine's title. As promised, the format is now 7½ x 5½ inches, the page count is 128, the price 1/6. Also, the Assistant is Leslie Flood, though that line is gone in issue **8** and the only editorial name is Carnell's. The colophon of **7** now bravely asserts "Published Quarterly." On the other hand, the masthead merely says "1954," no season indicated. But things are looking up. **8**, **9**, and **10** proclaim "Published Bi-Monthly" and have unobtrusive publication dates (5/54, 7/54, 9/54) hiding in the lower right corner. The covers of **7-9** are all by Quinn, agreeably composed and colorful but a bit crude in detail—though how much of this is the artist and how much the constraints in reproduction, I don't know.[16] Interior illustrations continue competently but without distinction from the usual suspects.

7 is fronted by Quinn's portrayal of Martian ruins. This illustrates Francis G. Rayer's lead novelette "Seek Earthmen No More," a quietly nonsensical story in which the protagonist, a space buff, suddenly speaks out against Mars exploration, sways the audience and ruins his employer, who fires him. He decides to go to Mars himself to atone—not bothering to explain to anyone that his "let's stay home" speech was actually telepathically dictated by an alien entity. And that's not because he thinks no one will believe him. It just doesn't seem

16. See these covers at http://www.sfcovers.net/mainnav.htm or http://www.philsp.com/mags/sciencefantasy.html.

to occur to him. Of course he gets to Mars and comes up with the completely uninteresting solution to the mystery; colonization will resume.

§

The lead novelette in **9**, "This Precious Stone" by H. J. Murdoch (pseudonym of J. T. McIntosh), is of similar ilk to Rayer's story. This one had been announced for publication in *New Worlds*, but was diverted to *Science Fantasy* after *New Worlds*'s long hiatus in publication. (See volume 2 of our companion survey of that magazine, *Building New Worlds*, chapter 4.) Martians and Earthfolk are fighting a war on Mars for water. The Earth types need water to fuel their spaceship, so they can go back to Earth and find out why nobody has showed up from there and brought them more water in quite a long time. A fighter pilot engages in a dogfight with Martian who turns out to be female, they nearly kill each other but manage to get to the citadel of the Healers, who offer a deal: we'll save you if you go on a mission to destroy the propulsion unit of the Earth space ship. They take the deal (it beats dying), and plot mechanics work themselves out mechanically. The big revelation from the old and wise Healers is that sooner or later the spaceship propulsion unit will start a chain reaction that wipes out all life, and *that* is why no one has heard from Earth recently.

Both of these stories amount to denatured *Planet Stories*, going through the pulp adventure motions without conviction. In general that's the problem with these early issues of *Science Fantasy*: there's almost no fantasy, just mostly dilute, derivative, and/or poorly rationalized SF.

"Dilute" is not a word that fits the lead story in **8**, E. C. Tubb's "Tomorrow," as over-the-top a piece of *noir* as has ever appeared in an SF magazine, or maybe anywhere. It's after the Blowup, not described in any detail but seemingly a limited nuclear war ("He glowered at me [over the videophone], his flickering image streaked and marred with the trails of radioactive particles blown from the mainland, and I twitched with unconscious reflex action to the mind-disturbing radiation from the wind-blown debris."). Destruction is uneven: there are a lot of ruins but there is still electricity (and videophones), and still diners (though sometimes staffed by mutants), and Carter's building still has a doorman. Also there are still private detectives, of which Carter is one.

And here's the theme: "This was a free world, had been since the Blowup, and a man did what he wanted, when he wanted, and how he wanted. That was freedom, and I was free." The tone is set in the first three pages, in which Carter objects to his neighbor's loud music and the neighbor takes exception when he complains ("The room behind him was full of smoke and stank of stale liquor and the heady scent of marijuana.") What to do? "I shot him three times in the body." Official reaction: the doorman says, "Next time do your killing outside the building, it saves a lot of work."

Carter has an assignment: to track down some papers stolen from Atomic Power Inc., perhaps by agents of the dread "Antis" (anti-what is not much explained). With a brief pause to kill the three vengeful friends of the noisy guy he had already killed, and for appropriate medical care ("The surgeon clucked like an old woman as he saw my arm."), he throws himself into his work, taking up en route with Lorna, the mottled-skinned mutant waitress from his local café, whom he takes on a date to the fights. ("The bout was between a middle-aged man and a lithe young girl. They fought naked with knives and the man was outclassed from the start...the girl slashed him to ribbons within five minutes... I glanced at Lorna from time to time, and when it seemed that she was about to vomit, I decided that it was time to go.")

He receives the obligatory blow on the head about halfway through ("Then the pavement opened beneath me and I was falling, falling, falling. Falling into a black eternity.") The story continues in this vein as we learn that everyone is double-dealing, and Lorna of course is dead by the end. The moral:

"'Yeah,' I said, and didn't recognize the sound of my own voice. 'Freedom—it's wonderful.' Softly I kissed the dead lips."

§

The short fiction in these three issues, overall, is a bit better than in the earlier ones, with fewer of the clumsy botches of the earlier issues—though also with little that is memorable. Those of greater interest include "Stranger from Space" by Gene Lees (**7**), about the emotional travails of a spaceman's wife who has come to hate him because of his long absences. It's quite well done up until the end, where it turns conventionally sentimental and O.Henry-esque. The blurb says "Miss Lees, a Canadian, captures the feminine angle in a manner no masculine author can hope to emulate." Gene Lees did not appear again, but one Eugene Lees contributed an article, "Utopias—A Few Years Later," to *Science Fantasy* **33** (February 1959). The blurb for that article acknowledges the earlier story by "Canadian journalist Gene Lees," and adds: "Now working for an American newspaper, *he* has been on a European tour for his employer and is currently working from Paris" (emphasis supplied). Nothing is said about the earlier gender mis-assignment, so it's unclear if Lees was engaged in a masquerade at the time or if Carnell simply assumed that anybody writing halfway competently about a woman's emotional life had to be a woman. As Carnell revealed in his editorial in *New Worlds* **25**, he learned the true state of affairs while attending a SF convention in Manchester, and met Lees, who had coincidentally checked into the room across the hall while stopping to visit a friend en route to a journalistic assignment.

Also interesting are a couple of pretty good stories by J(onathan) F. Burke (1922-2011), "Detective Story" in **7** and "Once Upon a Time" in **8**. The former is a good-natured private eye spoof ("Jackson and I were on Mars at the time. We had been dealing with that grisly little business that was known on the telecasts for a week or two as The Case of the Corpse in the

Canal. It was all tied up—the case itself, I mean: the corpse was too widely distributed ever to be thoroughly tied up, though we had done our wretched best.") The latter is about a couple of kids from a benign and enlightened psi-powered future who get whisked into the paranoid and manipulative past (still our future) by somebody there trying to compose avant-garde music on his electronic instrument. It's sort of at the intersection of "Mimsy were the Borogoves" (Lewis Padgett)[17] and "The Skills of Xanadu" (Theodore Sturgeon), and very pleasant.

Brian Aldiss appears in **9** with "Criminal Record," his first published story (not first sold) in the SF magazines, about some old record buffs who come upon a police recording about a criminal "smoof" accused *inter alia* of "timesliding," and who make the mistake of placing an advertisement inviting the smoof to drop over. It is inconsequential but clever and well executed. Arthur Coster—who had two stories in the Nova magazines, and is the pseudonym of Richard deMille, who had four stories in assorted other magazines—contributes "Family Secret" (**9**), which in its way anticipates the Whitley Streiber school of alien abduction accounts, except it is the abductee's wife who wields the rectal thermometer. Captain Semper, of the Air Force Flying Saucer Investigation, has bad dreams: he keeps waking up in the body of Omarpeff, who seems to be an alien crew member in Earth orbit (so the hints suggest) and is under interrogation for espionage, until his superiors finally believe him and sort of exorcise him. The story oscillates cleverly between the nightmarish and the domestic sitcom-ish. This, and Aldiss's story, and the two Burke stories, display the kind of quirkiness and idiosyncratic voice for which *Science Fantasy* eventually became known.

What is surprising in these issues is how unimpressive are the stories by writers who had big reputations at the time. E. C. Tubb has one fairly trivial story, "Unfortunate Purchase" in **7** (a kid buys what he says is a heat ray at a junk shop, dad sees

17. Pseudonym of Henry Kuttner and C.L. Moore.

whatever it is needs fixing, and it *is* a heat ray—a story much like Aldiss's except less lively), and one silly one, "Occupational Hazard" in **9** (spacemen commiserating in a bar about their wives being pregnant—space travel makes you sterile).

John Christopher's "Death Sentence" in **7** starts as a sort of police-procedural about a space murder committed by the protagonist, but the real story is that in the absence of capital punishment, murderers are sent into the past, and he arrives just before the start of nuclear war. It's well written enough, but gluing these pieces together doesn't make them a story. A. Bertram Chandler's "Six of One" (**9**) is a protracted pun story with a long windup and not much delivery.

And J. T. McIntosh's "Beggars All" (**7**) is another story that convinces me that either McIntosh had a thought disorder, or I do. Space explorers arrive on a planet where colonists have been isolated for centuries living hand to mouth. They beg piteously for whatever technological boons might be available, incurring the Earth folks' disdain. Meanwhile, there's a beautiful female crew member (named Pretzel, for no discernible reason) for whom the ship's commander has the hots, but he has suffered what he thinks is humiliating rejection. There is a revelation of why the colonists behave as they do which is then connected up with the romantic dilemma and its solution in a way that is as utterly uninteresting as it is strained and tenuous.

The remaining stories in these issues are mostly reshufflings of familiar material at various levels of competence. There is a pod of space epics. Lan Wright's novelette "The Conquerors" (**8**) starts out in the territory of John W. Campbell's "Forgetfulness" and Eric Frank Russell's "Metamorphosite": space explorers land on a planet of Sirius and find a road with a good-looking young woman sitting by it. She escorts them to her father's house, where our boys learn that (handwaving) certain elements in the atmosphere destroy metal, so the natives have developed along very different lines from us. They teleport, don't really have bodies but just make the humans think they do, and have already infiltrated Earth. But unlike the usual outcome in this subgenre, muscle wins out: one of the Earth humans reveals that their spacedrive, which is too big and heavy for their hosts to teleport, is decomposing fast, soon to blow up half the planet unless the aliens play ball with us. It is charmless but competently executed. The first of two stories by Margaret Lowe, "The Shimmering Tree" (**8**), takes place on a Venus mainly populated by poisonous plants. Exploring Earthfolk are disappearing, either not to return or to come back babbling about the "shimmering tree," which turns out to be hypnotic and to enslave its catch. The protagonist gets away, but wonders if he really did get away as he awaits return to Earth. Smooth matter-of-fact writing mitigates the clichés, the protagonist's rescue by his pet dinosaur aggravates them. Less well done is Peter Hawkins' "Haven" (**9**), as clumsy and overlong as his earlier "Outsider," about some Earthfolks who find an inhabited planet after their warship blows up; it will take a long time to get back to Earth and the war, and the question is which of the crew members will desert and go native and which will go back. The contrived ending spares the duty-bound captain from the choice.

"The Trojan Way" (**7**) by Francis Richardson (pseudonym of Lawrence Edward Bartle & Frank H. Parnell) is a smoothly written piece in which the characters flee Earth's velvet-gloved totalitarian Welfare State (sic) for a distant planet, cleverly avoid detection and repatriation, and then come to a pointless bad end. Francis G. Rayer's "Space Prize" (**8**) is another tiresome exploit of the canny space trader Mactavish. P. W. Cutler's "Take a Letter" (**8**) is an epistolary story involving a supposed government agency sniffing out extraterrestrials and a supposed solid citizen who is helping them out; whatever shred of cleverness it displays is smothered by excessive length and archness of tone and gimmick.

There are two contenders for Prize Bummer in these issues. John Ashcroft, who had ten stories and a guest editorial in Carnell's magazines and their nearest competitors, *Nebula* and *Authentic Science Fiction*, appears with his first story, "Dawn of Peace Eternal" in **8**. This is an overwritten variant on "and then

I woke up"—our hero is a captive of the terrible alien Thruna, but at the end we learn he's really in a mental institution, and it's just been mostly destroyed in a nuclear war. W. P. Cockcroft, a veteran of *Wonder Stories, Tales of Wonder*, and the 1939 fanzine version of *New Worlds*, contributes his last story, "Last Man on Mars" (**9**): an explosion kills everyone but the astronomer protagonist, who sits in his observatory drinking whiskey and listening to classical music and getting crazier with isolation, until a spaceship from Earth crashlands and the one surviving crewman lasts just long enough to tell him that war has started up on Earth again and that's it for space travel and our hero's prospects. It's just as bleak as Ashcroft's, but less noisy.

§

The Guest Editorials continue, and now they are beginning to display a bit more substance than before. John Wyndham is the Guest in **7** with "The Pattern of Science Fiction." The blurb notes that Wyndham is "yet another member of the International Fantasy Award panel," and I wonder if this is a talk he gave at an IFA function. He starts by mourning the low repute of the field and its name, though it's hard to tell whether his complaint is more about perceptions of the field or the reality of large amounts of bad material. But some are keeping the faith. Which is?

> Well, primarily, perhaps, that [stories] keep the rules...
> One of them is that a tale must proceed from its premise
> with adequate reason and logic... [I]n the imaginative
> story there must be a wholeness and a logic which is
> not cut across either by silly assumptions used simply
> to make a situation more exciting, or by silly inven-
> tions called up on the spur of the moment just to get
> the characters out of a jam. The unities of likelihood
> must be preserved to the best of the writer's ability.

Now there is a nice line that articulates a point of SF aesthetics as succinctly as I've ever seen. Another nice passage, though debatable: "Then there is the science itself. It has to be there. It is the backbone. Backbones, however, are worn inside, not outside." Returning to the former theme:

> Invention, then, cannot afford to lunge out wildly. If it goes far beyond the known, or at least the suspected principles of its age, the reader no longer has common ground with the writer... There is plenty of this kind of thing where the author has got himself into such a state of utter confusion that he falls back on aggressively tough remarks of great stupidity leading to a series of pointless fights to keep things going, and, unfortunately, it is this kind of thing also that has now come to be commonly thought of as the pattern of science-fiction.
>
> The object, then, of an annual Fantasy Award is to pick out the best exercises of controlled imagination—imagination working from data or theory within accepted limitations—work in which the writer has thought honestly, written carefully, and refused to abuse the logical implications of his theme.

Up next, in **8**, is Wilson Tucker's "Science into Fantasy," which points out that yesterday's apparent science in SF (about Mars and Venus, e.g.) is today's fantasy, and so are some of the assumptions in contemporary SF, like the physical ease of space travel. ("The daily visit to the water closet is another ingenious booby-trap.")

The Guest in **9** is J. T. McIntosh, whose "Something New Wanted..." is considerably more incisive than his stories of the time. "My experience of science fiction is that *you*, readers and editors of science fiction and fantasy magazines, are not really very keen on anything new, no matter what you say." So how do we get new ideas? "...[S]omeone puts them in a story which does not go very far, but which is at least published somewhere.

It comes in last or second-last in the magazine's reader-rating, if any... Someone else sees the story and decides that it's a good story gone wrong, and there's no reason why it shouldn't be used again the right way this time." I.e., more conventionally. And so on. "You get what you deserve—but more than that, you get what you *want*. That's why there are so few new ideas in science fiction." McIntosh includes himself in this discussion, asking "is there anything new about these?" of a list that includes his *One in Three Hundred*. He does claim to have had a new idea once, but he won't say what it is—he hasn't been able to sell it, but still hopes to figure out how someday.

§

In other developments or non-developments, outside advertising continues at a low level. Most of the ads are house ads, which are growing: there are two-page spreads for Nova bookplates and big splashes for the Nova Science Fiction Novels, which fell flat despite big plans. (Five of them—including James Blish's *Jack of Eagles*, Theodore Sturgeon's *The Dreaming Jewels*, and A.E. van Vogt's *The Weapon Shops of Isher*—made it into print.)

There is an ad in **7** for The Globe Tavern. It appears that proprietor Lew Mordecai, for whatever reason, left the White Horse for the Globe, so: "Habitués of the White Horse agree that sentiment goes deeper than panelled walls and, together with Mr. Mordecai," have shifted the London Circle meetings to the Globe. A full page is devoted to this! Either that's dedication, or the ad was free, or advertising space was *really* cheap in *Science Fantasy*. There's also an ad for a "Fantasy Secretary"—apparently not a double entendre in that innocent age—who "will type, correct, and lay-out your Science Fiction story, technical article, etc., ready for you to submit to British and American professional markets." And, most promisingly, half the back cover of **8** is an ad for the Royal Air Force Flying Review. New revenue frontier? No; this ad did not recur.

4: *SCIENCE FANTASY,*
VOLUME 4 (ISSUES 10-12)

Volume 4 (issues for September and December 1954 and February 1955) starts with two innovations: One is a new cover artist, Partridge, who quickly flew the coop. That's no great loss. **10**'s cover looks stiff and cluttered and the use of color is unimaginative compared to the usual Quinn.[18] The other change is a story title and author on the cover. Since **3**, the first Carnell issue, there had been no lettering on the cover other than title, issue designation, and price. There is a new printer, F.A.H. & Son of London being replaced starting with **11** by Rugby Advertiser of, you guessed it, Rugby.

§

Mike Ashley said in his Tymn/Ashley essay: "I don't think there's a bad issue from about **10** onwards." Certainly in these issues the magazine definitely turns a corner. Though there is still material that is inane or trivial or both, overall the quality and the originality of the fiction is significantly improved and the magazine as a whole begins to read like something other than a collection of everybody else's rejects.

The lead novelette honored on the cover of **10** is J. T. McIntosh's "Five into Four," and McIntosh's thinking continues

18. See these covers at http://www.sfcovers.net/mainnav.htm or http://www.philsp.com/mags/sciencefantasy.html. Another disagreement from Broderick, who finds this rendering quite charming, in a comic strip way.

to rub me the wrong way.[19] There's a matter transmission accident, and five people set out from Mars to Earth but only four arrive. The negligent technician is brought up on homicide charges. But wait! The four lucky survivors all realize that they are subtly...changed. So the fifth traveler wasn't lost. He was merely redistributed into the other four.

Charges are dropped, since the alleged victim is still alive, sort of, and the survivors all commence new lives, the leaven of new personality being just what they needed. (There is no mention of any weight gain.) But the idea that a redistribution of matter would result in a redistribution of personality (or anything else other than a nasty explosion) is silly beyond words. It might be made to work in an outright fantasy, but not, as here, in any supposed context of science. Or as John Wyndham put it a few issues previously: "The unities of likelihood must be preserved to the best of the writer's ability... Invention, then, cannot afford to lunge out wildly."

McIntosh also has the lead novelette in **11**, "Live For Ever," and here my beef is not so much with the premise (arbitrary and implausible as it is) but rather with its development. The secret of immortality is discovered, and it's just a matter of modifying your ideas. If you can follow an argument, you can read the instructions in the newspaper and you're in. (Too bad if your IQ is below 88, you'll just have to die.) The story purports to follow the social consequences over a period of years, which initially feature more hate killings, not fewer, because it is now more worthwhile to kill an enemy, and more necessary to remove anyone who might be dangerous. There are more strikes and labor trouble, more traffic accidents, more people who won't do their jobs, because now that everybody's immortal, everybody

---

19. In fairness to McIntosh, I should add that the problems of plausibility and logic in his stories about which I repeatedly complain are much more pronounced in his stories for *Science Fantasy*. He contributed several much superior stories, and one excellent one, "Bluebird World," to *New Worlds* during the 1950s, as described in volume 1 of our survey of that magazine, *Building* New Worlds.

is somebody and won't be pushed around.

But the violence eventually dies down because it's mostly criminals killing each other and soon enough they're mostly dead. The meek inherit. One can argue about how likely this scenario is, but the main problem is the author's complete failure to address the other obvious and huge problems of humanity's suddenly becoming immortal without becoming sterile: a population explosion starting very quickly and the precipitous collapse of the medico-thanatic-industrial complex with all its economic consequences. The complete neglect of these issues, in a story that purports to look panoramically at the results of immortality, is a vastly bigger plausibility problem than the flimsy starting premise, and a fatal one for me.

The lead story in **12** (announced for **11**, but postponed allegedly because of its length), is A. Bertram Chandler's "The Wrong Track," under the George Whitley pseudonym. This genial first-person story starts recursively at a session of the Circle of the Globe, the successor to the White Horse Tavern, and mentions John Carnell, Arthur Clarke, Peter Phillips, and Bertram Chandler as being in attendance. On the train home, the narrator and his wife feel odd, as if they are somehow facing or moving in the wrong direction. Trying to visualize things differently, they wind up in a series of parallel worlds. First the train is full of German newspapers and swastikas. They visualize themselves out of that and find themselves pulling into the Place de Trafalgar station (Napoleon won). Then they wind up in a train full of gray and beaten-down people living under the mental domination of thuggish extraterrestrials whose strings are pulled by a central intelligence. Avoiding capture, the couple hook up with the underground, people whose minds can't be dominated (mostly redheads, including the counterpart in this world of the narrator's wife). They participate briefly in an uprising and help blow up the central intelligence, and are fleeing for their lives when they are precipitated back into Hounslow Central. This unpretentious and entertaining pulp adventure story is made particularly enjoyable by the contrast of outré incident and homely detail.

§

The short fiction in these issues continues to get quirkier—not always better, but at least more interesting and less like imitations of the bottom of the rest of the market. **10** features John Wyndham's "The Chronoclasm," a clever, lightweight time travel story that I think might be the first much-reprinted story published in *Science Fantasy* after the Arthur C. Clarke stories in the first two issues. It is immediately preceded by Martin Jordan's "Zone of Youth," a peculiar story about a war between Youth (holed up in the Asteroid Belt) and Age, which for some reason makes me think of David Masson.

There is "Unborn of Earth" by Les Cole, a well-known fan of the time; this is the first of a dozen or so stories and articles he published in the SF magazines, under his own names and pseudonyms Les Collins and Colin Sturgis. It is a rather rambling story about extraterrestrials monitoring Earth scientists. The female passes for human, marries the main scientist they're interested in, and is relieved from duty on grounds of pregnancy. And it gets more complicated from there. Again, not necessarily good, but a bit unusual. Also unusual for different reasons is Francis G. Rayer's "Dark Summer," which consciously or unconsciously recapitulates the plot of Lewis Padgett's "Jesting Pilot" and anticipates Stanislaw Lem's *The Futurological Congress*. E. C. Tubb's "Bitter Sweet" is another of his sentimental mini-epics, this one about an old forgotten spaceman nostalgizing over his mothballed spaceship. John Ashcroft is present with his second story, "Stone and Crystal," in which a sensitive young man rebels against a brutish future society, and loses.

Highlights of **11** are G. Gordon Dewey's "The Tooth" (reprinted from *Fantasy & Science Fiction*, August 1952), which is told in reverse chronology and whose characters find a wish-fulfillment device and figure out how to make good use of it; Tubb's "The Enemy Within Us," about a mental patient who says his body is out to get him; and Joseph Slotkin's "The Mailman," involving mail deliveries from the future and a cad who marries women for their money and contrives to kill them. Slotkin published ten stories in the SF magazines from 1953 to 1956, three of them in *Science Fantasy*, and then was gone. Also present: Richard Rowland's "Where's the Matter?", about a crank inventor but not as funny as it should be; Eric Frank Russell's "I Hear You Calling," a lame vampire story; Francis G. Rayer's "Co-Efficiency Zero," a pleasantly earnest story about an alien cop from a world of extremely high temperatures who tracks down some malefactors from his home world, while helping and being helped by some human children; Sydney J. Bounds' "First Trip," about the first Martian colonist to return to Earth; and "Dimple" by John Kippax (pseudonym of John Hynam, 1915-74), Damon Runyon with a tinge of Amos 'n Andy on Mars. Kippax had a career arc similar to several of the writers who became regulars: about three dozen stories 1955-61, without exception in Carnell's magazines, *Nebula*, and *Authentic*, then a couple later in *New Writings in SF*. After that, nothing—another writer who seemingly had nowhere to go after Carnell's era.

12, in addition to the Chandler lead story, includes Alan Barclay's well-turned "The Dragon," in which a man scouting out the post-nuclear countryside encounters a village whose people are much exercised about a dangerous dragon. He finds the dragon, who turns out to be a mutant of the sort he's looking for, makes friends with it, and brings it back to the village to work for them. In E. C. Tubb's "The Last Day of Summer," a man who has passed the point where longevity treatments work is ready to be euthanized, and enjoys his last day; I think it's the best Tubb story so far, and Judith Merril thought it worthy of inclusion in her first annual "year's best" anthology.[20]

"Auto-Fiction Ltd." is attributed to Wanless Gardener, which

20. Judith Merril (ed.), *SF: The Year's Greatest Science Fiction and Fantasy* (Gnome Press, 1956).

I assume is a pseudonym and suspect is also a pun (along the lines of "I'm quitting my day job"). A businessman and writer are in a bar, talking about how hard it is to get rich with a new idea. "Why not mechanize my trade?" suggests the writer. Discussion turns to cardboard plot-finders, the police identification system, etc. They start out with a card file and move to computers, with the author laying about him satirically. E.g.: "We'd be cutting out the three main time wasters: research, continuity, and inspiration." Soon enough all the human writers have been driven out of the market and are turning to, e.g., "nihilinguistics" ("'We nihilinguists,' announced the Striped Monk, 'have dispensed with all physical impedimenta, even language itself.'") As the computer becomes more and more powerful the farce becomes broader and broader. Also amusing is "Free Will," a sort of shaggy robot story by Australian Dal Stivens featuring a robot and the ghost of a robot.

Surprisingly, the least worthy stories in the issue are by William F. Temple and Brian W. Aldiss. Temple's "Eternity" is identified by Mike Ashley in the Tymn/Ashley volume as the first *Unknown*-type fantasy to appear in the magazine (which I think is not quite right; its predecessor is Temple's "Double Trouble" in **3**, about the man haunted by the bad luck spirit.) In "Eternity," people start sprouting halos, for no apparent reason, without visible correlation to their virtue. Eventually, everybody develops one except for the protagonist, whose life is consequently ruined. When the aliens in charge of the experiment get tired of it, everybody's halo drops eight or ten inches and cuts their heads off. The idea is only workable as farce, but Temple treats it with earnestness, and then brings the story crashing down with a pointless ex machina ending. Aldiss's story "Breathing Space" is a heavy-handed one about people who don't know they are living in the remains of a moon base dominated by an out-of-control computer. There are rebels, bent on breaking out, who unfortunately succeed.

Overall, this issue **12** is the first one in which my reading enjoyment clearly outweighed my irritation. It's also nice to look at. My appreciation for Quinn continues to grow. This cover in one sense is crude and ought to look muddy. But the more I look at it the more I appreciate the composition and use of color. It's worth checking out, though this is one that doesn't look quite as good on the screen as it does in the flesh.[21]

§

The Guest Editorials skip a couple of issues but resume in **12** with Alfred Bester's "What's the Difference?"—between American and British SF, he means. It is odd to see this appear in *Science Fantasy*, since most of the talk about Britishness has been in *New Worlds*. Bester starts out by asserting that there is no difference in merit among writers, it's all a matter of taste, but collectively....

> The American and English cultures differ tremendously. We in the States are a nervous, high-strung people, anxious, insecure, generous but confused, painfully eager to get places but not exactly sure where we are going....
> Our science fiction reflects this. It is nervous, high-strung, generous but confused. It is a painful striving for The Answers. We in the States want The Answer to Everything. It must be definitive, short and quick. Eternity must be explained in a sentence, our galaxy in a phrase, our place in it in a formula—and then off to other important Answers.

By contrast, the English culture revealed in its science fiction is "assured, relaxed, aware of its own value, conscious of a long, honorable history, and doubtful but not too alarmed about its future. It is too sophisticated, or at any rate too well-bred to run and shout." Hence, says Bester, English SF's quiet tempo,

---

21. See this cover at http://www.sfcovers.net/mainnav.htm or http://www.philsp.com/mags/sciencefantasy.html.

leisurely development, emphasis on character rather than action. "I have the feeling that it has been fabricated by a people who have forgotten the terrifying violence which we accept as everyday commonplaces in the States"; the "unmerciful warfare between human beings" that Americans take for granted "has long been bred out of English civilization."

As a result, "American science fiction is exciting. To read it is like being cooped up in a room with an hysterical stranger." But the bad news is its "devotion to The Answers"—defining God and man, ending war, perpetuating peace, and settling the fate of the cosmos. "American authors have a tendency to reduce life to round numbers."

This is fine if you like tension and pat answers, but if you don't, English SF will be more to your taste. "It is calm, slow, relaxed. It does not search for The Answers. It attempts to explore human behaviour, and brings to its exploration a mature sense of values and a confident courage. It makes a realistic appraisal of the future undistorted by the infantile dreams and delusions that afflict America." But that's a bug as well as a feature:

> I have struggled through scores of English stories, chest deep in cliché, continually tempted to give up in disgust. Almost always I have been glad that I didn't give way to the temptation because I have found, tucked away in the stereotype plot, a fresh and interesting idea. Just to balance the equation I might add that I've ripped through scores of American stories, enchanted by the air of excitement, only to be bitterly disappointed in the end to discover that they were all excitement and no idea.

5: *SCIENCE FANTASY*, VOLUME 5 (ISSUES 13-15)

Dated April, June, and September 1955, respectively, issues **13-15** confirm the impression of a magazine that has largely settled down in physical format and has also hit a stride in content—albeit a quirky and unpredictable stride, occasionally suggestive of the Ministry of Silly Walks. The magazine stays at 2/- and 128 pages. The advertising is limited to house ads except for about a third of a page in **13** and **14** for the Fantasy Book Centre, much reduced from their full back cover ads in earlier issues. The interior illustrations remain undistinguished, some reasonably competent and some pretty lame.

13 leads off with Quinn's least interesting cover so far, a spaceship against a background of two-thirds-full Mars. Quinn's weakness is precision of detail and his strengths are a pleasing balance of form and selection and vividness of color. This one plays to his weakness, looking overall pretty stiff and crude (look especially at the shadowed part of the planet and the terminator).[22]

14's cover is uncharacteristically cluttered, of interest mainly for the trivial reason that the male figure in the foreground is said in a brief note to be a self-portrait of Quinn, who—like the protagonist of the story illustrated—is an Irishman.[23] (More of

22. See these covers at http://www.sfcovers.net/mainnav.htm or http://www.philsp.com/mags/sciencefantasy.html.

23. Broderick finds it far more interesting than that, one of Quinn's best covers.

that later.) In **15** he is back in form with a much better composed and more interestingly colored picture of an artist (clearly another self-portrait) at his easel, which also is another example of the recursive theme becoming common in this magazine: in the foreground is a stack of copies of *Science Fantasy*. They are all the same nonexistent issue of *Science Fantasy*, and moreover they bear the same cover painting that the artist is executing on his easel.

§

The lead novelette in **13**—one of the longest the magazine has yet published, running fifty-two pages—is "In a Misty Light" by Richard Varne. This is a sort of proletarian space opera that reads like a truncated Ace Double, pretty entertaining if you don't mind that it makes no sense at all.

Sands is mourning his lost Laura, who mysteriously disappeared. An Earth spy on Mek, Sands receives from an extraterrestrial femme fatale a secret to be brought back to Earth (we don't know what it is, it's in a recording capsule), just before the secret police bust in and kill her. Sands escapes and stows away in a stolen spacesuit in the hold of an Earth-bound spaceship. When the cargo is loaded he is buried in grain. The Meks try to search and detain the ship, the Terran Consul gets in their way, the ship takes off. It apparently does not occur to Sands that it would have been simpler to give the Terran Consul the secret capsule.

The Meks are in hot pursuit and eventually overtake the Earth ship, the Terrans resist their boarding, people are killed. Sands knows the Meks will find him in the cargo hold, so he skulks around the tailfins until he has an opportunity to shoot them. Meanwhile the Terran captain, who has been exposed as a coward and is humiliated, leaps across the void with a quantity of explosives and blows up the remaining Meks and their ship. It occurs to the now much reduced Terran crew that they have paid a pretty big price in deceased working stiffs to keep this man alive; just what's in this information capsule worth getting excited about? So they put it in the information capsule reader. It's the secret of immortality. Sands is quite chuffed. He ought to get a pile for it from the government.

Back on Earth, he wakes naked in a gravityless metal sphere, and learns that the government doesn't really need the secret of immortality. They've had it for 900 years and suppressed it because of its adverse effects on human evolution. Only a few can be trusted with immortality, and they join Earth Intelligence and are sterilized. That happened to his lost Laura; Sands, too, accepts the treatment. Then they tell him that Laura was extensively modified and sent to Mek to become...the agent who gave him the capsule with the secret of immortality, and was shot down in front of him. Fade to black. ("Consciousness went.")

Now wait a minute. Why did this secret agent disguised as an extraterrestrial summon the person she must have known was her old boyfriend to hand him a useless and superfluous secret to carry on a perilous journey back to an Earth government that already has it and is trying to suppress it? Ring Lardner had a line for it: "'Shut up,' he explained."

There is a recursive motif in this story too. When Sands goes to meet the mistress of disguise, the password is "Null-A" and she answers "Korzybski." Later on, one of the characters utters the epithet "Great Ghu." Could the whole thing be a spoof? If so, it's beyond poker-faced.

The lead novelette in **14** is a horse of a more florid color, "Sheamus" by Martin Jordan. Sheamus lives by himself, except for his ferret, and for all he knows he is the last human surviving. Michael Doonan, who reared him, has disappeared. A Martian describes the ridiculous catastrophe that has befallen the world:

> "It's certain," Dardanus was saying, "that the cobalt bomb, so incontinently exploded twenty-five years ago in the Pacific Ocean, robbed the planet of its atmosphere for at least thirty minutes. There's no need for me to recall the causes—superheating of the

ionosphere, followed by elevation of the heavier atoms and a partial band of vacuum encircling the globe. It's possible that at least half the molecules existing at that time reached escape velocity and were lost into outer space...."

Sheamus is an Irishman. We know this because the author tells us and also because Sheamus talks like this:

"Now it's a woman entire, all white and warm where a man seeks, and enough love in her, would make you sing for all with the taste of one only hour. And so fixed on a man's comfort, with the table's ribs boned white by the scrubbing and pots ashine better than beacons. Fine and busy she is, greeting a man with lips so clinging and red, you'd think she'd lain all day idle with wishing, yet there's a stew on the hob to twitch the stone nose of the Bellacragh itself."

Sheamus has never actually met a woman, though he has made a clay figure of one (portrayed on Quinn's cover), which is the only audience for the quoted remarks. Shortly he meets the Martians, who have set up shop on Earth. But these Martians originated on Earth, and have been transformed over 200 years by the thin Martian atmosphere (in Lamarckian fashion, but let's call it genetic engineering) into a three-gendered species. There are males, females who are really neuter, and Vivippies—short for viviparous—who are sexy but usually dumb. Reproduction is mostly by decanting. Nonetheless males and neuter females continue to marry, for professional reasons. In other futuristic developments, the Martians subsist on food pills, though they chase them with roughage.

When the Martians find Sheamus, a female anthropologist—a Vivippy but of Neuter status, it says—goes to check him out. She travels in a personal conveyance called an Immuny (for Immunity Suit) but is forced to abandon it when Sheamus tosses his ferret inside. Hence she is exposed to Earth's air, which contains a substance called Aphrophon that tends to restore conventional sexuality, and of course she finds Sheamus the answer to her newly constituted maiden's prayers. A subplot has them outwitting the Martians' robot chaperones.

Shortly thereafter, cruising around the local islands, they find Michael Doonan, who never intended to abandon Sheamus but got marooned. The reason Sheamus talks like a stage Irishman is that he was taught by one: Doonan is a former actor who mitigated his forced post-catastrophe retirement by child-rearing according to Synge and Yeats. "You're the last Irishman," he tells Sheamus. "*And I made you.*" And a bit later: "The last Irishman? Maybe the *first*. Maybe you never really existed before outside dreams." This prematurely postmodern motif is not elaborated. The Martian female and Sheamus are eventually captured and brought back to the Martians' dome, where they promote a rebellion and a hole in the dome that exposes the Martians to Earth's air and leads to a jailbreak of Vivippies. At story's end, the latter are preparing to scour the Earth for more surviving Earthmen, whom they deem fitter company than the etiolated Martian men.

To what extent this confection was meant as a serious and responsible deployment of genre materials (oh, stop), and to what extent a lampoon—and of exactly what—is impossible to tell. One suspects some lurking agenda related to Irish literary and cultural issues; one might think of Flann O'Brien's *The Poor Mouth*, but, one hopes, not for very long. Or maybe he's just having on the whole of SF. "Sheamus" is expanded—considerably, by three or four times—from a story in the UK *Argosy* (January 1954), titled "Sheamus and the Immuny" and labeled that month's "Science Fiction Choice." That version is quite rudimentary, starting with the arrival of the Immuny and mainly concerned with the struggle to escape the robot chaperones, with no sign of Michael Doonan or the loftier themes of identity and the like. It is the first of several Jordan appearances in that magazine; he had one other story in *Science Fantasy*, discussed earlier, and several in *Authentic Science Fiction*, but was gone from the field after 1955.

The lead story in **15**, John Brunner's "The Talisman," rolls along very pleasantly, slicker and more assured than either "Sheamus" or "In a Misty Light," as long as you don't stop to notice that it doesn't make any more sense than they do. Sinclair, a struggling professional artist getting by on book jackets and the like, finds a strange-looking egg-shaped piece of bric-a-brac in a junk shop, takes it home, discovers his artist's block is gone and his book jacket is turning into a masterpiece. He invites Shirley, an art critic he knows, to come look, and she's deeply impressed. That night he finds a dead man with a terrified expression in his flat, and the talisman gone. By morning he can't remember what happened (though he is sure something did), but the art critic's card reminds him.

He calls the police and asks for the inspector who came the previous night. They've never heard of Inspector Forster or of Sinclair. Sinclair calls Shirley, who assures him he isn't crazy. A policeman arrives with a message from Inspector Forster and is puzzled at the account of Sinclair's call. Shirley recalls the poet Christopher Bacon, first promising, then a genius, and whose work suggests he had the talisman for a while. Might the dead man and the missing talisman imply there were *two* intruders, one of them frightened to death? Sinclair finds that even without the talisman his artistic gift is still enhanced. He's painting "alien dream-pictures"; Shirley sees that he has also painted a portrait of Christopher Bacon, whom he's never met but dreams about.

Off they go see Bacon, who is now in a mental institution, writing things that no one can understand—but they can easily communicate with him. He had the talisman for a year, was thoroughly genius-ified, but can't convey what he perceives. Sinclair tells him he should stop trying to recapture what he had with the talisman; the talisman has changed him and he can resume being a genius in real time. (Unfortunately Shirley only touched it briefly so she has to stay second-rate.) Exeunt omnes, wondering where and with whom the talisman is now.

Here's the problem: half the story (the disappearance of the talisman, the dead man, Sinclair's disappearing-then-returning memory, the is-he-is-or-is-he-ain't police inspector) is a collection of dead ends and false leads that distract and create the illusion of something happening, but do not actually advance anything in the story, while the other half is just too damn easy. It's the sort of thing a more mature writer might have turned into a much better and longer story—as Brunner did, many times, later on.

§

The shorter fiction is an equally mixed bag, though definite trends are in evidence. There is much less earnestly amateurish science fiction, a generally lighter touch, a bit of outright fantasy, and several stories that are just about paradigmatic for the title *Science Fantasy*. For example, A. Bertram Chandler's slickly turned "Late" (**13**) is about a man working by himself at an orbital research station. There's some commotion on Earth, the radio goes dead, and his relief doesn't show up. The research station started life as a space vehicle, so he manages to improvise and get back to Earth, which he finds deserted by humans. He's missed the Last Trump and been Left Behind. This appeared later in the US as "Late Arrival" in *Imaginative Tales*, March 1956.

Then there's "Dear Ghost" by Alan Guthrie (pseudonym of E. C. Tubb) (**15**), which posits what amounts to relativity fatigue. You can only travel superluminally for so many hours before you turn into an invisible ghost, and that goes for your spaceship, supplies, etc., too. The protagonist is recruited on a quasi-suicide mission to deliver vaccine to a plague-stricken planet: he's probably too close to his retire-by date, the ship's pretty old too, but he rises to the quasi-suicidal occasion. Once embarked, he discovers that the ship is haunted, apparently by the ghost of a female pilot, whose picture is lying around, though it must be from a long time ago. After delivering the vaccine and being hijacked by colonists trying to escape, he "goes ghost" and finds her waiting. She's a babe! Of course.

Now for some outright fantasy. Helen M. Urban's "Pass the Salt" (13) reads like what might happen if a 1953 issue of *Fantasy & Science Fiction* were shipwrecked on a desert island and had no one to talk to but itself for several years. Sample: "He didn't know she was a witch. There was no sign on the back. No mark on the forehead or witchlike actions to shout a warning. A nice sort of girl who was fire and some refrigeration and a lot of looks. Not too expensive. Not inexpensive either, but just tolerable to the paycheck." He begins to suspect when she teleports the salt into his hand. Nonetheless he marries her. She gets annoyed when an old girlfriend calls him up, and casts spells she can't undo, causing him to look so weird he can't go out in public. So he listens carefully when she talks in her sleep and figures out how to cast a spell neither of them can undo making her invisible. Helen Urban had half a dozen stories scattered around the SF magazines—including *Fantasy & Science Fiction*—from 1955 to 1962.

Less annoying but also less interesting is Douglas West's "The Dogs of Hannoie" (15), about a man whose car breaks down in a remote small town, where they revere a pack of semi-wild dogs who are allegedly clairvoyant and howl at distant catastrophes. Here's the harbinger: "Le bombe atomic, it is not good, no?" The dogs are howling at nuclear tests on the other side of the world.

That's about as outright as the fantasy gets. Everything else has at least a veneer of rationalization. Jonathan Burke, noticeably improved, is back with "The Adjusters," a member of the same subgenre as Theodore Sturgeon's "Yesterday Was Monday," Damon Knight's "You're Another," and Philip K. Dick's "Adjustment Team": reality is maintained by a bureaucracy of dubious competence. Here it's the Ministry of Adjustment, which alters the past to improve the present, except there is always collateral damage. The two main characters meet cute at the Ministry's Complaints Department. Their respective spouses have disappeared as a result of the Ministry's adjustments. Getting no satisfaction, they eventually get married to each other. One of the original spouses reappears as a result of another Adjustment by the Ministry. The farce isn't quite as broad as it could be but overall it's a pretty amusing story. Burke also has the Guest Editorial in **13**, to which we'll return.

In a similar vein of metaphysical lampoon, but decidedly stranger, is "Double Act" by Howard Lee McCarey (pseudonym of Richard Rowland, who had a few other stories in *Science Fantasy* and *New Worlds*) (**14**), which starts out with Dockett and Kroyd performing a dismal comedy act. They are arrested, charged, and convicted of "F.B.S.—Fell Below Standard." ("Their script-writers were sent last week; good job too if you ask me.") They are sentenced to time travel, choosing the future, and find themselves walking across an endless plain, until they see a bunch of people suspended in the air, performing normal activities except that they are not visibly clothed and, e.g., the chairs they seem to be sitting in are not visible. They accost someone who says, "Go away! I don't wish to see you!" and is suddenly clothed. Later he says "Excuse me while I change" and his baggy trousers go from mauve to deep pink while a hat of curious design appears on his head.

Eventually Dockett and Kroyd find their way to Reception, where they learn to make things (and, indeed, people) with their thoughts. They move into a town full of similarly talented people and play a lot of golf on imaginary courses, getting younger. They feel a compulsion to go back to Reception, which turns out also to be Departure, and then find themselves children, back in our world, talking about what they want to be when they grow up. If there's a subgenre for this, it's represented by Gene Wolfe's "Forlesen." Shaggy metaphysics? This one would fit into the imaginary anthology *Great SF And Fantasy About The Metaphysically Absurd*, along with Howard Schoenfeld's "Built Up Logically," Frank Belknap Long's "To Follow Knowledge," and James Blish and Virginia Kidd's "On the Wall of the Lodge."

At the other end of several spectra is E. R. James' "Smoothies Are Wanted" (**13**), an earnest and labored psi story. In the future, telepaths will be used as labor relations officers, nicknamed "smoothies" because they smooth things over by figuring out what the contending parties *really* are after. This one, like Richard Varne's story, is hampered by ultimately making no sense at all. The Mars colony is threatened by a wildcat strike of the men who make the air. The smoothie's efforts to head it off are hampered by another unknown telepathic presence. But it turns out he's fighting himself ("You've been a schizoid—two people in one."), though he manages to pull it together in the end and keep the air circulating. So what happens? He (or they) gets a promotion, not a psychiatric leave. Nonetheless this is an improvement over James' previous efforts, which were pretty boring reshufflings of clichéd material. This is a more readable story with a fairly original idea.

Equally earnest but more polished is James White's "Dynasty of One" (**15**), in which the immortality treatment only works for people who can tolerate an intense heightening of conscience.

Recursive themes keep popping up. Here's "Mossendew's Martian" by John Kippax (**13**), a sort of "Don't Look Now"[24] variation about an astronomical artist who gets a chance for a big score doing effects for a Moon landing movie. He can't possibly get it done on time, but a man he meets in the bar says he can help and produces some really fine fake Moon photos very fast, except of course they aren't fake. At the end of the story it's casually revealed that this contact was made at the Globe Tavern, where London's SF crowd was then hanging out.

A different kind of recursion appears in Gavin Neal's "Reluctant Hero" (**14**), in which the author of the Rocket Brydon books, films, and comic strips goes to the Moon and is made the butt of practical jokes by the crew, but saves their bacon in the end.

E. C. Tubb appears in all three issues, with "Poor Henry" (**13**),

24. Reference is to the much-anthologized story of that title by Henry Kuttner.

a sour-tasting misogynist domestic-in-space about a poor sucker whose selfish and manipulative wife leaves him to be eaten by Martian sand-ants; "The Agent" (**14**), a variation on "To Serve Man"; and "The Predators" (**15**), a novelette about advertising types whose cynicism keeps Earth out of the Galactic Empire. These display capable professionalism but no particular charm. Tubb also has a Guest Editorial in **14**.

Wilson Tucker is in two of the issues with "My Brother's Wife" in **14** (previously in *Fantasy & Science Fiction*, February 1951) and "The Job Is Ended" (from *Other Worlds*, November 1950) in **15**. Both stories are well turned and both are about women who prove to be something different and altogether more repellent than they appear. Draw your own conclusions. Tucker, too, had his Guest Editorial in **8**, discussed above.

Other stories not accounted for include John Kippax's "Special Delivery" (**14**), another of his egregious Damon-Runyon-on-Mars stories featuring the narrator's dog Dimple and his black friend Satchmo; Kenneth Bulmer's pleasant enough "Psi No More" (**14**) (find the poltergeist? She's working for you); "Hilda" (**14**) by W. B. Hickey or H. B. Hickey, depending on where you read (it's really H. B., and this story about a literal-minded robot was in *Fantasy & Science Fiction*, September 1952); John Brunner again, as Keith Woodcott since he had "The Talisman" under his own name in the same issue, with "No Future In It" (**15**), a clever story about a fake wizard who accidentally summons a time traveler, the title story of Brunner's first story collection (by Gollancz in 1962 and Doubleday in 1964); and Charles E. Fritch's inane "Birthday Present" (**15**).

§

These issues of *Science Fantasy* contain two Guest Editorials and, wonder of wonders, a letter column. The editorial in **13**, "Ever Been to Uranus?", is by Jonathan Burke who, consistently with his practice, wants to get the science out of science fiction, or at least out of his face. After ploughing through technical material, he says,

> I found—as did so many others—that I preferred good writing to equations, and imaginative situations to extracts from text-books. Who cared whether the hero wore a space suit on Mars or not? Myself and my colleagues [whom he doesn't identify] no more demanded full mechanical details of a space ship than we demanded a potato-by-potato account of farm life in a Thomas Hardy novel. Liberation of the imagination was the essential.

Indeed, Burke complains of a bad review of one of his books which cited the fact that the characters did not wear space helmets on Mars. "To which I can only reply that Dante does not refer to the inhabitants of Hell as wearing asbestos suits. And in Dante's day scientists had pronounced views on the literal existence of Hell." He goes on to cite editor Carnell for telling him "People can't live on Uranus. We *know* that," and his own lack of enough temerity to ask Carnell if he had ever been there. After more mockery in this vein, he says sales of SF are falling off because

> [t]here are no human beings in science fiction...their behavior is governed by gadgets and plot gimmicks.... What goes on in the hearts and minds beneath those space suits? [The reader] is not told. And who can maintain enthusiasm about the actions of depersonalized space suits walking on alien worlds? ...Perhaps we had better forget about space travel for a while. Certainly if the intelligent reader is to be drawn back once more to science fiction instead of permanently rejecting it, he must be offered work that is mature *artistically* rather than ploddingly accurate according to the current scientific theories.

Clearly a man ahead of his time. Which is not to say he is entirely right.

In **14** we have E. C. Tubb's "Follow My Leader," a different but familiar brand of polemic: SF has lost its sense of wonder! Or as Tubb puts it: "I do not regret the mutation of those early stories into the far better written and presented ones of today, but one thing I do regret. I regret the variety and loss of vision, the touch of the impossible and the incredibly wild concepts." But now? "Now authors seem to write for the sole reason that they want to sell." That is, they "study the market" and send editors more of what the editors have (or a particular editor has) been buying. "How many magazines now give the impression that all the stories have been written by the same man? ...Exaggerated? It wasn't so long ago that a top-line American magazine chose to warn all authors that a certain type of story would no longer be accepted, no matter how well-written." (This is presumably a reference to John Campbell's notice that he was tired of atomic doom stories.[25]) Contra Burke, Tubb says: "True, science is catching up with us all the time, but what of it? Science fiction is a form of prophecy and we should be the last to grumble because of the increasing demand for accuracy." Even fantasy must follow its inner logic.

Tubb cautions: "Don't misunderstand me here, I am the last to advocate sex or sadism as the means to liven up the stories. Science fiction has so-far remained clean, let's keep it that way. There is nothing clever or desirable in taking advantage of the freedom of the field to exploit our own wish-fulfillments, erotic dreams, and frustrations." (J. G. Ballard's first publication, "Prima Belladonna" in *Science Fantasy* **20**, is about eighteen

25. Campbell wrote in response to a reader's letter in the September 1948 *Astounding Science Fiction*: "We have specified to our authors that the 'atomic doom' stories are not wanted, for precisely the reasons you give." Reader W. N. McBain had complained: "People are getting atomic warfare thrown at them from all angles these days. I for one am heartily sick of it. You are no longer a prophet crying in the wilderness. I've been reading enough of this type of story to have a reasonable idea of what ravening energies lie in the heart of the atom, and I want a bit of pure escapism."

months away—the beginning of the end, in Tubb's terms.)

In **15**, we find "Dear Editor" by "The Readers," which comprises one long and one very long tirade against Jonathan Burke's editorial. The introductory note indicates that Burke's editorial "touched off some spirited replies" and it's only fair to let the readers have a say. The very long tirade is by none other than Helen M. Urban of Hollywood, California, author of "Pass the Salt" in **13**, the militantly cute one about the man who married a witch. Here, however, she takes up the cudgels of scientific accuracy, taking a passing side-swipe at the reference in a John Kippax story to the "dark side" of the moon and energetically explaining to Burke that spectrographic analysis is quite sufficient to demonstrate that you would need a space suit on Mars. And further: "Burke! Part of the *fun* of writing s-f is thinking about the details which you denounce."

Burke's other assailant is Ed Luksus of Gary, Indiana, who says: "I've read enough of this 'take the science out of science fiction' to gain an ill temper. Messrs. Crossen and Tenn have been answered on this side of the Atlantic by the question 'What science?' I choose to query Mr. Burke in the same manner. The last story with any science in it was *Mission of Gravity* by Hal Clement which was serialised in *Astounding Science Fiction* two years ago."

6: *SCIENCE FANTASY*, VOLUME 6 (ISSUES 16-18)

Science Fantasy continues along in the groove the magazine reached in the previous several issues, with uneven but interesting lead stories, a reliable contingent of capably done short stories (original and reprint), and an equally reliable contingent of the bloody awful in each issue.

Interior illustrations continue nondescript. Guest editorials have disappeared and there is no other nonfiction. Advertising has completely disappeared except for house ads. The price stays at 2/-, publishing remains at Derwent House and printing at Rugby Advertiser Ltd., and the schedule remains aspirational. It says "Published Bi-Monthly," but the dates appearing unobtrusively in the lower right of the contents page say 11/55, 2/56, and 5/56, respectively. Another constant is the proofreading. There doesn't seem to be much. In one story, for example, a character is "Deidre" or "Deirdre" depending on what page you're looking at.

§

Issue **16** starts out with another pretty striking Quinn cover depicting a couple of walls decorated with trophy human (and alien) heads.[26] This illustrates the lead novelette, E. C. Tubb's "The Wager," an engagingly barbaric yawp about some deca-

---

26. See this cover at http://www.sfcovers.net/mainnav.htm or http://www.philsp.com/mags/sciencefantasy.html.

dent aliens dropped on Earth for a spot of urban sport hunting. Bad luck, they've picked the city where Gort, a member of the equally alien Guardians, is vacationing among the primitive Earthfolk. The viewpoint shifts among Gort, the bad guys, and the local police, and things move along quickly and bloodily in capable pulp fashion.

However, the outstanding items in the issue are two US reprints, C. M. Kornbluth's "The Mindworm" and Jerome Bixby's "It's a *Good* Life." Interestingly, the former is credited as coming from Kornbluth's UK collection *The Mindworm and Other Stories* (Michael Joseph 1955) and not from his previous Ballantine collection *The Explorers* (1954). Its original appearance in *Worlds Beyond* in December 1950 is not mentioned. The blurb to "It's a *Good* Life" (first published a couple of years previously in Frederik Pohl's anthology *Star Science Fiction Stories* 2 [Ballantine 1953]) hints that it's a reprint but isn't explicit.

In addition, there are three pretty good original fantasy stories. John Brunner's "Death Do Us Part" is a clever and amusing *Unknown*ish story about a ghost who wants a divorce. Equally lightweight and almost as clever is Duncan Lamont's "The Editor Regrets..." in which a magazine editor receives a ms. titled "The Perfect Story," which changes according to who's reading it, and which always comes true.

"Heart's Desire" by Niall Wilde (pseudonym of Eric Frank Russell) is about a nasty and unattractive Irishman who makes a deal with the Devil—excuse me, the Divvil—to make him irresistible to women. As usual in deal-with-the-Devil stories, he wasn't careful enough about what he wished for. (This is the same story later published in *Fantasy & Science Fiction*, January 1960, modestly revised, as "A Divvil with the Women.") I am surprised to see that Russell was capable of controlling his own mannerisms long enough to bring off this pretty smooth stage Irish performance.

Bringing up the rear are John Kippax's "Hounded Down," another piece of tiresome whimsy and Runyon pastiche about

Dimple, the Martian dachshund ("Cor stone me through an airlock I say," etc.), and William F. Temple's labored and tedious "Uncle Buno," about a kid who has a Martian math tutor who also develops into the solar system's greatest painter. The story bounces back and forth among nostalgia, moralism, irony and outright bitterness until it batters itself to death. But on the whole, I imagine the readers of 1955 thought they were getting their money's worth from this issue.

§

Issue **17** starts with one of Quinn's worst covers, crude and stiff-looking, illustrating Brian W. Aldiss's "Non-Stop."[27] Aldiss didn't think much of it either: he referred to "a cover illustration by Gerald Quinn, a cover to my mind as unconvincing as his enigmatic cover of orange shapes had been convincing" in *Bury My Heart At W. H. Smith's* (Hodder & Stoughton 1990), chapter 8. (I can't figure out what this "enigmatic cover of orange shapes" refers to.)

"Non-Stop" is of course the first cut at what became Aldiss's first novel. It is much shorter—thirty-seven digest-size pages—and it's quite interesting, in the sense of "may you live in interesting times." Frankly, it grated on me like fingernails on a blackboard. You know the story: primitive people obviously living in a generation-spaceship. The protagonist and company rebel, leave their community, and find out they've actually been in Earth orbit for generations. Their culture is dominated by the "Teaching," a quasi-religion based on the idea that people are despicable. ("You know what the litany teaches us, father. We are the sons of cowards and our days are passed in fear," says the protagonist to the priest who is trying to persuade him to leave. So the priest tells him that it's really cowardly to run away, and then he's game to go.)

27. See it at http://www.sfcovers.net/mainnav.htm or http://www.philsp. com/mags/sciencefantasy.html. As usual, Broderick disagrees, finding it quite pleasing.

The revelation at the end is that they won't be permitted on Earth, because they are an insane society, and are being kept alive on the starship only for study. The protagonist decides that he'll give up any grander goals and just be a big shot in the insane society, but he's thwarted in that too, and dismissed as "harmless" by the woman he aspires to. It's well enough done but seems rather pointless and mean-spirited, reminiscent of the complaints people would make about the New Wave ten years later.

What a difference there is between this short version and *Non-Stop* the novel—like day and night, or more aptly, in Mark Twain's phrase, the lightning and the lightning-bug. It's not just a matter of length but also of attitude. *Non-Stop* is not a great novel but it's a pleasure to read, full of incident and detail, free of the contempt for the characters that marred the shorter version. The Teaching is still there, but it no longer dominates. It's now a minor element in the depiction of a society of some complexity, and it's also explained away as originated by a crackpot. The characters are given considerably more depth. We learn the tragic history that has led to the present degenerated situation. And the end of the story carries a weight commensurate with the preceding events, rather than trivializing them and the characters as did the shorter version.

Maybe Aldiss matured enough in that interval that he no longer felt a need to prove himself superior to his characters. In any case, he seems to have found his way as a writer between the two versions. He says in his memoir *The Twinkling of an Eye*[28]: "Telling myself the story gave me great pleasure; I was absolutely sure of what I was doing." That's exactly how it reads. Of the earlier version Aldiss says only that he wrote it in late 1955 and Carnell told him: "Since I am short of material for *Science Fantasy*, I am going to publish your story, but frankly you are wasting a great idea on such short length. If you would like to turn the story into a novel, I will advise you and will try

---

28. Little, Brown, 1998, chapter XVIII.

to sell it for you in the United States." Carnell mustered more enthusiasm for the magazine blurb: "It is a great pleasure for us to present the first novelette by Brian Aldiss insofar as we believe that, like several other British authors, he has a long and successful future in front of him as a fantasy writer." Well, now that I think about it, he doesn't really say anything good about the *story*....

There's nothing in **17** as good as the reprints in **16**. The short stories range from the capably clever and amusing to the obligatory bloody awful. The US reprint in this issue is Judith Merril's "Connection Completed" (from *Universe*, November 1954), a psi period piece. A telepathic guy is trying to hook up with a telepathic gal. Is it really she across the table from him, both of them trying to ask without really asking "Is it you?" It's well enough done if you can accept the fantastic premise that people in such need wouldn't just blurt it out, since if they were wrong they would only have embarrassed themselves before a perfect stranger. I suppose this reflects the more reserved social mores of the time (in fact, the story can and probably should be read as a fairly obvious allegory of sexual repression).

John Brunner, very quickly the seasoned professional, again has two stories, both smooth but minor. "The Biggest Game," under the Keith Woodcott pseudonym, is about a professional philanderer and exploiter of rich women, who muses about their being the biggest game of all. Of course someone turns out to be hunting him. The even slighter "The Man Who Played the Blues," under Brunner's own name, is told by a semi-professional jazz musician to a police officer who is investigating the disappearance of Ribble, who sat in on piano with the band and played blues like nobody ever heard before, until a severe-looking man showed up, ushered him away, and made him disappear with some alien gadget. It probably seemed pretty hip at the time. Now it's mainly quaint.

Probably the best of the lot is "Loouey," by Alan Barclay, in which a London fixer gets wind of an apparent flying saucer landing and an alien on the loose, and learns that someone seeming to be the alien is holed up in a rural area racking up patents. So he and his muscle go to take possession, and get their deserved comeuppance. The story is told with great gusto and one gets the sense of an author having a really good time— not the case with most of Barclay's other work, especially his stories in *New Worlds*.

As to the "bloody awful" category, they all have one thing in common: they jumped, they weren't pushed. That is, they are not just ineptly executed but deeply misconceived. The least dire is John Mantley's "Uncle Clem and Them Martians," which appears to be a sort of pastiche of Henry Kuttner's Hogben stories by a writer who can't quite lose his stiff upper lip. Think of a Masterpiece Theatre remake of "The Beverly Hillbillies." The plot (bottom line, omitting the cameo appearance by Albert Einstein): Uncle Clem deduces that the menacing and seemingly invulnerable extraterrestrials are based on water soluble crystals inside an impervious skin that doesn't feel pain, so he contrives to have their shoes lined with sandpaper and holes punched in them and then gets the aliens to walk through water.

Proceeding downhill, we have "Proof Negative," by Trevor Staines (pseudonym of John Brunner), in which the mysterious stranger proves to be Santa Claus. Next is "To Touch the Stars" by Joseph Slotkin, blurbed: "Ever since life began the forces of Good and Evil have been delicately balanced in mortal conflict, yet few writers in recent years—except the late H. P. Lovecraft—have managed to capture the macabre setting." Suspicions confirmed: the story is a Lovecraft pastiche, value added negligible. Somebody brings a peculiar old console radio to the weird radio repair man to get it fixed. The repair guy discovers that he's got a direct hookup to the Things Man Was Not Meant To Know. In fact, he gets taken right over, just like that nice Mr. Charles Dexter Ward, and is bent on bringing the Things over for tea. Sample: "There, before his uninitiated eyes, the green arm of ghastly perdition reaches around the yielding body of a glowing creature, half human, half unnameable monster, dragging it back with it through a shattering screen into the dread beyond." Pretty eldritch, huh?

Of Len Shaw's "Syllabus" Carnell blurbs: "During the past five hundred years the English language has changed out of all recognition—and is still changing. The following story could well be written in the twenty-first centry, perhaps by one erstwhile descendant of Will Shakespeare." Well, you be the judge, here's the beginning:

> Scrinch open sleep-leaded lids, John Smith. Savour sunbeam-flooded morn. Survey marital bedchamber in preprandial hour's pellucid clarity. Consider accoutrements of mid-class domesticity—off-white ceiling, vitreous walls, nylon drapes, deep-piled fibre-glass fitted carpet. Eye-caress dressing table, top a-riot with erotically containered beautician's magi-products, brushes, combs and oh-so-common curlers.

Just goes to show that the sins of the New Wave were not the least bit original. There is a plot here, dimly visible through the undergrowth. Parents are supposed to sign their teen-age girl up for her irrevocable education and career path. She's made and backed off several choices, now she's fixed on marine zoology, except that Daddy keeps having dreams and visions of her being eaten by a whale. It turns out she's really psi-talented and trying to hide it while manipulating herself out of *any* career choice, but now they are on to her and she will go into Advanced Psionics, like it or not. One is tempted to ask the author, "Well, why didn't you just say so?"

§

Issue **18** has a cover by a new artist, Terry (F. J. Terence Maloney), who did a number of covers for *New Worlds* from 1956 through 1958, but only this one for *Science Fantasy*—at least under his own name (see Chapter 8 for elaboration). It's a pleasant enough alien landscape (reddish, so it must be Mars) with spaceship in the background.[29] Closer scrutiny of the foreground shows several men in spacesuits standing around what looks like a flagpole, two of them in consternation, one of the two apparently shaking his fist. One could surmise that these intrepid space explorers are expressing rage and frustration that somebody else has gotten there first and raised their flag. Unfortunately, the title banner obscures whatever is at the top of the flagpole, if anything, and the third spaceman appears to be looking at his watch, so it is impossible to confirm this hypothesis. The cover doesn't illustrate any of the stories, so there's no help there.

The lead novella is John Brunner's "This Rough Magic," the best to date of his contributions to the magazine. The protagonist, hearing the sound of a good guitarist, walks into a Soho club that proves actually to be the locus of a sort of voodoo cult. He befriends the guitarist but manages to offend the cult leader, and finds himself on the bad end of various magickal gambits. With the aid of his intrepid semi-girlfriend, the guitarist, and the guitarist's glamorous Jamaican witch-friend, he first tries to avoid and then to engage and defeat the magician. The story ends in a burst of quite well-turned melodrama.

There's a lot that's attractive about the story. The women characters are unusually prominent and well drawn for this era. The story is unusual for its time in its acknowledgement of the existence of black society in London. Brunner draws interestingly on the anthropology of magic and the story presents a point of view on it that's unusual for fantasy (though not surprising for Brunner the rationalist), and refreshing to my taste: yes, magic is knowledge, but that doesn't mean it should be preserved. It's not neutral knowledge because it can only be used for personal gain. The sooner it's forgotten and replaced by medicine, scientific agriculture, etc., the better off we'll all be.

As with "The Man Who Played the Blues," there are touches that now seem quaint, like Brunner's slightly ostentatious hip

29. See it at http://www.sfcovers.net/mainnav.htm or http://www.philsp.com/mags/sciencefantasy.html.

knowingness ("Reaching behind him, he picked up the guitar again and played a little silvery run ending in the E minor seventh harmonics produced by half-stopping the strings at the octave fret and lifting the barre while they are still sounding"), and the careful articulation of good liberal views of the time ("I had a high respect for the negro race—it wasn't their fault that they got themselves stranded on a continent whose climate was too equable and where game was too abundant for them to develop a technological civilisation.") But he did push the envelope a bit, with his protagonist approving interracial marriages: "It'd solve all our racial problems if we all mixed up into one uniformly coloured species." Then, at the end of the story, the white protagonist's white semi-girlfriend, with whom he is hopelessly in love, turns up at his hospital room engaged to the black guitarist. But when she leaves, the glamorous Jamaican witch enters, and romance is clearly in the air. Not bad for 1956, probably unpublishable in the US then.

The story was expanded into *Black is the Color* (1969), a non-genre novel described as "a thriller involving black magic." This version, however, is unequivocally fantasy—while the effectiveness of magic seems to depend to some degree on the victim's belief in magic, it doesn't depend on the victim's knowledge of the particular magical acts.

The cream of the short stories is Brian Aldiss's "The Failed Men" (a.k.a. "Ahead"), one of his best early stories, though it had never been anthologized, just reprinted in Aldiss's collections, until it appeared in Broderick's *Earth Is But a Star*. Far-future humanity has literally buried itself and gone comatose, for reasons unintelligible to anyone else, and time-traveling civilizations including ours have banded together to rescue them and start the species up again. And the rescuers are losing their minds. It's as downbeat a story as anyone has ever written, but impressive and moving in its brief length. One might congratulate Carnell for appreciating a story so contrary to the conventionally cheery and positive assumptions of the genre, but in fact Aldiss recounts:

Carnell was honest down to the last half penny, and brought his magazines out regularly. He had no literary taste. When I submitted to him one of my best early short stories, "The Failed Men," he wrote back saying, "This will make you laugh. I hated your story and couldn't make sense of it but, since we were going to press and I was short by five thousand words, I shoved your effort in. Here's the cheque." I didn't laugh. One wants appreciation as well as money. Particularly money on Carnell's miniscule [sic] scale.[30]

Jack Williamson's "Guinevere for Everybody," reprinted from Frederik Pohl's anthology *Star Science Fiction Stories 3* (Ballantine 1954), is certainly topical these days. A fellow finds a woman for sale for $4.95 in an airport vending machine. She's manufactured from the cells of the winner of a contest to identify "the woman that every man wanted." He needs information about her background but she won't talk unless he buys her, at which point she persuades him he also needs the $19.95 accessory kit. He's on a mission to figure out what has gone wrong with Athena, the computer that runs the factory that has started producing the Guineveres. (It was sabotaged by a disgruntled ex-manager whom Athena automated out of a job. The sabotage consisted of programming it to do something that would provoke its destruction, i.e. manufacturing Guineveres.) When he gets back to the motel where he has installed Guinevere, she is horribly aged—it's planned obsolescence, intended to insure replacement demand, and he can get a nice trade-in on her if he wants. And that's not all. The story flails out in several other directions as well. I don't think I've ever seen this kind of clear-the-decks satire from Williamson. It's a mess, but a sharp and vigorous one.

Lan Wright's "Wishes Three" is an *Unknown*ish rehash of the "be careful what you ask for" theme, trivial but redeemed by

30. Aldiss, "The Glass Forest," http://www.solaris-books.co.uk/aldiss/html/glass_forest_4.html (visited 10/19/11).

lively writing, not always a feature of his work.

After those, it's downhill as usual. Peter Phillips' brief "First Man in the Moon" is merely inconsequential, while Julian Frey's "Head First"—about some alien children enrolled in a school where the headmaster's name is Wilmar P. Quagmire, which is probably all you need to know—is actively silly. (Frey was a penname for John Hynam, who usually wrote as John Kippax.) A more baroque sort of lameness may be found in John Kippax's "Fair Weather Friend," admittedly a merciful improvement over the Dimple the dachshund on Mars stories. Here the characters run a rainmaking operation in the United States—authentic local color is provided by a "sherriff" who says "Well I'll be hoodooed," and a farmer named Eb Doorbell. Their materials are being stolen by a time-traveling magician from ancient Egypt who needs to steal the thunder (as it were) of a competing rainmaker back home. The real-time rainmakers oblige him by providing him a new, improved rainmaking agent. His competitor, by the way, is named Noah.

In a similar vein is Dan Morgan's "Beast of the Field," in which a miserable man comes to a psychiatrist with the delusion that he is an alien. Of course, he *is* an alien, and he's trying to track down another shipwrecked alien, and now he has. The psychiatrist admits that he's the guy, but he doesn't want to go home because the crash destroyed his telepathic centers and he'd be a cripple. So the investigator leaves him, saying, "Goodbye and good luck—Doctor Freud." What next? Adam and Eve?

7: *SCIENCE FANTASY*, VOLUME 7 (ISSUES 19-21)

These issues are most notable for the first appearance of J. G. Ballard. Outwardly the magazines look a bit shabby, since the covers by Quinn remain below standard, suggesting an artist who has lost interest—and indeed, these are Quinn's last covers for *Science Fantasy* for several years. Overall they look rather pointlessly busy (though the cover of **20**, depicting a damaged child levitating high above a crowd in a plaza, almost comes off).[31] The problem is compounded by the eye-grabbing bright yellow now used in the logo strip on top of the cover, which competes for attention with the cover picture and contributes to the overall air of cheesiness. Fortunately Carnell or his art director (if he had one—none is listed) thought better of it and returned to a more neutral frame in later issues.

Quinn at this point is the only interior illustrator, and the number of illustrations has plummeted. Only the lead stories and a very few others are illustrated now, with a few filler drawings in particularly conspicuous empty spaces. There is another ill-considered visual innovation in **19**: frisky typography in story titles. The title of "The Unharmonious Word," a story about Scrabble, is printed as the words might appear in a Scrabble game; "Stair Trick" is printed diagonally so the letters are offset like stairs; "Tiles" is printed vertically rather than

---

31. As usual, Broderick disagrees, finding it rather impressive for its epoch. See these covers at http://www.sfcovers.net/mainnav.htm or http://www.philsp.com/mags/sciencefantasy.html.

horizontally. Fortunately these creative impulses were quickly strangled and things are back to normal in the next issues.

The schedule ("Published Bi-monthly," says the colophon) remains notional. Issues **19**, **20**, and **21** are dated August and December 1956 and February 1957 respectively, though this chronic irregularity is about to change. After this volume, the magazine is pretty steadily bi-monthly. There are inside front cover ads for *Forbidden Planet* in **19** and **20**. Otherwise, it's house ads only. The contents follow the now-established pattern of one long lead story backed up by seven or eight short stories, made possible because there is no non-fiction and no significant space taken by advertising.

§

The lead story in **19** is Marion Zimmer Bradley's "The Climbing Wave," reprinted from the February 1955 *Fantasy & Science Fiction*. It's familiar territory: a spaceship approaches Earth on the first visit from a several-generation-old star colony. But where are the cities, the spaceports? Not much call for them these days. "'Do you rule Earth?' The man's mouth dropped open. 'Do I rule... Ha, ha, ha!'" This is the tendentious pastoral tradition of John W. Campbell's "Forgetfulness," Eric Frank Russell's "Late Night Final," Jack Williamson's "The Equalizer," later on Theodore Sturgeon's "The Skills of Xanadu," etc.

Kearns, who was ship captain when the interstellar drive was on, is a Type A progress buff who is outraged at this decadence and more outraged at his shipmates' desire to get with the program, build themselves country houses, and go to work making vegetables and babies. Gradually he gets seduced by the joys of, e.g., making spectacles for his shipmates, who can't get used to the sunlight (it's red where they come from), and then is entirely disarmed by the locals' response to a medical emergency, when it is revealed that actually they do have quite a bit of technology—they're bombing a tornado right now—but they only bring it out when they really need it, just as you keep your fire extinguishers out of sight until they're needed. (Oh? Mine is right there in plain view, and staying there.) The story ends as several of the characters fly past the remains of a spaceport: "Yet behind them the mighty symbols remained, cold and masterful, a promise and a threat: eight great starships, covered from nose to tail with green-growing moss and red rust." I wonder if J. G. Ballard noticed.

On the whole, it's not too bad a story, and pretty ambitious for someone whose first story had only appeared ten months before the initial publication of this one. But a few things here are a bit hard to take. E.g.: "It is impossible to shrug one's shoulders in free fall. The motion sends you flying across the cabin...." Heads up, Newton! Also, the crew is all young but they are rigidly segregated by sex for the five-year voyage, because in space no one knows how to deliver a baby.

One might think a space-traveling civilization would have other solutions for that problem, but no: if it did, there would be no occasion for scenes like the confrontation between the protagonist and an illicitly amorous couple whom he finds canoodling in the ship's lounge, a scene it is hard to avoid visualizing as a cover from *Soap Opera Digest*, the young studs facing off with their craggy profiles, their women cowering but avid-eyed behind them. Such impressions are not contradicted by dialogue like: "She whispered, 'Then we're almost there! Oh, Brian!' and her eyes were a double star, first magnitude."

Then there is the rest of the gender politics. The folks from the colony practice gender equality, and "wife" is a dirty word. (This is not quite explained.) On Earth, however, when the landing party encounters the talking head for the new Arcadian world-view, he regrets that there is no woman in the house to entertain the female crew member while the men talk business—and she gets up and offers to help the kid with the dishes. On Earth, it appears, natural women confine their interests chiefly to babies, and the returned colonists suck it right up.

The next two issues have lead stories by John Brunner, who has displaced E. C. Tubb (now occupied editing *Authentic*) as the magazine's mainstay. Intellects vaster and cooler than mine have observed that Brunner's true métier was as a pulp writer, and "A Time to Rend" in **20** (later revised to become the title story of his 1966 Compact collection *No Other Gods But Me*) is 90% of a textbook demonstration of the point.

Colin Hooper takes refuge from the rain in a doorway, and there's Vanessa (a "girl," as women were routinely called in the 1950s even by the liberal Brunner) already there. He's seen her around town several times. The door behind them opens and they are invited into a mysteriously large room containing a glowing disc hanging in the air and a robed man who calls them both by name. They look at the disc, lose consciousness, and wake up a few hours later in a dusty room in the same location with their watches stopped. One Kolok appears, calls them by name, and warns that they must stay away from each other. He appears again, they flee, wind up at a rally of a humanist religious cult called Real Truth, are rescued by Kolok from pursuing black shapes, and are then captured in another more primitive world run by a robed character named Telthis. He also knows their names and likes to burn and melt his retainers when they annoy him.

Again they are rescued by Kolok, and finally learn what's going on. This parallel world is run by an elite with genetically determined mental powers approaching omnipotence (the words "psionic" and "mutant" interestingly do not appear), and Telthis is the bull goose godling. Everybody else lives lives of serfdom in low-tech poverty. The elite doesn't need technology because their mental powers plus a lot of cheap labor give them everything they want. But Telthis, the Alexander of his cosmos, is bored and seeks new horizons—ours. The Real Truth cult will be the means of invasion. Hooper and his new girl friend have been manipulated together because they carry the fateful genes and in some not-too-well-explained manner can be used to facilitate the takeover.

Telthis's posse is closing in. Our guys are desperate. Hooper rages at Telthis and suddenly there's a portal open back to our world. It seems that Hooper has just enough of the power to save them in time of need, and they escape. But it's too late to stop the invasion, about to start at the Real Truth's rally at which their messiah, the Perfect Man (Telthis), is to appear. He does appear, and—

—nothing happens. These mental powers don't work so well on Earth, where people have had to do everything the hard way, wrestling with physical reality.

This story is a pretty good exemplar of pulp virtues—as noted, 90% of the way. A lot happens. It's told with great economy but even pace. The action is cogently directed toward gradually revealing what's really going on without a bunch of pointless fistfights and shootouts. The characters are intelligent and engaging ordinary folks (despite their genetics) who rise to the occasion. It's reminiscent of some of the better lead "novels" in *Startling Stories* or *Thrilling Wonder*, for example Henry Kuttner's.

And the end is a big letdown. The problem, rather than being solved, just goes away, as in, say, *The Andromeda Strain*. Brunner plays fair with the reader, in the detective novel sense. The characters' watches stop when they go to the parallel world, and their cigarette lighters also don't work, strongly hinting that if technology doesn't work in Telthis's world, his powers might not in ours. But it still kicks the props out from under the story, rather than delivering the powerful climax that Brunner skillfully leads the reader to expect.

The story is interesting for its attitude. As noted, it's about psionic mutants without using the words. It has the look and feel of fantasy and the McGuffin is as indistinguishable from magic as Brunner can make it. And the story's argument is essentially the same as in "This Rough Magic" in the previous volume: Magic sucks. It gives arbitrary power to the adepts and terrorizes and immiserates everyone else, and we're much better off without it. The characters' genetic endowments are meaningless in this world—and a good thing too.

In **21** the lead story is Brunner's "The Kingdoms of the

World," which has never been reprinted or novelized, and it's easy to see why. Unlike the tightly wound "A Time to Rend," this novella is an exasperating collection of false starts and loose ends. If Brunner had something coherent in mind he didn't manage to get it on paper. Howard, a Jewish man trying to escape his background, encounters Bell, a Mephistophelean figure who asks him what he wants and seems to want to make a deal. Howard throws him out. Weird things begin happening to him, such as finding himself in a truck full of Jews and Gypsies being taken away by the Nazis, and being told by his wife that he has invited Bell to dinner and later finding Bell and his wife in passionate embrace.

His very intelligent secretary Julie takes him in hand and to bed and tells him there's no such thing as good and evil, just the way the world works. He learns she is a former psychiatric patient, and then finds her with Bell, and they engage in some sort of titanic mind battle, which he wins, leaving them incapacitated. By this time Howard has somehow figured out that they are not human, but some sort of parasitic being that co-evolved with humans. He calls Julie's psychiatrist, who comes with a couple of orderlies to take the pair away and try to "do what we can" for them.

What can that possibly mean? And what were these creatures hoping to get from Howard? And what did his Jewish background have to do with anything, except perhaps to shape his hallucinations, if they were hallucinations? Maybe there is some scheme of Biblical references behind all of this. The obvious one is the title, which seems to refer to Satan's taking Jesus up to a high place and offering him all the world's kingdoms. But Bell never actually offers Howard anything concrete, and Howard never says what he wants, except late in the story when he tells Bell and Julie that he wants "three thousand years of revenge," an idea that immediately submerges again. It's all quite baffling, and all the more irritating because it seems as if Brunner might have had something interesting on his mind if he could only have pulled it together.

§

In hindsight, the big news in Vol. 7's issues is J. G. Ballard's debut, in **20**. By cover date, Ballard had two first stories: both "Prima Belladonna" in this issue of *Science Fantasy* and "Escapement" in *New Worlds* are in magazines dated December 1956. Most likely "Prima Belladonna" hit the streets first, since *Science Fantasy* was published bi-monthly and had no November issue. (Ballard thinks "Prima Belladonna" was written first, Carnell says "Escapement" was submitted first.) "Escapement" and "Build-Up," which was published in the next issue of *New Worlds* (**55**, January 1957), are discussed in this book's companion volumes dealing with *New Worlds*.

The gaudy and extravagant "Prima Belladonna" recounts the affair between Jane Ciracylides, a lounge singer, and the narrator, proprietor of Parker's Choro-Flora—that is, he sells singing flowers. Exactly how a flower sings, or knows what to sing, or what it could possibly sound like, isn't too clear, but Ballard milks the idea for some glorious nonsense, possibly a sly parody of some of the tech-gibberish in other SF of the time: "...I was in the shop tuning up a Khan-Arachnid orchid with the UV lamp. It was a difficult bloom, with a normal full range of twenty-four octaves, but like all the tetracot K3+25C5A9 chorotropes, unless it got a lot of exercise it tended to relapse into neurotic minor key transpositions which were the devil to break." (Ballard thought better of some of this in later publications; in the *Complete Short Stories* (Flamingo 2001), the phrase "but like all the tetracot K3+25C5A9 chorotropes" is omitted from the sentence.) Normally this orchid doesn't sing—Parker uses it to tune the other flowers—but it makes an exception when Jane comes into the shop. She and the orchid are hot for each other. Or maybe she's just a tease. Either way, all hell breaks loose whenever she comes into the shop.

It wasn't the noise, which only a couple of dozen people complained about, but the damage being done to their vibratory chords [sic] that worried me. Those in the 17ᵗʰ Century catalogues stood up well to the strain, and the moderns were immune, but the Romantics burst their calyxes by the score. By the third day after Jane's arrival I'd lost $200 worth of Beethoven and more Mendelssohn and Schubert than I could bear to think about.

Later, she sneaks into the shop for a private session:

The Arachnid had grown to three times its size. It towered nine feet high out of the shattered lid of the control tank, leaves tumid and inflamed, its calyx as large as a bucket, raging insanely. Arched forward, her head thrown back, was Jane.

Parker tries to pull her away, yells "Get down!" (Why?) "She flung my hand away. In her eyes, fleetingly, was a look of shame." So he steps out (why, if he was yelling at her to "get down" as if there was some danger?), and keeps his friends out, and later Jane is gone (permanently) and the Arachnid is back to normal size (it dies the next day).

There's also a paranormal subtheme in the story, quite conspicuous but completely undeveloped: Jane's singing is hallucinogenic. The first time Parker and his friends see her (watching her mostly undressed through her window from his balcony), when she notices them an illusory scorpion appears among them. At her singing debut in Vermilion Sands, everybody hears something different (St. Louis Blues, Bach's Mass in B Minor). When they're out for dinner, Jane would "sing honeybirds and angelcakes to the children who came in across the sand to watch her."

Carnell's blurb for the story is amusing: "In particular, we cannot remember having read such an intriguing idea about singing plants before, although there have been stories that have referred to such a possibility." As is Judith Merril's in her anthology *SF:'57: The Year's Greatest Science Fiction and Fantasy* (Gnome 1957): "This is Mr. Ballard's first published science-fiction, and contains one of the very few entirely new s-f ideas of the last few years." If ever there was an SF story that turned on style and imagery and not "ideas," this is it.

Stylistically, it's a bit of a mess: the contrast is pretty incongruous between the bizarre imagery and goings-on and the cocktail-hour archness of the story's frame. The narrator, describing Jane's arrival at the beginning, says the prospect that "there was a good deal of mutant in her...didn't bother either myself or any of my friends, one or two of whom, like Tony Miles and Harry Devine, have never since been quite the same to their wives." At the end of the story is the lame coda: "So if any of you around there keep a chloro-florists and have a Khan-Arachnid orchid, look out for a golden-skinned woman with insects for eyes. Perhaps she'll play i-Go with you, and I'm sorry to have to say it, but she'll always cheat."

In between this master-of-ceremonies patter, one repeatedly trips over harbingers of the writer Ballard became. There are the sharp-sounding phrases that when you stop and think about them don't really mean much, such as the description of the game i-Go as "a sort of decelerated chess." (And how do you cheat at it?) There is Ballard's fascination with the interstitial detritus of technological civilization: "Reclaiming some of the tanks, I'd come across the Arachnid, thriving on a diet of algae and perished rubber tubing." Certain images pretty plainly foreshadow (or fore-illuminate) his preoccupations of the early 1960s: "She was a walking galaxy of light." "On the balcony opposite, wearing a gown of shimmering ionized fiber, the golden woman was watching me." "Light dazzled in the street outside." "...I listened to her voice, like a spectral fountain, pour its golden luminous notes into the air." "Sometimes in the late afternoons we'd drive out along the beach to the Scented Desert and sit alone by one of the pools, watching the sun fall away behind the reefs and hills, lulling ourselves on the heavy rose-sick air." (So this *is* the first Vermilion Sands story.)

So why does this jerry-built story work as well as it does? Ballard wrote very smoothly, even at the beginning. The characters are vivid, presented with enough circumstantial detail to give them texture, at least, if not substance. And all the story's colorful unlikelihoods are asserted matter-of-factly and with great conviction.

§

The other short fiction in these issues has regressed toward the mean. Volume 7 lacks both the excellent stories and the bloody awful ones of previous issues. The range of variation now is from well-turned trivia, usually by established writers, to the merely lame, usually by the less established. The reprints, other than "The Climbing Wave," are Mildred Clingerman's "Stair Trick" (**19**, from *Fantasy & Science Fiction*, August 1952), a gimmicky story about true love discovered in a bar, and Richard Wilson's "Friend of the Family" (**20**, acknowledged to be reprinted from Frederik Pohl's *Star Science Fiction Stories 2* (Ballantine 1953)), a routinely well-meaning story about an alien helping out some ordinary country folk in their time of need.

Other examples of well-turned trivia are Bertram Chandler's (sic—there is no A. in his byline, unlike previous appearances) "The Unharmonious Word" (**19**), which posits a Scrabble play using all the most difficult letters, which when pronounced summons a demon into the pentagram conveniently left over from the previous night's magic show. In John Brunner's "When Gabriel—" (also **19**, a sequel, no less, to "The Man Who Played the Blues"), the protagonist, a jazz trumpeter, has a mysterious golden horn thrust into his hands on the way to a gig, which happens to be in a crypt. When he plays it the dead start rising, and Gabriel falls by to get his horn back. This story later appeared in the April 1957 *Fantastic Universe.*

Chandler has another smooth product in "The Maze" (**21**), this one published in the US, but not a reprint—it appeared almost simultaneously, in the April 1957 *If*. People go into a mysterious structure on Mars, but never return, with a clever if contrived explanation.

Brian W. Aldiss has two stories, which serve to remind that this prolific writer produced a lot of stuff that's just as well forgotten. "With Esmond in Mind" (**20**) is a modestly clever story about a man who repairs illusion machines, which manufacture scenes from the owner's memory. He gets his head between the electrodes of one, and suddenly the machine's owner is present in all his memories. In fact, he's present in everybody's memories, because the machine's faulty grounding let Esmond's personality loose into the "muon screen" that permeates everything in the future. "No Gimmick" (**21**) is tiresomely recursive: an SF writer is locked up and interrogated by Asian invaders who want to know what SF is all about and just don't get it. There are many passing in-group references, e.g.: "They must have seized even the minor writers, Hawkins, Aldiss, Morgan."

E. C. Tubb appears in **21** with "A Fine Day for Dying," which reasonably cleverly puts the proposition that life in Heaven will be quite boring. Carnell notes disingenuously that Tubb stories are "few and far between now that most of his time is taken up as an editor"; in fact, Tubb has three more stories under pseudonyms in these issues, and two more in the pipeline to appear in issues **22** and **23**. In the well-meaning but talky and overlong "Breathing Space" (**19**), as by Alan Guthrie, a campaign of automation-driven layoffs stops hastily when a peculiar electronics company employee engineers the company's newest radio design to stop all nearby electronic devices when turned on. Looks like they'd better keep a staff on after all. The middle management types who find him out don't turn him in, just sedate him and call for an ambulance when he acts paranoid—and leave too quickly to hear the employee's extraterrestrial masters calling, a pointless revelation under the circumstances. Tubb's sober point is that people need time to get ready for automation, though he doesn't say much about "what then?" "Mistaken Identity" (**20**), as by D. W. R. Hill, a name used only once in the SF magazines, is without redeeming social or other value: aliens who look and act like Japanese beetles land in the garden of a fanatical rose-grower who has just bought a new pesticide. "Special Pleading" (21), as by Philip Martyn, doesn't qualify as SF or fantasy: it's a jokey barroom conversation between a frustrated salesman and a guy who thinks it's just great for people to drink and smoke, and since the salesman is driving, why doesn't he have a double before he leaves? It is revealed that the garrulous fellow is a mortician.

One odd item is "Meeting Mr. Ipusido" by Sture Loennerstrand. There's no translation credit, so it's not clear whether it was written in Swedish or English. It starts on a Kafkaesque note, the narrator expressing great fear of someone he sees on the street, who turns out to be a character from a story he wrote and who takes great umbrage at the terrible fate to which the author has condemned him. It's not badly done at all, at least until the end when we learn that Ipusido is an anagram for Oidipus (sic, closer to the Greek spelling). Loennerstrand is described as "a Swedish author and journalist who has been interested in fantasy writing since 1935 although it was not until 1942 that his first story was published. Since then he has had over 60 published and in 1954 wrote the Swedish prize-winning novel 'The Spacehound' which was published by Bonnier's of Stockholm." He has no other stories listed in the Miller/Contento magazine index. The *Encyclopedia of Science Fiction* mentions that he was a co-editor of *Hapna!*, the Swedish SF magazine. He seems to be remembered now, at least in English-language sources, only for *I Have Lived Before: The True Story of the Reincarnation of Shanti Devi* (Ozark Mountain Publishing 1998, Swedish publication 1994).

Idiosyncratic in a different direction is Mike Nevard's "Tiles" (19), a surreal vignette about a seemingly deranged man who has come to kill a stranger lying in his bed; and then he woke up! And finds himself waking up in bed to find a stranger approaching to kill him. This one also has the virtue of brevity.

It would have fit perfectly into the Bonfiglioli-edited magazine of a decade hence. Mike Nevard, described in Carnell's blurb as "yet another London newspaperman," had no other appearances in the SF magazines.

Harlan Ellison's "Rain, Rain, Go Away" (**20**) is a lame fantasy about a nebbishy guy who has one talent—he could always chant "Rain, rain," etc., and it would work; but now "another day" has come and he can't make it stop. This was about Ellison's tenth published story. Carnell's blurb says, "There will be more stories by Harlan Ellison in the near future," but there weren't, at least not in *Science Fantasy* or any of the other Nova magazines (he did appear in the post-Nova *New Worlds* with "A Boy and His Dog").

John Kippax has two stories. In "Finegan Begin Again" (**21**) the protagonist rescues a leprechaun, who grants his wish to be protected against predatory women; when danger strikes, he is transported to a beach 80 miles away. This becomes inconvenient when he meets a woman he *wants* to marry, and the rest is reasonably clever slapstick. In "Cut and Come Again" (**20**), Piotr Lugan, "re-creator" by profession, is approached by some strange- and menacing-looking people in archaic dress and retained to re-create a guillotine, with which they apparently do away with one of their number, though Lugan falls and hits his head and misses the festivities. Then somebody else shows up at his door saying he was referred by the victim. It's competently enough done but the point is elusive.

John Boland's "Herma" (**20**) is introduced with a drumroll by Carnell: "It is a significant fact that many leading novelists have used fantasy as a background to their plots and it would appear that there is something intriguing about such possibilities when the author is not bound by any hard and fast rules." Boland had by then published two borderline SF novels, *White August* and *No Refuge*, and later turned out a large flock of crime novels. But "Herma" is more of a kazoo solo, featuring a milquetoasty scientist with a caricatured overbearing wife. He occupies himself creating life in his home laboratory, and he makes his wife a domestic servant, asexual but highly competent, except that it turns into a beautiful complaisant woman in the lab at night.

The rest of the short fiction consists mostly of gimmick stories of varying triviality and familiarity, mostly by familiar names. E. R. James' "Too Perfect" (**19**) is a silly but amusing recursive story about a writer who writes a novel so compelling that no one can put it down, and the literal consequences thereof; it displays an unexpected sense of humor for James, and also is not a word too long. Joseph Slotkin's "The Coffee Pot" (**19**)—his last story in the magazine, indeed in the genre—is a benignly inane sort of shaggy-god story in which a young married couple discovers that their coffee pot is never empty; they start to make big plans to open a restaurant but somehow never bring it off; after they are old and gray, regretting that they never really made any money, they actually take the lid off and look into the coffee pot for the first time, and see that it's perpetually full of diamonds. Sydney J. Bounds' "Random Power" (**20**) proposes a shopgirl with the psychic power of wish-fulfillment who is recruited for military purposes, to counter similar Soviet effort; what happens when she figures out she's part of a war and doesn't like it? Lan Wright's "Vanishing Trick" (**21**) rings yet another variation on the powerful aliens frightened away by human hokum, in this case a truant child's display of stage magic. The only new name is that of J.E. Tomerlin, whose "Alienation of Affection" (**21**) starts out as a parable of McCarthyism, with a scientist in the dock accused of being an alien, found guilty on no evidence, and then lynched; his defense attorney barely gets away, and it is revealed that he *is* an alien, who warns his kin to stay away from Earth. Tomerlin had two more stories in the genre in 1963 and 1966.

8: *SCIENCE FANTASY*, VOLUME 8 (ISSUES 22-24)

Volume 8 comprises issues dated April, June and August 1957, and they look a lot better than their immediate predecessors because of the advent of a new cover artist, the idiosyncratic Jose Rubios—later revealed actually to be a pseudonym for Terry (F. J. Terence Maloney), who under his name did the cover for **18** and a number for *New Worlds*. Unlike his NW work, mostly very literal space and other-planet scenes, these suggest he might have a background in advertising art, now gone pleasantly awry.[32] As Rubios, Terry did four consecutive covers for *Science Fantasy* and two for *Science Fiction Adventures* and then ditched that name, possibly to reappear as Jarr, of whom more later.[33] Interior illustrations have quietly vanished (gone with the Quinn).

Non-house ads have crept back. In these issues we have the Science Fiction Postal Library, Psychic News, the World SF Convention, the return of the Fantasy Book Centre, which also traffics in Jazz ("All speeds, all makes"), and the "Solascope"

---

32. See these covers at http://www.sfcovers.net/mainnav.htm or http://www.philsp.com/mags/sciencefantasy.html.

33. Jarr is identified as a pseudonym of Maloney in the artist index of www.sfcovers.net. However, in *Science Fantasy* **43** (October 1960), an article titled "The First Decade" says that Jarr was "a team"—but of whom or what, it doesn't say. (The article is bylined Kenneth Johns, himself (so to speak) a pseudonym for "a team" comprising John Newman and Kenneth Bulmer.) Desultory inquiries have failed to resolve this mystery and we leave it for later generations of interested scholars, if any.

Giant Rotary Guide to the Solar System, which is claimed to show "PLANETS AND ORBITS to scale." Neat trick, or else made for people with very large living rooms. Wait a minute, it says it's twelve inches square. Hope it came with a magnifying glass. There's also a new house ad, for bookplates by Gerard Quinn, joining the ads for *New Worlds* and the Nova SF Novels. And with **24**, Nova Publications moves from Derwent House on (in) Arundel Street to Maclaren House in Great Suffolk Street. They're still printed by Rugby Advertiser, still proofread by no one who will own up to it. Most notable gaffe: the cover of **23** boasts at the bottom "HAWKINS * ALDISS * BALLARD * BOLAND." There is no Boland story in the magazine. Price, size, pages, look and feel remain the same.

§

The fiction is another mixed bag: there is quite a range of quality both in the lead stories and in the short fiction—the bloody awful is back in the latter. So is Ballard, with "Mobile" in **23**.

Chief among the lead stories is Peter Hawkins' never-reprinted "The Daymakers" (**23**), which is the sort of thing that makes plowing through these old magazines worthwhile. It's not a great story, but it's a vigorous, well-visualized, and reasonably intelligent one that deserves better than its present obscurity. Hawkins had a few stories in very early issues of the magazine. They were clumsy and amateurish but indicated that he at least had some idea what a story is. In the interim he had a few more in *New Worlds* and seems to have figured out how they work. "The Daymakers" is in the tradition of Sturgeon's "Yesterday Is Monday," Heinlein's "They," Knight's "You're Another," Dick's "Adjustment Team," etc., but is better than merely derivative.

Trevor North runs a small electronic engineering company but is bored and dissatisfied with his own limits. He consults his psychiatrist Purdy, an old friend. He opens a door in Purdy's suite and sees "blackness, utterly incredible blackness, against which floated myriads of hair-fine threads of literally thousands of colors and shades, some bold, some pastel, some phosphorescent, some satanically dark, others glowing with almost saint-like purity." Purdy tells him he just needs a vacation. So he leaves, recursively: "Briskly he turned down Arundel Street, walking past the offices of Nova Publications...."

A series of bizarre accidents and coincidences befall him and he sights the multi-colored hair-fine threads again. Purdy introduces him to Adrian Hammond, who has painted scenes of the multi-colored threads. Next day he wakes up to discover that his alarm clock stopped at midnight, there's no power, no people about anywhere, and the Thames has dried up. He finds Purdy dead and a tape left for him, which tells him that the world isn't what he thinks it is. Each day is separately constructed, used once, and then over time it is dismantled and its parts used in building other days. However, human life is getting too complicated for the Daymakers to keep up, so they are looking for a few good managers.

Apparently North is stuck in a used day that's being scavenged for parts; Nelson's Column and other monuments are missing, and as the days pass more and more pieces of London (including North's companion, the one live human he's found) fall upward into the sky and vanish. (That's what is going on in the otherwise puzzling and rather pleasing cover painting.) Then North falls up too, finally flying through a trapdoor behind which he finds Hammond and later wakes up in a hospital bed. The painter advises him to think of the Daymakers' activities as analogous to keeping tropical fish (humans being the fish), and by the way he can't go back—they've already manufactured a simulacrum of North to run the electronics factory and incidentally to marry North's secretary.

Meanwhile North gets a cushy job helping the Daymakers manage their props. To accomplish this, he sits in a comfortable chair and undergoes a sensation like doors opening and closing in his mind. At least, that's the training. (Nice work if you can get it.) Hammond explains that the bizarre events that befell North were fallout from a struggle between Hammond and Purdy. Then the apparently deceased Purdy appears, and says he's not really a Daymaker, and apparently neither is North—"Your talents, Trevor North...make you the moulder of the final, absolute Reality... May we go now, sir?" Did I mention that Hawkins seems to have been a bit influenced by van Vogt? While the story's cosmogony is a bit, er, contrived, the initially bewildering plot is well handled and the vision of life in a deserted London being stripped for parts is pretty entertaining.

The other lead stories don't measure up as well. Richard Wilson's "It's Cold Outside" (**22**, also published a few months earlier in the December 1956 *If*) is a well-meaning and well-written but ultimately botched dystopian story. The protagonist and his wife live in the City-state of Greater New York, which is becoming more and more totalitarian in a velvet-glove sort of way—the government issues Suggestions, not edicts, but it's not too smart to blow them off. One of the public faces of conformity pressure is a comedian named Jerry Hilarious, who is constantly making fun of Outside and Outsiders, people who live in barbarism outside the City-states.

Our characters run afoul of the government in connection with the wife's pregnancy (the Suggestion is to have your kids decanted), and they decide they've had enough when it is Suggested she check into a hospital for the last month and that the child be made a ward of the state until it's clear he's OK. They bolt, make it to the outskirts of town, check into a hotel so they can reconnoiter for their breakout, and who else checks in but...Jerry Hilarious. Yes, he's a secret agent of the Outsiders (who are not barbaric at all) and his act is really directed at encouraging doubters to defect from the City-states.

This sort of cheesy rug-pulling revelation is all very well in a story like "The Daymakers," which pretends to be no more than the metaphysical adventure story it is, but it wrecks the tone of a story like this that aspires to be a humanistic think-piece. This is a characteristic failing of ambitious genre SF, the inability to wrap things up with the same gravitas with which the problem is stated and developed. Melodrama becomes the last resort of the not-quite-up-to-it writer (though admittedly Wilson was on other occasions very much up to it).

Robert Presslie's "Plague," the cover story of **24**, wrestles with the challenge of... Dope! Not "the true narcotics—morphine, heroine, cocaine, hashish, marijuanha" (sic passim), but manufactured "pep drugs, boosters, and tranquillisers." Everybody is suddenly using them, society is falling apart, the protagonist is one of the last functional members of the Narcotics Bureau and gets sent out to investigate the trade. After a lot of mostly tiresome hugger-mugger it's revealed that what's really at the bottom of things is a disease imported from Venus, the cure for which is alcohol. This is another kind of trivializing limp ending, except that the story was pretty trivial to begin with.

This issue has a second story labeled as a novelette, Margaret Lowe's "Blind Chance," a considerably better story. It's about a rebellious young man in a city where everything is copacetic because humans are served by emotionless androids, and if you don't agree, that's OK because the Examiners will condition all your discontent out at age 18. Clave flees his appointment with the Examiners and goes in search of the underground Starmen, who study forbidden physics and astronomy in hopes of getting off-planet. But the Starmen don't want him because he's an untried kid. They send him back out marked as an android and he lives as one for a while, then escapes and finds the Starmen again, where now they welcome him as a person of substance and inform him that he really *is* an android—an unconditioned one. Androids are really no different from anybody else if you let them develop naturally. By the way, the Starmen don't really want to leave Earth until they bring justice to it. This of course is a string of clichés, but much more capably written and realized than in Presslie's story. This story is the second and last under the Margaret Lowe byline, following "The Shimmering Tree" in *Science Fantasy* **8**, in 1954.

§

The most striking feature of the short stories is the resurgence of lame and archaic science fiction. Some of these stories read as if they fell behind Walter Gillings' file cabinet before the War, or maybe Gernsback's. John Mantley's "The Black Crucible" (22) is a chief offender. Mantley's earlier story "Uncle Clem and Them Martians" suffered from not being as funny as intended. This one has the opposite problem. It begins after a nuclear war, with the entire surviving population of the Earth assembled by the shores of the Great Slave Lake—896,744 of them, to be precise.[34]

This multitude is assembled for a pre-departure ceremony for the crew of the spaceship that is about to launch for Venus, which the protagonist has decided to call Grail. The ceremony is a presentation of wings, no less, for which the crew is all standing at "rigid attention." These are "clear-eyed, determined youngsters between the ages of twenty and twenty-six. Each physically perfect, mentally sound, morally dedicated." Etc., etc. The story recounts the grueling space voyage of these intolerably superior caricatures, including the one woman, a creature of impossible beauty, sensitivity, etc., all but one of whom are dead by the time they reach their destination, to this reader's considerable relief. The story is also interminably long—36 pages, longer than some of the stories labeled as novelettes.

E. D. Campbell's "The Hybrid Queen" (22) is about the man who pioneers beekeeping on Venus, to his considerable regret when his bees hook up with radioactive plants. This one too reads like a rescue from the *Wonder Stories* inventory. (Though opinions differ; I see to my astonishment that Judith Merril gave it an Honorable Mention in the back of her year's best anthology.) E. R. James' "Galactic Year" (23) involves a telekinetic mutant who was orphaned as a child by the persecutions of the ignorant, but look at him now! He is presiding over the creation of new stars from dust clouds as the Emperor of the Galaxy looks on in admiration! James had a story in the first

---

34. Let us hope they had plenty of Porto-Sans.

issue of this magazine, and several thereafter, but unlike Peter Hawkins seems to have learned little in the intervening years.

Onward to better things. Brian Aldiss has two stories, the better one being "Let's Be Frank" (23), which Judith Merril picked up for her annual Best anthology. An English petty nobleman discovers that he shares a common consciousness with his son, and it breeds true, takes over the Old World, and then runs up against its rival in the New. The story is smoothly and economically done, a pleasure to reread. Interestingly, Aldiss seems never to have put it in one of his own collections, though it has been anthologized several times and seems to me one of his best early stories. "Flowers of the Forest" (24) is a more awkward affair. A man has mutilated his unfaithful wife, regrets it, goes to a South American witch to liberate his soul to go see how she's doing, and winds up killing the witch. Before he can get back into his body her pet leopard has occupied it, and she has occupied the leopard's body, and the leopard proceeds to kill his body. This kind of humorless and conventional supernatural story was never Aldiss's métier, and it has a certain embarrassed quality to it, like a man standing around in a really silly costume. This is another one that seems never to have been in an Aldiss collection, and for better reason.

Other standouts, for merit or at least idiosyncrasy, include Richard Wilson's "The Ubiquitous You" (24), about a mad or at least very cranky scientist who creates half a dozen clones (though he doesn't use the word) of his assistant, all of whom have drastically different personalities. It's essentially slapstick, brought off with near-Sheckleyesque aplomb. "Living? Try Death!" by Justin Blake (23) is a black comedy about a genius of generic advertising ("Hungry? Try Food!") who pushes matters too far. According to Miller/Contento, Justin Blake is a pseudonym of John Bowen (b. 1924), novelist and playwright, whose post-apocalyptic *After the Rain* was published by Ballantine in 1959. This story is his only appearance in the SF magazines.

Jonathan Burke's "Peter Preserved" (24) is a *Galaxy*-style fossil about, in effect, the evils of the VCR: a man's parents value their recordings of their now adult child more than the child himself, and don't much mind when they drive him to suicide. Robert Silverberg's "The Man with Talent" (**24**, first published in the Winter 1956 *Future*), a clever if contrived early story, is about an underappreciated poet on Earth who emigrates to a planet wholly owned and occupied by 16 rich families, all of whom prove to dabble in all the arts themselves. The poet's function, it turns out, is to be an audience.

E. C. Tubb has two stories. "Ad Infinitum" in **23** continues this magazine's frequent recursive motif: it's about a writer writing about a writer, and he's having a conversation about it with his wife, whose clothing, hair color, etc., change from paragraph to paragraph. The blurb says that Tubb advised Carnell to read it twice before commenting, and Carnell says that "after the third and fourth reading it begins to take on even deeper aspects of subtlety...." I am taking his word for it, though the story is amusing enough. Tubb's "The Bells of Acheron" (**22**) is a brief pulpy melodrama about a planet whose crystalline growths mimic the voices of deceased loved ones.

Bertram Chandler (still no A here) continues to display his adeptness at pleasant but utterly inconsequential stories with "The Principle" (**22**), a pub conversation story about probability, which subsequently turned up in *Science Fiction Stories* for September 1957. (In fact it appears to have had a sequel there: "'The Principle' Revisited," an article in the May 1960 *Science Fiction Stories*, the last issue.) The other Chandler story is "The Trouble with *Them*" (**24**), which posits that the reason you can't find things, and then they turn up where you've already looked, is that aliens are borrowing them to see if they can reverse engineer them. The protagonist manages to follow his watch through their portal and gets the grand tour.

Worth mentioning for eccentricity, if nothing else, is William F. Temple's "The Green Car" (**23**), which earnestly rings a change on the Weird Menace formula under which seemingly supernatural events always turn out to have a highly contrived but prosaic explanation. A green car comes whizzing down the road, runs over a child, and disappears. A similar-looking man driving a similar green car, which has the same license number, drove off a cliff in the area some years ago. The man in the green car appears again, is chased down. Turns out it's not a ghost driver and car. Beings from beneath the sea have salvaged the car that went off the cliff, put their own propulsion system in it, pressurized it with water, and are running reconnaissance missions, with the driver wearing a mask made to look like the deceased driver-off-the-cliff. The story ends with a solemn hope for peace.

John Wyndham's "Bargain from Brunswick" (**22**) is a lightweight Pied Piper of Hamelin variant recycled from the June 1951 *Fantasy and Science Fiction*. K. E. Smith's "Incident" (**22**), about physically damaged spacemen, adds not much to C.M. Kornbluth's "The Altar at Midnight." John Kippax's "After Eddie" (**23**) is routinely clever and vice versa—but eliciting an Honorable Mention from Judith Merril.

J. G. Ballard returns to *Science Fantasy* in **23** (June 1957) with his fourth published story, "Mobile," which is lightweight but well turned, without the thrown-together-from-mismatched-parts quality of "Prima Belladonna" and "Build-Up" (the latter discussed in the *New Worlds* companion volumes). Carnell has a typically off-the-point blurb: "Back in the early 1930's there was published a fascinating serial entitled 'The Death of Iron,' its title speaking for itself. It is certain that author Ballard has never read that story, yet by a reverse process he has produced as delightful an idea—sentient, growing metal. Written with a freshness and with touches of humour that typify the modern trend of fantasy writing." (Actually, for those who care about such things or are unable to dismiss them from their minds, the proper antecedent for this story is probably A. E. van Vogt's "Juggernaut.")

In "Mobile," the Monuments and Public Works Committee of Murchison Falls (hard by Moose Jaw, I suspect) has commissioned a statue which, when unveiled, fails to capture the townspeople's hearts and minds. It's called "Form and Quantum:

Generative Synthesis 3," and as described, it sounds a lot like something from one of Richard Powers' SF paperback covers. It has "a weird blighted look like a derelict radar antenna." Everybody hates it, so it winds up in the back yard of the protagonist, a member of the Committee, where he discovers it is growing. Where's it getting the mass? The air. A scientist reassures him that this allotropic reaction will shortly stop, and that pieces cut from it will be inert. The next morning it is fifty feet long (having started at twelve feet). They cut it up into scrap metal and have it hauled away. The sculptor, who has disappeared, sues them and wins. On the way out of the courthouse, which is still under construction, the protagonist realizes that the exposed metal is vibrating like the statue. The statue's pieces have been recycled and used in the construction, and the metalwork is already growing.

The story comprises a series of efficient scenes of relatively even (short) length, told in first person, and is advanced in large part through dialogue, chiefly between the protagonist and his wife. Ballard has gotten the knack of domestic back and forth which he didn't quite have in "Escapement" in *New Worlds*. The tone of detached good humor is maintained consistently and the whole thing is commendably economical though not terse. This is a writer who has started to figure out what he is doing.

"Mobile"—retitled "Venus Smiles," for no reason apparent to me—was revised considerably and published in the September 1967 *If*, then in Ballard's collection *Vermilion Sands* (1971). The revisions are entirely surface ones, with the events and much of the dialogue remaining pretty much the same. The main change was making it a Vermilion Sands story rather than a Murchison Falls story, which entails more than just adding references to Vermilion Sands: a certain cultural reorientation is required. Carol, the protagonist's conversational foil, ceases to be his wife and is now his secretary. She lives in his house but has her own bedroom and addresses him as "Mr. Hamilton." I think the point is not that she is sleeping with him, but that in Vermilion Sands no one of substance does anything so boring as be married.

And here's another point of re-orientation: In the first version, the narrator observes ruefully: "What might be perfectly acceptable in Rockefeller Plaza, the Festival of Britain or the Venice Biennale was all too obviously a long way ahead of Murchison Falls." In the revision, he says: "What might be perfectly acceptable at Expo 75 or the Venice Biennale was all too obviously passé at Vermilion Sands."

Ballard also took the opportunity to work in a dose of his preoccupations and characteristic imagery. In the original, the sculptor is one Lubitsch, "a small wiry man of about forty, subdued and distant—subdued, as we now knew, only because he was still recovering from his first traumatic encounter with Neo-Futurism." In the Vermilion Sands version the sculptor has become a woman, Lorraine Drexel: "This elegant and autocratic creature in a cartwheel hat, with her eyes like black orchids, was a sometime model and intimate of Giacometti and John Cage. Wearing a blue crepe de Chine dress ornamented with lace serpents and other art nouveau emblems, she sat before us like some fugitive Salome from the world of Aubrey Beardsley." And later: "A dream-like smile gave her the look of a tamed Mona Lisa."

Ballard has also gussied up his McGuffin, appropriately I suppose, since Vermilion Sands is at least in the near future while Murchison Falls appears to reside in the too, too solid present of 1957. In Vermilion Sands they are not commissioning just a sculpture, but a sonic sculpture. Now it's called "Sound and Quantum: Generative Synthesis 3," and it gives auditory rather than visual offense: "The statue was now giving out an intermittent high-pitched whine, a sitar-like caterwauling that seemed to pull apart the sutures of my skull."[35] This of course

---

35. Ballard may have been inspired in part by his conversation with William Spencer, a friend who wrote several stories for *New Worlds* and who also dabbled in sculpture. He had the idea of incorporating a theremin, an early electronic musical instrument played by moving one's hand or other body part of choice nearer to or further from it, into sculptures, "which would then emit varying sounds as the spectator moved around them. I mentioned

gives Ballard free rein for his favorite pastime of culture-dropping: "Fragments of the *Nutcracker Suite* and Mendelssohn's 'Italian' Symphony sounded from it, overlaid by sudden blaring excerpts from the closing movements of Grieg's Piano Concerto. The selection of these hack classics seemed deliberately designed to get on my nerves."

"Mobile" was one of three stories spread out over a nearly two-year dry spell in Ballard's writing, following Ballard's traumatic encounter with an SF convention, as discussed in the second *New Worlds* volume.

Bottom line: I like the jokes in "Venus Smiles," but I think the more innocent and less cluttered "Mobile" is actually the better story.

---

this project to Jim Ballard and he said that he thought the sculpture should be at least six feet high and of a menacing appearance!" Spencer was not able to reduce this idea to practice for technical reasons, but it appears that his mere description of it may have captured Ballard's imagination. "The Sonic Sculptor: William Spencer Interviewed by David Pringle," *Interzone* 194 (January 1994), p. 44.

9: *SCIENCE FANTASY,* VOLUME 9 (ISSUES 25-27)

Science Fantasy's issues for October 1957 through February 1958 are immediately notable for the departure of Jose Rubios as cover artist and for the advent of Brian Lewis, who did almost all of the next twenty or so covers and then disappeared. He was almost as dominant at *New Worlds*. His initial *New Worlds* covers displayed a sort of cartoony hyper-realism, but those on *Science Fantasy* were blatantly abstract from the beginning. Indeed, the contents page credit for these first two on **26** and **27** say "Symbolic cover painting from...." I suppose this was to ward off puzzled inquiries about precisely what scene was being illustrated. Lewis seems to have gotten the message from Richard Powers without being taken over by it, and the results are pleasantly gaudy. These covers certainly must have grabbed the newsstand browser's eye more effectively than most of their predecessors.[36]

Aside from the change in cover artists, the look and feel of the magazine remain the same. The closest thing to innovation is that in **25** the last story is completed on the inside back cover. In content, these issues, even more than any of the preceding ones, are dominated by a group of regular contributors. Bertram Chandler has four stories, one under the George Whitley pseudonym; John Kippax has three; John Boland, Robert Presslie, and Robert Silverberg each have two. There's one each by

---

36. See these covers at http://www.sfcovers.net/mainnav.htm or http://www.philsp.com/mags/sciencefantasy.html.

Brian Aldiss, John Brunner, and Richard Wilson, who featured prominently in recent issues. Also Edward Mackin and John Rackham, soon to be regulars, make early appearances. Ads are as usual, with *Plus* Books joining the Fantasy Book Centre.

Bi-hemispheric publication continues. Whitley's "The Tie That Binds" (**26**) later appeared in the June 1958 *Fantastic Universe*; Silverberg's "Hidden Talent" (**25**) had earlier appeared in the April 1957 *If*; William Tenn's "Wednesday's Child" (**26**) had been in the January 1956 *Fantastic Universe*; Silverberg's "Valley Beyond Time" (**27**) had appeared in the December 1957 *Science Fiction Adventures*; Aldiss's "Judas Danced" (**27**) appeared about simultaneously in the January 1958 (and only) issue of *Star Science Fiction*, as "Judas Dancing."

§

Overall, the fiction contents of these issues are unimpressive. Kenneth Bulmer's "Reason for Living," the lead novelette in **25**, is a pleasantly hokey but insubstantial story in the *Startling/ Thrilling Wonder* vein. Dick Janvrin periodically finds himself disappearing into a violet haze and appearing in a castle where he has to fight off various lethal perils. This interferes considerably with his daily activities, such as flying a jet aircraft, so the RAF sends him to a psychiatrist, whose daughter's friend turns out to have similar visions. It is revealed that Janvrin is the grandson of the illegitimate child of a member of an older super-race, whose repellent matriarch can't stand the idea that any of their heredity is running around loose. While it's nice to see some actual fantasy in *Science Fantasy*, this one suffers considerably by comparison to the John Brunner stories of the previous couple of years, with their vivid characters and interesting settings. Janvrin is too much the intrepid fighter pilot, the daughter's friend is too sweet and beautiful, etc., etc., to seem anything but competently turned clichés.

Brunner is back in **26** with "Lungfish," an earnestly well-meaning SF story about a semi-generation starship. The trip takes about thirty-six years, so there are "earthborn" and "trip-born" factions, and when they get there the tripborn don't want to land. They're the next evolutionary step—more homage to Lamarck, or maybe epigenetics—and they want to stay in space. Characters and situation are well sketched but the plot becomes turgid and busy at the end. This one later appeared in *Fantastic Universe*, March 1958, and was revised for Brunner's collection *Entry to Elsewhen* (DAW 1972),

The best of this volume's lead stories is probably Silverberg's "Valley Beyond Time" (**27**), reprinted, as noted, from the US *Science Fiction Adventures*, December 1957, and later the title story of a 1973 Silverberg collection from Dell. A man is minding his business in the valley where he's lived all his life, and some strangers come by and point out that he hasn't lived there all his life, he just got there like they did, and he hasn't gotten over the conditioning yet. It turns out something called the Watcher has snatched a small group of humans from their ordinary pursuits around the galaxy and has in effect put them in a very pleasant private zoo. It's told them that if one of them leaves, all of them have to, and most of the plot is driven by that conflict. It's a very smooth piece of adventure fiction, several degrees better developed and characterized than Bulmer's story.

§

Not much stands out in the short fiction. The biggest news is probably the development of a couple of relatively new contributors. Robert Presslie, author of the noisily ineffectual Evils of Dope story "Plague" in the previous volume, returns with "Comeback" (**25**), about a corrupt television producer who decides he will bring back The Great Gustav, a stage magi-cian famous long ago for making young girls disappear and not bringing them back. Now, decades later, he brings them back: "The next thing they saw was a line of nine horrors, nine rotted corpses which had made a comeback from other worlds and other times. And the smell that stank from the sensories was a smell that put Clarion out of business, a smell that put an end to all cheap sensationalism, a smell that ushered in an era of clean, sane entertainment." Well! Come home Savonarola, all is forgiven! Following on the heels of "Plague," this story establishes Presslie as the premier moralist of *Science Fantasy*.

Less risibly, Presslie contributes "Dial O for Operator" to **27**, and that one's pretty good: it's a taut suspense story about a telephone operator who gets an emergency call from a woman who has been trapped in a telephone booth by some sort of menacing creature. He stays on the line with her trying to help her survive while the cops look for her—but the booth's empty, in this continuum anyway. Presslie (b. 1920) published about three dozen stories from 1955 through 1963, without exception in the UK magazines (with one reprint in the US *New Worlds*). Then he had a couple in Carnell's *New Writings in SF* in 1965 and 1966, and that was it for him.

John Kippax's "Solid Beat" (**25**) is another irritatingly jokey and inconsequential story about a jazz bassist from the future who presents the band's drummer with a kit from 2055—a log and a couple of shinbones. Recursiveness surfaces briefly here when the characters refer to Theodore Sturgeon's "The Education of Drusilla Strange." Kippax's "Send Him Victorious" (**26**) is clever and less irritating. An egotistical academic type suddenly finds himself in a parallel world that at first seems to have better recognized his merit than the one he started from. "Me, Myself and I" (**27**), Kippax's first novelette in *Science Fantasy*, is a more piquant kettle of fish. An ineffectual man finds a book called *BE YOURSELF* on the train. It shows him how to visualize his ideal self, who first gives him advice, then offers to substitute for him at crucial moments, and then of course takes over his life. This one is nightmarish rather than jokey as its premise might suggest, the skull beneath the smirk. Judith Merril gave this one an Honorable Mention. But then she gave one to "Solid Beat" too. (And, more understandably, to Presslie's "Dial O for Operator.")

There are several other stories by established authors.

Aldiss's "Judas Danced" (27), one of his better early stories, might be described unfairly as a reprise of Damon Knight's "The Country of the Kind," this time as farce. After that it's downhill. Richard Wilson's recursive "Time Out for Tomorrow" (26) is an amusing story about a time traveler who appears at a meeting of SF writers (this appears to be a Hydra Club story, like Knight's "A Likely Story"). Silverberg's "Hidden Talent," as noted, also appeared in *If*, and I suspect was written with *Astounding* in mind. In the future, the psi-talented will be sent by the Esper Guild to planets where they have to conceal their talents or they will be burned as witches. That's so they will learn self-restraint. Exactly why they have to learn self-restraint is not too clearly explained. A telekineticist spends some unsatisfying weeks as a farmhand trying to suppress his talent, then figures out that he can pretend to be a stage magician and hide his talent in plain sight. This is a pretty well executed story about a completely contrived situation, one that couldn't possibly be of much interest to anyone not already steeped in the genre. It's SF talking to itself.

William Tenn's "Wednesday's Child" (26) is about a woman who seems to have been negligently designed, maybe a prototype for a discontinued model, with a tacked-on horror ending. It is a sequel to Tenn's famous "Child's Play"—whatever happened to the little girl that the protagonist made from the Bild-a-Man Kit? Tenn says of the story, "And it was bounced. My God, how it was bounced!"[37] It is not one of his better stories.

The prolific Bertram Chandler's "Ghost" (26) is above his average—a pleasant story about a time paradox occasioned by a Mannschen Drive malfunction. The other Chandler stories are notable only because two of them feature cannibalism: in "How to Win Friends" (25) the Terran apprentice diplomat serves his wife for dinner, and in "The Converts" (27) a couple of annoying interstellar missionaries wind up as the main course,

---

37. William Tenn, afterword to "Wednesday's Child," in *Immodest Proposals: The Complete Science Fiction of William Tenn, vol. 1* (NESFA Press 2001), p. 287.

with crackling and applesauce. The last, "The Tie That Binds" (**26**) as by George Whitley, is a milestone in Chandler's something-from-next to nothing methodology: the narrator and his wife have an argument about neckties and their iconographic significance in Britain (school, club, regiment); next day he buys an odd necktie, and shortly bumps into one of the extraterrestrials whose spaceship crew is solely entitled to wear that tie. Double-recursively, they recognize the name Whitley as that of an SF writer, and ask if he wrote "Drift"—which in fact was published under Chandler's own name (*Astounding*, June 1957).

John Boland's "The Wire Tappers" (**26**) posits that aliens or somebody jigger the telephone system so the person at the other end hears what you are thinking, not what you are saying, resulting in the collapse of civilization, and a good thing too. This is essentially a reprise of Fredric Brown's "The Waveries." Boland's "Straight from the Horse's Mouth" (**25**) less interestingly recounts the woes of a man who offends a gypsy and is slowly turned into a horse

One notable debut in these issues is "Criffle-Shaped" by Edward Mackin (pseudonym of Ralph McInerny, b. 1929) (**26**), best described as industrial slapstick, the first appearance in *Science Fantasy* of his series character Hek Belov. Mackin had a few stories in *Authentic Science Fiction* before it folded, and then became a regular in the Nova magazines, publishing a dozen more Belov stories and a few others; after their demise his career was over with a few minor exceptions. Another debut is John Rackham's "Drog" (**27**), a three wishes story that doesn't redeem its formula. This is Rackham's first story in the SF magazines; he became a mainstay of the Nova magazines for the rest of their existence, a pillar of *Analog* for some years under his real name John T. Phillifent (1916-76), and a prolific producer of Ace Doubles and other original paperbacks under both names.

John Brody, previously known for some pretty bad stories in the early *New Worlds*, reappears with "Bored to Death" (**25**), a heavy-handed story about a too-safe future in which gladiators entertain the public by manipulating robots, and one gladiator challenges his rival to a real fight. The remaining loose end is "Headnoises" (**27**) by Leonard Hildebrand (no other SF magazine credits), which reads like fanzine fiction.

10: *SCIENCE FANTASY*, VOLUME 10 (ISSUES 28-30)

Science Fantasy volume 10 (April, June, and August 1958) is fronted by three Brian Lewis covers, clearly influenced by Richard Powers but less ethereal. One of them (**29**) is particularly striking; I think it's appeared in more than one SF art or history volume, and a more modern version by Anders Sandberg features on the cover of Broderick's anthology *Earth Is But a Star*.[38] It's also the only one that purports to illustrate anything. The band at the top of the cover disappears with **29**, considerably improving the magazine's looks. The band at the bottom now lists the lead story, compared with earlier issues where it often listed several authors' names.

The prior outside advertisers are gone, but now there are ads for the UK SF Book Club, the Blue Centaur Book Company in Sydney ("A Science Fiction Service on Your Own Continent"), plus an inside front cover ad in **30** for Planned Families Publications ("Worries and upsets between husbands and wives are so frequently caused because they lack knowledge of modern family planning... Please send me, under PLAIN COVER, a free copy of 'Planned Families.' I am an adult.")

§

---

38.   http://www.amazon.com/Earth-but-Star-Excursions-Through/dp/1876268549 (visited 10/19/11). See all these covers at http://www.philsp.com/mags/sciencefantasy.html or http://www.sfcovers.net/mainnav.htm.

The lead stories in **28** and **29** are labeled "Short Novel" rather than the usual "Novelette" and are considerably longer than those in earlier issues (57 and 79 pages respectively). Non-fiction is back, of a sort: Brian Aldiss has two "articles," "The Carp That Once" in **28** and "Smile, Please!" in **30**. These issues are much more British than their predecessors. Only two of the stories were also published in the US, and both are acknowledged as reprints: Lester del Rey's "Little Jimmy" (**30**), from *Fantasy & Science Fiction* in 1957, and Harry Harrison and Katherine MacLean's "Web of the Norns," which Carnell says is "considerably revised and shortened" from its first appearance (in *Fantasy Magazine* in 1953, titled "Web of the Worlds").

The good news is that these issues are much more *Science Fantasy*-ish than a lot of their immediate predecessors. That is, the stories (mainly the lead stories) have more of the off-trail and idiosyncratic character that the magazine is known for.

In "Web of the Norns," the "short novel" in **28**, the title is meant literally. The Norns are sitting around bickering as they work, and one of them accidentally dislodges a thread from its proper place. Once past that prologue, the plot is essentially a misogynist retelling of a Charles Atlas ad. (But don't let that put you off.)

A maternally over-protected young man is about to get married. He steps out momentarily because he is starting to have one of his spells of immobility and unconsciousness, and finds himself in the midst of a murderous brawl in a primitive inn, which he escapes after helping the mighty-thewed barbarian who was about to be mobbed and killed. He survives in the snow-covered wilderness by making himself useful fetching and carrying for the M.T.B., a mercenary heading off to the nearest war. Becoming stronger and more self-reliant by necessity, he begins to realize how over-protected and manipulated he has been.

In the middle of the war, involving the Independent Free State of the Tyrant Helbida, the negligent Norn corrects her mistake and our protagonist finds himself back outside the church, minus his recently developed muscles but retaining his new, manly personality. He tells off his mother and fiancée and declares himself in control of his life. There's not a lot to this substantively, but it's pretty entertaining, capably and wittily written and well visualized. I wonder if the psychologizing here—and/or the misogyny—is owed to Dianetics (with which MacLean was involved): "Why had he ever believed he was an invalid? Because his mother had told him, and because he had those fits of immobility." As far as I can tell this story has never been reprinted since its two magazine appearances.

Issue **29** features John Brunner's "Earth Is but a Star," which I believe is the longest piece of fiction yet to appear in the magazine, and also one of the best-executed, even if it is teeth-grindingly twee in places. It's a decadent-far-future epic that obviously owes a lot to Jack Vance's *The Dying Earth*. In fact, it starts more or less where *The Dying Earth* leaves off, in that the protagonist tries to answer that book's final question "What shall we do....?" He's discovered that a small star is heading Earth's way and will arrive to destroy the Earth in about 300 years. But his society is dominated by Historians, people who almost literally live in the past, and he can't get anybody's attention. So he sets out—to find a fellow mourner!

This comes easy, and of course she's a babe, though in most respects the story is ostentatiously sexless. Their mission is quickly transmuted from mourning to stopping the star. Their quest is mainly a travelogue through a very old and transformed world. Brunner displays a nice talent for matter-of-fact strangeness: "A solitary tavern grew from the beach." "...in the distance, over the calling and the music of the city going about its affairs, he could faintly discern the insane laughter of the next day's meat as it assembled on the gentle slopes of the hills inland prior to descending to the shore and dying there." (That dates it: by, say, 1970, any effete far future would of course have been vegetarian.)

As quest stories go, this one covers a lot of territory but remains unusually laid-back, which is just as well, since it makes less jarring the revelation at the end that there never was a problem and the star has always been under control; it's piloted by returning space travelers from an earlier and more vigorous civilization. Had Brunner seriously jacked up the tension along the way, this would have been a severe letdown, but given the story's dreamy and lackadaisical manner, it's a fairly soft landing. This became *The 100th Millennium*, half of an Ace double and one of Brunner's first US books, a year or so later, and then in 1968 *Catch a Falling Star*, with a significant degree of revision, especially to correct some earlier reflex misogyny.

The lead story in **30** is John Kippax's "Destiny Incorporated," never reprinted, and a nice try. It's another "what's-real" story, like Peter Hawkins' "The Daymakers" of a few issues back. Matsumura Tomokatsu works in a private laboratory. His employer is visited by menacing characters from a large corporation. Carrying a locked briefcase, he is dispatched by his employer on vacation. A little girl runs out into his path and he swerves into a boulder, waking up in a hospital and being told that he ran her over. At that point things get bizarre.

Shirley, a Japanese-American nurse, is on the night shift but nobody else seems to know about her. Out the window at night, he sees...nothing...and during the day he notices that cars on the visible roads drive off towards the horizon, and just disappear. Cars coming toward town pop into existence. When he tries to leave, he finds himself driving back into town, finds Shirley by the roadside with a suitcase, picks her up, heads out again and the little girl runs in front of his car again.

Eventually, explanation time: he's in the clutches of the Predestinators, who manage the lives of various species around the universe, but they've never encountered anything like the denizens of Sol III, who are destined to go to the stars. Matty's employer had developed a mind control technique, which Matty knows about because he opened up the briefcase, but he has no dreams of power and is prepared to renounce it and go back to his previous life-line, where he loses his memory but is rewarded with Shirley, and humanity won't be diverted from its destiny. This really doesn't explain everything, and the great revelation is annoyingly telegraphed by excerpts from the subsequent addresses of the Chief Predestinator at the beginnings of chapters. But the bizarre events of the plot are crisply and effectively told, and overall it's quite a readable story by a writer who is suddenly getting better after a series of jokily inconsequential ones. There's an interesting sub-agenda, American prejudice against Japanese-Americans, but Kippax doesn't press the point—the romantic interest he provides his protagonist is of the same ethnicity. This story has apparently never been reprinted.

§

The short fiction is the usual very mixed bag, with the by-now-venerable E. C. Tubb coming off best with a couple of well-turned sardonic fantasies. In "Return Visit" (**28**) he actually restores some semblance of life to the deal-with-the-devil plot, positing that over time, human society has progressed faster than demonkind, so they're pretty backward by now and don't really have that much to offer. Tubb's protagonist teaches his demon to smoke cigarettes and drink whiskey before coming to his inevitable bad end. In "Fresh Guy" (**29**), which Judith Merril picked up for her annual Best anthology, the ghoul, the vampire, and the werewolf are hanging around waiting for the survivors of a nuclear war to emerge from underground, when a recently minted vampire wakes up from suspended animation and starts making plans for his future.

Brian Aldiss's "Blighted Profile" (**29**) is another of his better early stories, involving a benignly deluded old man who is victimized by one of SF's legion of innocent child monsters. This cruel plot is laid out against a sort of pastel pastoral post-nuclear-war future, the whole punctuated with sharp and self-consciously arty observations that nonetheless work pretty well ("Age had her in its web. Only her eyes were not grey.") It's a nice mix of contrasting elements, almost more like a painting than a story. It is interesting to find it in the same issue as "Earth Is But a Star," and Carnell comments: "Both have caught the atmosphere of the far future in such a manner that the setting is believable if alien to our present-day senses." Well, not really believable, but both pretty good performances, if turned to very different ends.

Del Rey's "Little Jimmy" (**30**) is an intelligent and effective semi-ghost story, a notch above this journeyman's usual product. "Life Size" by Julian Frey—Hynam/Kippax—(**30**) posits that your television, refrigerator, etc., are really operated by very small people incarcerated inside them. The protagonist learns too much and is shrunk to join their numbers. This one gets by on sheer audacity.

From there we proceed to the lame, the halt, and the misconceived. "An Affair of Gravity" by Edward Mackin (**28**) is another ponderously jokey story about Hek Belov, the conceited, impecunious and fraudulent cybernetics bum; it features an antigravity machine. Kenneth Bulmer's "Out of Control" (also **28**) proposes that in the future, when some people have mastered levitation, they will be employed as taxi operators, carrying people from place to place in harnesses, and in this instance, acting out a very tired suspense/gangster plot against the backdrop of what is probably the least adventurous psi premise ever aired.

Robert Presslie's "The Champ" (**29**) flails around about boxers who have the styles of the great pugilists of the past impressed into their brains and select one (or several, seriatim) in the ring. The narrator is a promoter whose boxer gets stomped by an android, and is revealed at the end to be his son, now brain-addled. Jonathan Burke's "New Folks at Home" (**30**) starts promisingly—most of humanity has teleported itself to another planet, leaving the elderly behind, and the kids can only visit them by astral projection, and they're losing interest—but it turns out Earth is being taken over by sinister mutants who Cloud Men's Minds.

New writer Clifford C. Reed—another British magazines-only writer, seventeen or so stories, whose career did not survive Carnell's departure—has two stories. "What Happened to Lodwick" (**29**) is a thoroughly dull story about an Australian farmer who discovers a talking sheep and eventually kills it because it's unnatural. "A Sense of Proportion" (**30**) is more interesting, but for unfortunate reasons. Mysterious men come to a new advertising agency because they want to sell a pill that makes people feel good but isn't addictive. For no discernible reason, the protagonist speaks in what the author seems to think is a translation from stage Yiddish or something: "Like duck's water off my back such claims you make," etc.

Brian Aldiss's "articles" are pretty inconsequential too. "The Carp That Once" (**28**) is described by Carnell as "a brief piece of nonsense"; just so. "Smile, Please!" (**30**) is about sorting out his photographs to put in a scrapbook, with a couple of sharp observations about old photographs, e.g.: "What frightens me is the firing squad mentality they all suffered from in those days. Every man Jack and Jill of them confronts the lens like a hero, rigid at attention, lined up in chronological order. Profiles were not invented then....") They read like items dashed off in an hour in Carnell's office, either because Carnell was short on copy or Aldiss was short on the rent. There weren't any more of these in later issues.

Additionally: R. Whitfield Young's "The Locusts" (**28**), a creaky alien invasion story with an irrelevant adultery plot taped in; Francis G. Rayer's "Wishing Stone" (**30**), an equally creaky story about an alien wish-fulfillment device that falls into the hands of a miserable human child; Max Shrimpton's silly "Thermometer" (**30**); and John W. Ashton's innocuous "A Small House" (**30**), about a couple who have a view of Paradise out one of their windows but never manage to do anything about it.

11: *SCIENCE FANTASY,*
VOLUME 11 (ISSUES 31-33)

Science Fantasy volume 11, issues for October 1958-February 1959, is again fronted by three Brian Lewis covers, these displaying a variety of styles. Only one (**33**) is reminiscent of Powers this time, and that one is to my eye almost equally reminiscent of Frank Kelly Freas—an unusual combination. The cover of **32** is a disappointingly cartoony dragon-slaying scene, but **31** (illustrating Sturgeon's short story "The Graveyard Reader") is striking. The cover of **33** initiates the vertical strip with contents list on the right side of the cover, which remained the layout until October 1962.[39]

Otherwise, the magazine continues as before, with such minor innovations as an ad for the British Science Fiction Association in **33**, and an article (a real one, not the tossed-off japes by Brian Aldiss in the previous volume), "Utopias—A Few Years Later," by Eugene Lees, the object of gender confusion discussed in Chapter 3. There is more transAtlantic traffic in this volume than the last, with some seven of the stories also having US publication: Sturgeon's "The Graveyard Reader" (**31**), reprinted from the Groff Conklin anthology of the same name; Lester del Rey's "No Strings Attached" (**31**), from *If,* June 1954; Harry Harrison's "Arm of the Law" (**31**), which appeared about the same time in the August 1958 *Fantastic Universe*; John Brunner's "City of the Tiger" (**32**), later incorporated

---

39. See these covers at http://www.sfcovers.net/mainnav.htm or http://www.philsp.com/mags/sciencefantasy.html.

into *Telepathist* a.k.a. *The Whole Man*, and also published in *Fantastic Universe*, November 1959; Robert Silverberg's "The Man Who Never Forgot" (**32**) from *Fantasy & Science Fiction*, February 1958; and Richard Wilson's "Super City," the "short novel" in **33**, which was serialized in *Infinity*, January and March 1958, as "And Then the Town Took Off," and became half an Ace Double under that title.

§

The lead stories in this volume are all labeled "short novels" (ranging from 43 to 78 pages). "Super City" is the least of them, a limp and dispirited farce about a small town full of colorful characters that suddenly sails off into the air, taking with it a train containing a government messenger who learns that the briefcase chained to his wrist contains a secret high-tech communication device—sort of like a cellphone—that permits him to take orders from Washington. He eventually negotiates with the kangaroo-like aliens behind the levitation and gets the girl too.

Kenneth Bulmer's "The Bones of Shosun" is considerably livelier, even though it was nudged off the cover of **31** by Sturgeon's "The Graveyard Reader." It's a marked improvement over his previous long story, "Reason for Living" in **25**. It gives the strong impression that Bulmer has been going to school on John Brunner, which is not a bad idea, since Brunner at this point is the magazine's most reliable frequent contributor.

Justin is precipitated arbitrarily by a nuclear plant accident into a parallel world in which the "literati" lord it over the "sublits" and magic works, though it is couched in familiar technical terms (e.g., scrying is done through a "television set," which the mage contrives from running water). Justin immediately runs afoul of the law, is haled before a corrupt and arbitrary court, and sentenced to the most horrid punishment of all, the cybmatte. What's that? First, it's a regime of manual labor. But when Justin reveals that he can read, he's led into a big gloomy room to...a cubicle with a computer in it. Well, not quite the Dilbert scenario. Computational problems are set for the workers, who are provided slate and chalk and must solve them and think the answers into the screen in front of them.

Justin meets the obligatory babe and they make the obligatory escape involving the obligatory disguises, swordfights, etc., and the obligatory chase, which fetches up in this world's equivalent of the nuclear power plant, where power is converted to usable magical form by the equivalent of galley slaves. Justin has picked up enough magic himself to get them all (himself, girlfriend and a couple of other companions) back to our world in the nick of time.

Bulmer clearly expended a lot of hard work and cleverness on this story, but it falls short in major respects in the impossible-to-avoid comparison with Brunner. It's generally less subtle and more caricaturish, the physical settings less vividly conveyed, the secondary characters relatively flat. (One of the pleasures of the Brunner stories is the sharp and resourceful women in them. Obligatory they may be, but they're more than placeholders, unlike Bulmer's female lead.) Bulmer started publishing a year or so later than Brunner, but I suspect the difference is not in experience as a writer but in experience as a person; Brunner just seems to have got around more, to have been a more sophisticated individual and a closer observer of people and things around him than Bulmer.

And here is the man himself in **32** with "City of the Tiger," later in *Fantastic Universe*, November 1959. Brunner's protagonist, Hao Sen, comes to consciousness on camel-back heading into Tiger City, which seems to be located in a sort of magical Mongolia, on an unspecified errand. Brunner lays the barbaric splendor on pretty thick. They head for the Tavern of the Silver Fountain, on the Street of a Thousand Felicities, but to get there you have to take the Street of Many Kites. Et smoldering joss-stick cetera.

Hints begin to be dropped; Hao Sen is trying to figure out who is really the most important person in Tiger City. After various diversions including a dragon-slaying, lamely illustrated on Lewis's ill-advised cover, he fingers the magician Chu Lao, whom he defeats in a duel of magic...."and then," two pages from the end, "he was Gerald Howson, Psi.D, curative telepathist first class, World Health Organisation." This whole megillah is revealed as the fantasy of another telepath who has recruited some patsies and kidnapped them into his fugue state, and Howson has gone in to rescue them in the time-honored "Dreams Are Sacred" fashion.

"City of the Tiger" is followed in **34**, in the next volume, by "The Whole Man" (a.k.a. "Curative Telepath" in *Fantastic Universe*, December 1959), in which Howson is sent off on vacation and goes back to the slum from which he was rescued years previously, irrevocably stunted and crippled by the same brain hiccup that gave rise to his talent. He looks up past acquaintances and his mother and then falls in with a Bohemian crowd and rescues its most talented member from his philosophical/artistic/suicidal difficulties. The artist offers him a sort of temporary partial mind transplant that will permit his physical disabilities to be corrected, at the cost of the artist's staying flat on his back in hospital for as long as it takes. This offer, Brunner says in a brief bathetic crescendo that I think is designed (consciously or not) to echo the end of Sturgeon's *More Than Human*, renders Howson a "whole man."

All this is familiar to anyone who has read the subsequent massively modified fix-up novel published five years later, one of the books that put Brunner on the map as something more (or at least different) than a post-pulp adventure-wallah. The differences between magazine and book versions are significant. The entire 40-plus pages of "City of the Tiger" are shrunk to 14 pages in the book, and they appear almost two-thirds of the way through it. There's no rug-pulling surprise at the end of the section. What's happening has all been laid out in advance. The whole backstory of Howson's personal history, hinted at in the novellas, is spelled out in detail, and the Tiger City episode is only one of several such therapeutic ventures along the way.

By contrast, the material of "The Whole Man" appears more or less intact in the latter third of the book, albeit rewritten and expanded. In the two novellas, we see sequentially Brunner the unreconstructed pulpster and Brunner the earnest, well-meaning, and (let's face it) sometimes fairly boring writer he turned into, and in the book version Brunner leaves no doubt that it's the sober and statesmanly hat that he wants to wear. I should add that this is a late-formed perception. Back in 1964 *The Whole Man* seemed to me a commendable step toward SF's manifest destiny of becoming accepted as the Literature of the Future. (It was a Hugo nominee that year.) But I'm younger than that now.

§

The outstanding piece of short fiction in this volume is Sturgeon's reprinted "The Graveyard Reader" (**31**), about—what else?—a man who reads graves and teaches the protagonist, whose wife has run away and been killed in an automobile accident in the company of another man, to do the same. It's not one of his better-known stories, but it holds up very well on rereading, even in the company of the other stories he was writing during this period, the peak of his career. It's one of those unfortunately few occasions when Sturgeon managed to keep his mannerisms and sentimentality in check, with the usual fine result.

Its nearest competition is Brian Aldiss's "Intangibles, Inc." (**33**), a sort of agreeable shaggy fairy tale about a mysterious traveling salesman who peddles intangibles and who manipulates the rather dim protagonist into betting him that he won't move the salt and pepper shakers for the rest of his life. Aldiss liked it well enough to make it the title story of one of his collections and anthologize it in *Best Fantasy Stories* (Faber & Faber, 1962).

Robert Silverberg's "The Man Who Never Forgot" (**32**), from *Fantasy & Science Fiction*, February 1958, is about a perfect mnemonist whose talent has ruined his life, making it impossible for him to have any close relationships or even to stay in the same place for any significant period. He gets beaten up and winds up in a hospital in a small town close to where he grew up. When his mother finds out and comes to visit him, she lets slip that his grandfather had the talent also. He realizes he doesn't hate his mother any more. He's grown into his talent. And the notion that he might pass it on to children puts a whole new slant on things. As the story ends he is, as it were, taking a turn for the nurse. This is a pretty good early Silverberg story, rendered considerably more interesting by the fact that it's shaped a lot like the later *Dying Inside*, and perhaps also because it draws on his own remarkable powers of near-eidetic recall.[40] Silverberg himself later wrote: "Glancing through it now, I'm startled to see how strongly it foreshadows a much better known work of mine that deals with the hidden drawbacks of superior mental powers—the novel *Dying Inside*, which I would write fifteen years later."[41]

The other stories by name writers are pretty silly. Del Rey's "No Strings Attached" (**31**) is a gimmicky deal-with-the-devil (actually a demon). Harry Harrison's "Arm of the Law" (**31**) is about a robot cop delivered to the corrupt and inept police department of Nineport, Mars. The robot cleans things up right away, sort of Susan Calvin meets the Mayberry police force. Bertram Chandler's "The Underside" (**32**) is a jokey time travel story. E. C. Tubb's "Beware" (**32**) is a variation on the mysterious shop that appears and disappears: this one sells dreams, and of course the protagonist chooses the wrong one and is ruined, all told in windy stage-Irish.

The magazine's newer regular contributors are there in force, though it's not particularly well directed. Most notable is Edward Mackin's "Chaotics" (**32**), another story about the

40. In the header to the story in *F&SF* (February, 1958), the editor mentions that "Bob Silverberg has an almost freakishly retentive memory..."

41. *The Collected Stories of Robert Silverberg, vol. 1: To Be Continued* (Subterranean Press 2006), p. 275.

insufferable Hek Belov the repairer of computers—and this one is actually amusing, with Belov shanghaied to the Moon and jailed by story's end.

Wild-swinging Robert Presslie is back with one of his more florid productions, "Ladies' Man" (**32**), involving a conceited android genius who is also irresistible to women, his human secretary who is in love with him, two women who are or seem to be representatives of rival planets fighting over natural resources, and a ridiculously labyrinthine plot. It's impossible to tell whether he's serious or it's a parody.

Clifford C. Reed has stories in all three issues, of which the best is "The Misfit" (**31**) about Hell as a bureaucracy and a demon who doesn't seem to have much future with the company. "Who Steals My Purse" (**32**) is a jokey story about a nebbish who invents a matter transmitter and uses it to outwit the people who are trying to cheat him; it's chiefly a story about lack of imagination and narrow horizons, with a nicely drawn petty villain. "The Sweet Smell of Success" (**33**) is a labored story about an obnoxious journalist investigating a street peddler who he thinks is selling dope but who is actually selling success—just open the lid and take a whiff. This story is mainly notable for one of Carnell's most unintelligible blurbs: "The following story is of the abstract type Mr. Reed is beginning to develop so well. It isn't so much his fantasy atmosphere which stimulates the interest as much as the effects such an atmosphere have upon the human characters involved." Carnell sometimes seemed to be writing in some private language.

John Kippax contributes "Call of the Wild" (**33**), about a man beset by possibly delusional communications from insects (like Philip K. Dick's "Expendable") with a gimmicky ending (to the story, not the character). And here's Arthur Sellings, a *New Worlds* regular making his first of two appearances in *Science Fantasy* with "Limits" (**32**), a polite and well-written fantasy about an old theater that helps out actors by making their performances and their settings seem completely real—but this is not in fact a favor to them.

Finally, there is Eugene Lees' readable if glib article "Utopias—a Few Years Later" (**33**), which is actually about "gloomy utopias" and proposes that their success is proportional to their inaccuracy, i.e., the extent to which they have diverted history away from their vision. He discusses *Fahrenheit 451*, which he thinks had a role in the demise of McCarthyism; *1984*; and *Brave New World*. He describes Forster's "The Machine Stops" as "the least known, least influential, the most frightening, and, in some ways, the most ruthlessly logical" of the books he discusses. It reminds him of the air-conditioned apartment in which he used to live.

12: *SCIENCE FANTASY*, VOLUME 12 (ISSUES 34-36)

Science Fantasy volume 12, for April, June, and August 1959, maintains the newly established look, with the cover picture restricted to the left two-thirds and the contents listed on the right third. This layout works very well with Brian Lewis's colorful and well composed covers. He doesn't need more space. Lewis has hit his stride now, with three striking and confidently done covers in three different styles in this volume. At this point *Science Fantasy* is about as good-looking a magazine as you'll find among the SF digests of its time. Look at these issues and draw your own conclusion.[42]

The fiction contents continue the trend towards longer and fewer stories, with all the lead stories being "short novels" of 60 pages or more. There are five stories in **34**, four in **35**, and three in **36**. That's partly because the page count decreases from 128 to 114 with **36**, and stays there until the very last digest-sized issue, **64**, when it goes back up to 124. (Strictly speaking, it stays at 112 during the interim, since in **37** the front cover ceases to be part of the page count.) There is also more nonfiction. Each of these issues contains an article, and **35** has a real innovation for the Carnell *Science Fantasy*—an editorial, only the second, and the first statement we've seen about what Carnell thinks he

---

42. See these covers at http://www.sfcovers.net/mainnav.htm or http://www.philsp.com/mags/sciencefantasy.html.

is about in this magazine. There is more below on that. There are only two reprints from US sources in this volume: Arthur C. Clarke's "The Songs of Distant Earth" (from *If*, June 1958) and Fritz Leiber's "Space-Time for Springers" (from *Star Science Fiction Stories 4*, Ballantine, 1958). Advertising content is generally the same as other recent issues.

§

The short novel in **34** is Brunner's "The Whole Man," discussed in the previous chapter along with its predecessor "City of the Tiger" in **32**. Next up, in **35**, is the frequently irritating J. T. McIntosh, whose "200 Years to Christmas" (which later became half of an Ace Double, under the same title) is, to my taste, typically bland and implausible.

Two centuries along in a 400-year generation-starship voyage, a social cycle has been established: the Militarist Age is followed by the Freedom Phase, the Golden Age of Art, the Dark Age, Know-More, the Gay Phase, and Revival. The story starts at a pretty wild party, by the standards of 1959. But the Gay Phase is about over, and we see Revival start, first as a voluntary movement, then as a compulsory Puritan social order, which lasts until a couple of people are sentenced to death for fornication. Everybody's had enough, and Revival falls apart in the face of a rather mild rebellion. This all takes about four years, as I read the story's chronology. That seems to be part of the point. McIntosh declares at the end that the ship-dwellers "were compressing five thousand years of change into four hundred years. They couldn't help it."

And why are they doing this? "There could be no end to the swinging of the pendulum." This of course explains nothing and to my mind is even more ridiculous than Asimov's Psychohistory. The pleasing but rather cryptic cover by Lewis, which illustrates the story, is cryptic because, in addition to several severe faces and a dejected-looking male figure against a backdrop of stars, it bears the legend "J.C." and below it,

"Chronicles." This is not an anachronistic reference to Jerry Cornelius or You-Know-Who, but is completely uninterpretable without reading the story—an odd sort of thing for a cover. But it looks good.[43] (J. C. turns out to stand for Judgment Council, and Chronicles are a record kept by the ship's official historian.)

Things improve considerably in **36** with Brunner's "Echo in the Skull," a well turned piece of gritty post-pulpery which also quickly showed up in an Ace Double under the same title. It remains enjoyable. Some years later Brunner revised it and published the new version as *Give Warning to the World*.

Sally Ercott has fallen into a life of poverty and alcoholism in a cheap rooming house, seemingly mentally ill. She can't remember her earlier life and is tormented by bizarre visions. Nick Jenkins, self-employed inventor, runs into her (literally, in his car) and takes her for a meal, a bath, and new clothes. Clyde West, a West Indian denizen of the rooming house, discovers her sleazy landlord and landlady are following her and over-hears a disturbing remark about making her find another body. Sally is kidnapped back to the rooming house, Nick is brought back there at gunpoint, Clyde West intervenes.

The landlord/lady are not just sleazy, they are possessed by a Yem, a nasty sentient alien parasite bent on conquest whose main body is in the basement and is not too far from sporu-lating and enslaving us all. Sally's seemingly psychotic visions are (extra)species memories of other worlds transmitted by earlier victims of the Yem and triggered by her having come near the Yem on her way to the railroad station. So they...call the police! Ordinary folks are always saving the world in SF, but it's a refreshing change to see them do it in a run-down slum rooming house with the assistance of the cops from the local precinct. Brunner's talent for physical detail and setting, and for sketching appealing characters with economy, brings this unpretentious entertainment to much more life than you'd

---

43. Broderick adamantly disagrees about this one, which he regards as a deplorable mess: http://www.philsp.com/data/images/s/science_fantasy_195906.jpg (visited 10/19/11).

expect. This is one of Brunner's enduring skills.

One odd thing about this story is its indigestible first line: "By-products of the solar phoenix reaction, deprived of the majority of their ultraviolet components by the ozone layer in the upper atmosphere, punched yellow through the gaps at the edge of the curtain." Brunner justifies it on the next page—Sally was reading a science fiction magazine the previous night—but still.

§

The best of the short fiction is the reprints, Clarke's pleasantly sentimental "The Songs of Distant Earth" and Fritz Leiber's now very familiar cat epic "Space-Time for Springers" (a bit cloying, but it's *good* cloy) (both **35**). The rest are at best clever but slight. John Rackham's "Nulook" (**34**) posits a predecessor of Ubik, which returns things to a prior state—nonexistence if applicable. It's all in the titration. Chandler a.k.a. Whitley contributes "Can Do" (**34**) in which a djinn appears from a can of off-brand sardines, but the narrator's wife sets it free with a trivial wish, and that's why they are having off-brand sardines at every meal now. Surely there might be *another* djinn...

Arthur Sellings' "The Long Eureka" (**36**) is a reasonably amusing satire about a man who invents an immortality treatment in 1820 and is still trying to get someone to pay attention in the 2300s; unfortunately Sellings dissipates the story's bite with a trick ending (man catches a starship, hopes any aliens they meet will listen, but they turn out already to be immortal). E. C. Tubb's "Somebody Wants You" (**36**) is about a man so useless that he can't even sell his organs for transplantation. An extraterrestrial takes him home and gives him a job...catching rats. Edward Mackin has another contrived and formulaically silly Hek Belov story, "The Diagnoser" (**34**).

John Kippax's "The Lady Was Jazz" (**34**) is about a musician to whom appears one Lee Cayou, who identifies herself as the spirit of Jazz, and she don't need no badge because she talks like this: "Sounds like the boiler's puffing tonight." "Those cats of yours know what it's all about, but it's you I want to talk to." Kingsley Amis, ace jazz fan, would approve. It's all moldy fig, no sour Miles Davis or Ornette Coleman spoken here. She teaches him a lot, then he rejects it and finds his own voice, and she moves on to the next dude, er, cat. This is the cover story in **34**, and the cover looks pretty good especially if you don't look too closely.[44]

A special word is due the two Brian Aldiss contributions to these issues. In **35** "Fortune's Fool" is blurbed as a "lightly whimsical Aldiss piece—we nearly said 'of nonsense'—," and that's about right: it's apparently never been reprinted. In **34** there is the peculiar "Are You an Android?", which is also peculiarly left off the cover (at this point the entire contents are generally listed on the right-hand sidebar). What's peculiar is that, without reference, the story recapitulates Philip K. Dick's "Impostor" in a sort of first-as-tragedy-then-as-farce sort of way. The first-person narrator, named Aldiss, starts out by bemoaning the prospect of robots and androids, and specifically: "And tucked below the solar plexus...a bomb triggered to explode at a fatal key phrase, perhaps?" Aldiss becomes concerned that his wife is an android and contrives a series of daft tests of the matter, such as concealing a scale inside the front door (in case she really weighs a couple of tons) and dropping itching powder down her back (to see if she reacts organically). None are revelatory. Finally, he persuades her to recite "I am a robot," and she springs apart. Then he calls Scotland Yard, which is unsympathetic and suggestive, and:

"'You mean,' he says in puzzlement, 'you mean I—am—a—' Aldiss springs apart."

Neither of these stories has been reprinted, for good reason I'd say.

§
_____

44. And here Broderick agrees: http://www.philsp.com/data/images/s/science_fantasy_195904.jpg (visited 10/19/11).

As noted, **35** contains an innovation for the Carnell *Science Fantasy*: an editorial. For a bit over five years, he writes, he's felt that the magazine without an editorial is like a train keeping a schedule; you don't see the driver. Why he's felt this for five-plus years in a ten-year-old magazine without doing anything about it before is not explained. He says that he has never been able to define accurately the kind of material the magazine will publish. You'd think a magazine devoted to fantasy could flourish, but no: since the heyday of *Unknown* and *Weird Tales*, the American magazines calling themselves *Fantas** are now devoted mostly to science fiction. He expects *Science Fantasy* to "lean" more towards science fiction in the near future (witness the Clarke and McIntosh stories in this issue). Note that all this is said about five months before the November 1959 issue of *Fantastic*, an all-Fritz Leiber issue featuring "Lean Times in Lankhmar," arguably the beginning of the renascence of fantasy in American magazines, and a year before the first appearance of Thomas Burnett Swann and two years before the first of Michael Moorcock's Elric stories in *Science Fantasy*.

He claims *Science Fantasy* has achieved a high literary standard, higher than *New Worlds*, and the evidence he cites is anthologization and Honorable Mentions by Judith Merril. Finally, he announces a series of articles on fantasy writers by Sam Moskowitz—generally, it appears, the same ones that were running in *Satellite* in the US, moved to *Amazing* when *Satellite* folded, and eventually were collected in 1963 in Moskowitz's *Explorers of the Infinite*. These had actually started in **34**, the first one being about Mary Shelley but titled "The Sons of Frankenstein." By **36** the packaging is settled, and it's "Studies in Science Fiction 2. Arthur Conan Doyle."

There's also an article in **35** titled "Atlantis—a New Theory," by Arthur R. Weir, D.Sc., a well-known UK fan at the time, which proposes that everybody's been looking in the wrong place, and the Pillars of Hercules referred to by Plato are not the Straits of Gibraltar but the Straits of Messina. Whatever you say, Doctor.

13: *SCIENCE FANTASY*, VOLUME 13 (ISSUES 37-39)

Science Fantasy volume 13 continues as before, except that **37** is dated November 1959 rather than the expected October, likely because of the printers' strike that interrupted *New Worlds*' schedule that year. But the bi-monthly dating is back with **38**, dated December, and **39**, February 1960. Overall presentation is mostly unchanged, with pleasant if undistinguished Brian Lewis covers on **37** and **38**. **39** introduces a new cover artist, the appropriately named Jarr.[45] This cover is an annoying piece of whimsy titled "Alien on the Big Dipper," portraying a cartoony violet-skinned being on a roller coaster holding a hideous combination clock and vase with flowers, with stereotypical human couple in the front seat. I loathed this cover some 40 years ago, and time has only slightly mitigated my distaste. Jarr did only one other cover for *Science Fantasy* and a few more for *New Worlds* and *Science Fiction Adventures* before disappearing. The rest are perfectly acceptable, nothing like this.[46]

The trend towards longer and fewer stories is slowed. Only one of the issues has a "short novel" (Kenneth Bulmer's "Castle of Vengeance" in **37**), while the others each have two novelettes, along with two or three short stories, plus an installment of Moskowitz's "Studies in Science Fiction." These cover Wells, Poe, and Cyrano de Bergerac respectively. All of them had

45. See Chapter 8, n.32, concerning the mystery of Jarr's identity.

46. See these covers at http://www.sfcovers.net/mainnav.htm or http://www.philsp.com/mags/sciencefantasy.html.

appeared in *Satellite* a year or so before showing up here. The other American item is Silverberg's "Warm Man" (**38**), from *Fantasy & Science Fiction* for May 1957. Everything else is new and British. Despite Carnell's editorial warning of a few issues back that the magazine will "lean" more towards SF, there's a strong representation of fantasy in these issues.

The most interesting development in the fiction is the return of J. G. Ballard after a hiatus of more than a year and a half, with "Now: Zero" in **38** and "The Sound-Sweep" in **39,** and his contemporaneous return to *New Worlds* with "The Waiting Grounds" and "Zone of Terror." I'll discuss the first two below (the latter two are covered in our companion volumes on *New Worlds*); the four are extremely varied, interesting individually and collectively in terms of the development both of Ballard's craft and of his preoccupations and identity as a writer.

§

Issue **37** leads off pleasantly with Bulmer's "Castle of Vengeance"—hardly a great story, but improved over its predecessors, indicating a writer who is working at getting better. It uses the same device as his previous long stories in *Science Fantasy*, a protagonist arbitrarily precipitated into a dangerous magical parallel world. Masters works for an advertising agency. He has changed his name after being falsely implicated in an embezzlement, for which he was acquitted but his partner was convicted and died in prison. His enemy Baskombe, the boss's nephew, has found out his secret and is threatening to expose him.

Masters finds he needs a new tin of Cowgum (a transparent rubber adhesive) and one mysteriously comes sailing through the window. He dummies up his advertisement, a collage of a ruined castle, a gladiator, armored knights, etc., in the service of Socko soap. Suddenly he finds himself in the world of the advertisement, with an army advancing on the castle. He is brought back to safety by the telephone ringing.

Later, Baskombe shows up at his flat, where Masters is temporarily working, and himself falls into the advertisement world. Masters burns the advertisement, trapping him. But reconstructing the ad, he again falls into it, and it becomes clear that the flying Cowgum is the instrument of translation into the magical world; later it is revealed that the magic Cowgum was flung from Hell by his deceased co-defendant, who is bent on revenge and has enlisted Baskombe in his scheme. All ends well, and humanely: Baskombe has a change of heart rather than being dispatched to a horrid fate by the author.

On the way there are several nice touches; for example, everything pasted up with the Cowgum appears in the magical plane, including the cut-off picture of the front half of a tiger and the white paper silhouette of a woman that Masters has inserted while trying to find the right model. Both of these become horrible apparitions. One can actually imagine this story appearing in *Unknown*, which can't quite be said for Bulmer's earlier efforts. It does not appear ever to have been reprinted or to have been expanded for book publication.

§

38 starts with E. C. Tubb's novelette "Enchanter's Encounter," a well turned if not quite compelling *Conjure Wife* variation. A psychiatrist who despises superstition meets a pretentious magician, makes a bet, gets cursed, confronts the magician, reclaims the photograph, nail clippings, etc., that the magician has been using against him, and gets some of the magician's effluvia to hold hostage. Still denying that magic works he maintains that this is really just science. Meanwhile, the woman he is obsessed with has proved to be a witch herself, and confesses that she used a love charm on him. He declares his undying and non-induced love, burns the charm, and exits, now thinking only that someday she'll make somebody a nice wife.

The other novelette (the cover story) is William F. Temple's "Magic Ingredient," which has nothing to do with magic. A journalist encounters a self-made and fairly nutty millionaire (he devised an arthritis remedy), who is spending his money to create a gigantic advertising display visible from space. The journalist winds up working for him. The Martians land and demand to see the millionaire, having construed his ad as an invitation. They don't understand capitalism, so he sets them up in business with their own arthritis remedy, which shortly puts the millionaire out of business. Meanwhile the Martians have left, but they come back looking for the millionaire because they can't figure out the secret ingredient of his remedy, which restores Martian virility (it's dandelions). He swaps the secret for their arthritis business *and* for their hallucinogenic gas Somo, which at the end he is planning to pipe nationwide.

This story suffers from a fatal lack of focus. Some of the pieces are perfectly fine, but they don't add up. It starts as sharp and almost nihilistic satire, becomes quite plotty when the Martians land, and ends with a paean to "the common trader" who once again is leading the way, this time "across the seas of space." It seems to be the work of a writer who quite literally doesn't know (or can't decide) what he is doing. Frankly I have been underwhelmed by almost all of the Temple stories I have read in my trek through *Science Fantasy* and *New Worlds.*

The novelettes in **39** are Ballard's "The Sound-Sweep," which also has problems but is problematical at a much higher and more interesting level (we'll return to it), and J. T. McIntosh's "The Ship from Home," another brick in my personal wall of irritation at McIntosh's work. The characters are about the eighth generation of a group of forty interstellar colonists who have been isolated by the post-landing misadventure of their spaceship. A ship finally shows up, but it turns out there's a war going on between the Trues and the Newmen. The Trues are Earth-normal. The Newmen are "mutants," but here is what McIntosh means by that term. The protagonist patiently explains to his wife:

"When you go and live on another planet...you naturally become a little different physically. The air you breathe isn't likely to be exactly the same, the food you eat can't be quite the same, even the water is liable to have different deposits and bacteria and all the rest of it. The body changes because it lives on different things."

As a result, the people in the arriving starship are about eight feet tall and emaciated-looking, compared to the colonists, who are closer to standard height but typically have 13- or 14-inch waists.

Another spaceship shortly appears, blows up the first one, and proves to be inhabited by Trues, who kidnap protagonist and wife. The captain of the ship agonizes derangedly about the cruel war of extermination and what he is going to have to do to the colonists, who are Newmen and enemies regardless of their sympathies. But the problem vanishes when protagonist and wife start bulking up on the ship food. So they aren't really Newmen. The ship's doctor says that most Newmen would "mutate back to True type" after several generations back on Earth, but these folks, "though strictly Newmen, seem to change back in...say six months or a year. That's not mutation, it's simple adaptation." Whew! Problem solved!

A lagniappe of annoyance is provided by McIntosh's bludgeoning insistence on the gender stereotypes of his time. The women are flighty, not too bright, and preoccupied with their appearance. The spaceship is landing and the protagonist proposes to go meet it right away: "'Don't be silly,' said Honey, who was nothing if not feminine. 'How can I go in this old dress?'" And a few paragraphs later: "'I can't come,' wailed Paula, who was also feminine. 'I'm not dressed.'" And apparently just putting something on is not an option.

§

The short fiction is the usual mixed bag with nothing particularly outstanding. The better items include John Rackham's "Curse Strings" (**37**), about a witch devoted to doing evil who rewards a young man who rescues her with the curse of receiving-only telepathy. Years later, he's a successful psychiatrist and undertakes to cure her of being a witch. It's a very lively story for most of its length, though it reverts to tedious conventional sentiment at the end.

Silverberg's reprinted "Warm Man" (**38**) is about an empath done in by an encounter with an outcast child, an inversion of Katherine MacLean's "Defense Mechanism." E. C. Tubb's "The Window" (**37**) is blurbed: "The plot of this story is so simple that under ordinary circumstances it would not be acceptable, but author Tubb in one of his bursts of literary genius has turned it into a beautifully written piece of speculative writing." English translation: "This seasoned professional has once again made something out of nearly nothing." A man is obsessed with a lighted window he can see at night, but can't figure out where it is by day. Nor can he find the building at night because he always loses it in the urban glare when he's out on the street. Eventually he buys a telescope, triangulates, etc., and establishes that it's an empty field. The power fails, his light is the only one left on, he makes it there, demands entry and gets it, and then discovers he's been seeing a time glitch and now he's in the future.

W. T. Webb's "Not a Sparrow Falls" (**39**) would be a lot more effective if it weren't so overtly derivative of Pohl and Kornbluth's *The Space Merchants*. A man works in advertising. There are ads on the mirrors. His wife, overcome by subliminals, has bought brand name tea that won't work with their brand name teapot. Poor people have to wear free clothing with ads all over it. The man's boss says:

> "Diehard anti-advertisement cranks struggled to the last ditch. They fought tooth and nail to prevent us from appending advertisements to the pictures in the National Gallery. They demonstrated in their

thousands when we placed our hoardings in such profitable tourist spots as the Lake District and the National Trust areas. And they even got a certain amount of trade union support when we introduced the regular subliminal advertising on the television networks. But advertising is a force that cannot be beaten...."

Compare that to Harvey Bruner's speech in the first chapter of *The Space Merchants*. Otherwise the story is a well-written nasty satire in which the funeral of the corporate godfather is appropriated for the ad campaign for Sparrow's Tinned Asparagus. (Judith Merril gave it an Honorable Mention in her annual anthology.)

The drearier end of things is represented by the obligatory Hek Belov story, "Time Trap" by Edward Mackin (**37**). This one is actually reasonably amusing, less formulaic than most of them; Mackin seems to be getting the hang of this "humor" stuff. In Alan Anderson's "Strokie" (**37**), cuddly alien pets prove a menace to civilization, since they sap initiative and cause people to grow green fur. But they are psychologically addictive and people can't give them up, except that smoking cigarettes breaks the addiction. Alan Barclay's "Who Was Here?" (**38**) deals tediously with some college students determined to paint their school name ("Tech"!) on a space rocket and who encounter an alien with a different but equally uninteresting agenda.

Clifford C. Reed's "Suspect Halo" (**39**) presents a secretary who suddenly sprouts a halo and also levitates, spawning an investigation and an explanation too uninteresting to make it worthwhile trying to follow it. Carnell blurbs: "Eighteen years ago there was another halo story (written by Lester del Rey and published in *Unknown Worlds*) but please do not write and tell us about it!" This is quite different, he says, and new readers won't know the old story. I wonder how many people wrote to tell him that the *Unknown* halo story was actually "The Misguided Halo" by Henry Kuttner, in the August 1939 issue in both US and UK editions. Perhaps Carnell was thinking of "Hereafter, Inc." by del Rey, published in the 12/41 *Unknown* (though not until Spring 1949 in the UK edition). A quick riffle reveals no halo in that story, but the memorably ugly illustration for it in the Prime Press collection *And Some Were Human* adds one. Further, Carnell seems to have forgotten his own halo story, William F. Temple's "Eternity" in **12**, discussed in Chapter 4.

§

The second wave of J. G. Ballard stories commenced at the end of 1959 and the beginning of 1960, two each in *Science Fantasy* and *New Worlds*. They are "Now: Zero" and "The Sound-Sweep" in *Science Fantasy* and "The Waiting Grounds" and "Zone of Terror" in *New Worlds*. There was a hiatus of over 18 months between these and his last previous story, "Track 12" (*New Worlds*, April 1958), after Ballard's traumatic encounter with an SF convention, discussed in *Building New Worlds,* Chapter 6.

The thing that is striking about this group of stories, all published within a few months of one another and apparently written within a similar span, is how various they are, in scope, attitude, execution and merit. Two of them are trivial but the others are the most substantial stories Ballard had yet produced.

"Now: Zero" (**38**) is about as inconsequential a story as Ballard has published. The first-person protagonist discovers that if he writes about somebody's death, it will happen. He tests the power and confirms it, then uses it to remove people who are obstacles to his advancement at his workplace, but he overdoes it a bit and the company shuts down and lays everybody off. At the end of the story, the narrator broadens his field of fire to include everyone reading the story—we're all supposed to die when we read the end of it. This is interesting only as an exercise in narrative voice, and as such it's pretty successful. The story is told in a sort of buttoned-down Poe-ish style of restrained loony grandiosity (think "Cask of Amontillado," not "Tell-Tale

Heart"), and Ballard manages to maintain a nice consistency of tone, turning up the dial slowly as matters progress. But it's more of a finger exercise than a story.

"The Sound-Sweep" (**39**) is a different kettle of fish entirely. Though far from completely successful, it's a much more ambitious story (Ballard's longest to date by a big margin) and one which is more suggestive of his later preoccupations. Madame Gioconda is a former opera singer, displaced by the advent of ultrasonic music and constantly scheming about her comeback. She has befriended Mangon, rendered mute as an infant by a blow from his mother and then reared in an orphanage. His hearing is acute. Thus he is a valued operator of a sonovac, a device which sweeps away the stale residue of old sounds from walls, floors, etc.[47] Now this is all pretty ridiculous, but Ballard isn't embarrassed. He revels in it:

Ultrasonic music, employing a vastly greater range of octaves, chords, and chromatic scales than perceptible to the human ear, provided a direct neural link between the sound stream and the auditory lobes, generating an apparently sourceless sensation of harmony, rhythm, cadence and melody uncontaminated by the noise and vibration of audible music. The re-scoring of the classical repertoire allowed the ultrasonic audience the best of both worlds. The majestic rhythms of Beethoven, the popular melodies of Tchaikovsky, the complex fugal elaborations of Bach, the abstract images of Schoenberg—all these were raised in frequency above the threshold of conscious audibility. Not only did they become inaudible, but the original

_____

47. This is not Ballard's first use of this notion. A "sound-sweeper" figures in the beginning of "Passport to Eternity," one of his earliest stories (see his letter to David Pringle, December 20, 1993, at http://www.jgballard.ca/pringle_news_from_the_sun/news_from_sun22.html) (visited 10/19/11), though it was not actually published until 1962. The protagonist uses it to mute the voice of his argumentative wife.

works were re-scored for the much wider range of the ultrasonic orchestra, became richer in texture, more profound in theme, more sensitive, tender or lyrical as the ultrasonic arranger chose....

The earliest ultrasonic recordings had met with resistance, even ridicule. Radio programmes consisting of nothing but silence interrupted at half-hour intervals by commercial breaks seemed absurd. But gradually the public discovered that the silence was golden, that after leaving the radio switched to an ultrasonic channel for an hour or so a pleasant atmosphere of rhythm and melody seemed to generate itself spontaneously around them. When an announcer suddenly stated that an ultrasonic version of Mozart's Jupiter Symphony or Tchaikovsky's Pathetique had just been played the listener identified the real source.... But the final triumph of ultrasonic music had come with a second development—the short-playing record, spinning at 900 r.p.m., which condensed the 45 minutes of a Beethoven symphony to 20 seconds of playing time, the three hours of a Wagner opera to little more than two minutes. Compact and cheap, SP records sacrificed nothing to brevity. One 30-second SP record delivered as much neurophonic pleasure as a natural length recording, but with deeper penetration, greater total impact.

This is high concept as tall tale, a solemnly mischievous parody of Science Fiction, the Literature of Extrapolation. It's not Ballard's first offense in this respect either—he did the same thing with the singing flowers in "Prima Belladonna"—but now he has a clearer idea of how and what he's doing. Editor Carnell says, in a typically tone-deaf blurb: "Eighteen months ago in the April issue of *New Worlds*, Jim Ballard had a delightful short story entitled 'Track 12' which opened up the possibilities of sonics as a plot theme. Here, in this long novelette, he has extended his ideas into a high level and most unusual story."

These developments have put paid to the human voice as musical instrument, since (Ballard says) it can't be re-scored, being generated by "non-mechanical means which the neurophonic engineer could never hope, or bother, to duplicate." Now there's a failure of imagination, but without it, of course, there would be no story. Madame Gioconda's career is ended, and here we see the first appearance of one of Ballard's characteristic motifs:

> In a despairing act of revenge she bought out the radio station which fired her and made her home on one of the sound stages. Over the years the station became derelict and forgotten, its windows smashed, neon portico collapsing, aerials rusting. The huge eight-lane flyover built across it sealed it conclusively into the past.

Actually there are two characteristic motifs here, one the derelict radio station and the other Madame Gioconda herself, the first of Ballard's larger-than-life, theatrically obsessive characters. She and the perversely symmetrical relationship between her and Mangon are at the center of the story: she, silenced in passing by blind technological and economic forces, and never reconciled to it, devotedly served by Mangon, silenced viciously by his own mother but having found a practical niche in society, and an emotional one as the last worshiper of the discarded diva.

She contrives her comeback by blackmailing one of her old lovers, LeGrande, with considerable assistance from Mangon, who takes her out to the dump where the sound-sweeps empty their sonovacs and live in ramshackle cabins, and where they listen to the residues of LeGrande's private conversations. This is the first of the classic Ballardian landscapes, endless stockades among the dunes filled with sound-absorbent baffles.

A place of strange echoes and festering silences, over-hung by a gloomy miasma of a million compacted sounds, it remained remote and haunted, the grave-yard of countless private babels.... Occasionally, when super-saturation was reached after one of the sum-mer holiday periods, the sonic pressure fields would split and discharge, venting back into the stockades a nightmarish cataract of noise, raining onto the sound-sweeps not only the howling of cats and dogs, but the multi-lunged tumult of cars, express trains, fair-grounds and aircraft, the cacophonic musique concrete of civilisation.

Mangon, ecstatically engaged in the campaign to restore Gioconda's voice, suddenly recovers his own—though, as she becomes more preoccupied with her own affairs, he begins to stutter. Then she moves out of the radio station, leaving him a nasty message, shouted for him to hear its residue, and his voice disappears entirely. Of course she can't actually sing any more. The plan was for Mangon to start up a sonovac during her sup-posed triumphant return so no one could hear her but herself, leaving the orchestra to play unmolested. Instead he destroys the sonovac, the musicians begin to walk off, the audience is in an uproar. "But Madame Gioconda failed to notice them. Head back, eyes on the brilliant ceiling lights, hands gesturing majestically, she soared along the private causeways of sound that poured unrelenting from her throat, a great white angel of discord on her homeward flight."

The story doesn't come off perfectly. Part of the problem is that the notion of sound residues which affect mood and can be heard by the keen-eared is just too damned notional—we know it isn't so in a very concrete way. We know that about elves and demons, too, but that kind of fantasy presents us with a different and easier kind of demand for the suspension of disbelief than does "The Sound-Sweep." Also Mangon's regaining and then losing his voice, central to the story, is just a bit bathetic. But overall "The Sound-Sweep" might be described as the first fully Ballardian Ballard story in terms of theme, rhetoric, and image working together.

14: *SCIENCE FANTASY*,
VOLUME 14 (ISSUES 40-42)

Science Fantasy volume 14, issues for April, June, and August 1960, presents with three colorful and striking Lewis covers[48] and generally continues business as usual. The Rosicrucians and the Jazz Book Club have advertisements in **40**. The less said about the former, the better, but the JBC's presentation is interesting in light of Kingsley Amis's contemporaneous comments on jazz and SF. Amis goes on at some length in *New Maps of Hell*[49] about the parallels between the two, and their enthusiasts. The ad says:

> Do you believe in parallel universes? We do. We believe, for instance, that the worlds of jazz and sf are parallel, a little more than merely co-existent. Offbeatness, for people who somehow can't go all the way with the world they live in. Snobs, of course, parade on the fringes, but the true loonies, world-wise, are to be found at the dead centre, as often as not gyrating from one parallel world to the other with the greatest of ease. Naturally, you are an sf-addict, or you wouldn't be reading this. Why not explore the further joys we can offer, that is, unless you have already done so?

---

48. See these covers at http://www.sfcovers.net/mainnav.htm or http://www.philsp.com/mags/sciencefantasy.html.

49. Harcourt, Brace & Co. (1960), pp. 16-17.

In the next issue, both these advertisers are gone, replaced by Charles Atlas. Other advertisers include Digit Books and the SF Book Club, the latter announcing that Kingsley Amis is joining Carnell and Dr. J. G. Porter (identified in earlier issues as Dr. Porter, F.R.A.S., of the Royal Greenwich Observatory) in selecting the club's books.

Moskowitz's "Studies in Science Fiction" series soldiers on with A. Merritt in **40** and Edgar Rice Burroughs in **41**, taking a break in **42**. There is, quite unusually, a book review in **41**, of Mordecai Roshwald's *Level 7* reviewed by Leslie Flood. This is peculiar, since Flood is regularly reviewing for *New Worlds*, and *Level 7*—a high-minded nuclear war novel—is about the last book to single out for *Science Fantasy*. There is also an editorial in **42**, which praises John Keir Cross's *Best Black Magic Stories*, then notes once more the dearth of weird and macabre magazines in the US or the UK, which proves there is no reading public for them. Except that there are more such anthologies than ever before, proving that there *is* a reading audience "tucked away somewhere."

Then—drum roll—the statement of policy: "However, much as I personally deplore the passing of the weird story magazines, there is no intention of moving *Science Fantasy* towards that medium." In the beginning: "From the material submitted *Science Fantasy* began to build a personality of its own, ignoring the weird (we were flooded with ghost stories at one time) and concentrating on an overlapping policy of off-trail s-f and fantasy." The virtue of this policy is proved by the fact that the magazine is still publishing and is getting stories in Merril's annual anthologies. Carnell concludes, rousingly: "On the law of averages *Science Fantasy* is due for still further credits in the foreseeable future." What an optimist! Note, by the way, that two issues later, **44** will have blazoned on the cover "SPECIAL WEIRD-STORY ISSUE."

§

The trend toward longer and fewer stories resumes: the three issues contain four, three, and four stories respectively. The transAtlantic traffic in this volume, aside from the Moskowitz articles, is limited to Robert Silverberg's "Counterpart" from the October 1959 *Fantastic Universe*.

This volume begins inauspiciously with Kenneth Bulmer's "short novel" (fifty not-too-crowded pages) "Strange Highway" (**40**), a considerable step backwards for him: a dull and lifeless SF story about shiny globes that appear in the UK, flattening everything in their path, and the intrepid scientist who figures out that they are spaceships using another dimension's faster-than-light drive. This one was old-fashioned in 1960 and would have been ordinary twenty years earlier. It is completely without the flashes of wit and invention of his last fantasy short novel "Castle of Vengeance." It reads like the product of a bored author.

Things look up a bit in **41** with John Brunner's nicely titled short novel "The Gaudy Shadows," which begins with world-traveling Laird Walker and his friends discussing research on lysergic acid. One of the party, Terry, is terrified, passes out, then later tells Walker he should apply for a job where she works, a place that seems to manufacture movie scenery. Tileman, the company's maximum leader, eventually confides that it is manufacturing a hallucinogenic gas that delivers people into a convincing fantasy world with the assistance of suggestive props that the company manufactures. Tileman is coining money by charging decadent swells a lot to attend his séances. But he also has another gas that makes people so depressed they kill themselves. That's why Terry is terrified and standoffish.

When Tileman discovers Walker and Terry talking, he draws the correct conclusion. They flee, pursued; hugger-mugger ensues and Tileman gets a faceful of his own depressant and goes insane. This one is pleasant enough but doesn't measure up to Brunner's better previous work in the magazine. Not a whole lot happens and Terry is not as well developed as Brunner's usual female characters. It was expanded into a novel

(Constable, 1970), in which the idea and plot were considerably more developed. The novel retains the same title.

§

Issue **42** has two novelettes rather than a short novel, and it's J. T. McIntosh again, with "Planet on Probation," a member of a very small subgenre of SF stories that are driven by insurance. (Quick! How many can *you* name?) Blake is a Habitability Consul, the one who decides whether colony planets can remain colonies or are so dangerous they have to be evacuated. Habitability Consuls are hated because colonists always take out insurance policies that give them large payouts if they manage to stay on the colony planet for a term of years, but if they don't, they lose everything. (This makes no sense in insurance terms, but "the governments of Earth were behind it," so that's all right.) It's the Habitability Consul's job to determine whether the risks of the planet are too great to allow the colony to remain.

You might think that if government retained that kind of authority over colonies, it would figure out the risks *before* allowing any significant colony to be established. But no. This colony, Marlar, is in danger of being shut down by Blake for two reasons: its extremely volatile weather, and a nasty form of food poisoning called marlaritis. The weather is this volatile: Blake is having a pleasant conversation with a young woman who is sunbathing in her bikini (half of it anyway). Then, within seconds and without warning, they are in a blizzard which completely hides buildings 100 yards away.

Worse still, the Settlement Commission chief tells Blake that they have a terrible problem—a sudden drought—and he doesn't know what to do. The colony has been there for five years suffering these bizarre weather conditions but apparently nobody has planned for a drought; Blake suggests that they lay some pipe so places with more water can send some to those with less water. This has not previously occurred to the Settlement Commission chief. As for the food poisoning, the native plants, which people have to eat, become unpredictably poisonous and lots of people die from the resulting illness. Nobody knows why, and nobody knows what to do about it, as McIntosh sets out in terms virtually Fanthorpean:

> It wasn't that there were poisonous varieties....
> It wasn't the soil. Any variety could be safe anywhere or poisonous anywhere.
> It wasn't the weather. In a particular field a thousand plants would be all right and one all wrong.
> It wasn't the rough handling all Marlar's vegetable life got. For in fields protected at enormous expense from the vagaries of the climate, the proportion of poison plants was decidedly higher than usual.
> It wasn't transplanting.
> It wasn't too much water.
> It wasn't too much sun.

Small animals called betchels always know whether a plant has become poisonous, but there aren't enough betchels to go around. (Breed them? Nobody thought of that.) Blake is intrigued by the topless young woman, Lucille ("Blake had a tantalizing glimpse of two impudent little breasts which made up in quality what they lacked in quantity."), but she stands him up for a date. Later, she gets sent to him when he calls for a stenographer, leading to an argument, which leads in turn to one of the peak moments of twentieth-century romantic comedy: "Blake noticed that when she was angry her bust measurement was fully adequate."

Blake decides to save the Marlar colony by threatening to destroy it, giving the word that it should be shut down, but telling the colonists that they have a few months before the evacuation can start, during which they can stop exposing themselves to the weather and cut down the accident rate. Lucille, who by now has moved in with Blake because people are abusing her for going around with him at all, gets down on the ground and looks at a plant the way a betchel does, and discovers that when a plant goes poisonous, its stem looks different in some unspecified way when viewed against the sky. The day is saved, and Blake is going to "make an honest woman" (her term) of Lucille any day now.

This is all too silly for words. The best thing I can say for this story is that it is McIntosh's last for *Science Fantasy*, indeed his last for any of the Nova magazines. From here through the rest of the '60s, all of McIntosh's magazine publications are in the US.

§

John Brunner's "Imprint of Chaos" (**42**) is the first of the Traveler in Black series, which were very popular at the time and have remained among his best-remembered work. The traveler, who we are repeatedly told has "many names but one nature," unlike the rest of us who I suppose contain multitudes, has been appointed (by whom is not explained) as a sort of metaphysical supervisor over one segment of the universe, with a mission to help establish the primacy of order over chaos. As the story opens, he is riding fence. His big concern in this opening episode is that in the city of Ryovora, where people have traditionally had their heads screwed on right (Brunner's phrase), they think that what they need is a god, like other cities have. So the traveler nips out to our Earth and snatches the unsuspecting Bernard Brown, who is hiking in the woods and minding his business, tells him he's unlikely to find his way home but gives him directions to Ryovora, including a warning about magical hazards to be encountered en route.

There, to his great discomfiture, Brown is welcomed as a god, though not without doubt. The next city over hears about it and sends over *their* god, the giant Quadruple God of Acromel, so named because he has eight arms and legs, to call Brown out. Brown observes the Quad God, concludes that he's really an overgrown child, and has his people make a gigantic balloon in the shape of an even more fearsome apparition and shout in unison "Go away!" Quad God flees, the people say to themselves "We could have thought of that," and they conclude that they don't really need a god. Mr. Brown is excused after a final scene where he and the traveler bruit the futility and undesirability of magic.

We've seen this in earlier fantasies by Brunner the rationalist, who comes not to praise magic but to bury it, though only after enough colorful magical episodes to entertain the rubes. But here the contradiction is a bit more extreme, because the setting is exotically magical, as opposed to the well-grounded mundanity of, say, "This Rough Magic," and the story is told in the fey and pompous cadences of high fantasy. For example, from a conclave of the necromantic elite of Ryovora: "The Margrave nodded and made a comforting gesture in the air. He said, 'But this cannot be the whole story. I move that we—here, now, in full council—ask Him Who Must Know.'" Brunner seems unable to decide between wallowing in the cheap and easy FX of the genre ("Tyllwin [a particularly powerful magician] chuckled, a scratching noise, and the flowers on the whole of one tree turned to fruit and rotted where they hung.") and outright parody of it. So it's an interesting try that doesn't come off: having it both ways is too long a stretch when the story is so completely grounded in a magical world.

Interestingly, even though the story is clearly set up to support sequels, and Brunner continued to appear regularly in *Science Fantasy* for the next two or three years, the next Traveler in Black story did not appear for almost six years ("Break the Door of Hell," in the second—April 1966—issue of *Impulse*, *Science Fantasy*'s successor). I wonder if Brunner felt some of the same difficulties writing these stories that I had in reading the first one. If he did, he doesn't seem to have done anything about it retroactively with "Imprint of Chaos." The version in his collection *The Compleat Traveller In Black* (1986) shows a lot of line edits but no major reworking of the story.

§

A significant event is Thomas Burnett Swann's first appearance in *Science Fantasy* (he will become an important contributor in later years of the magazine): the short story "The Dryad-Tree" in **42**. Not that there's much to it: a woman moves into her new husband's house, there's an orange tree next to it, but it doesn't like her much, so it rearranges its branches to deny her shade and drops fruit on her when it has the chance—obviously it's jealous. So when her husband is out of town, she has the tree surgeon come and strip off all the leaves. But never underestimate a supernatural tree. Shortly the wife is beset with a barrage of lightning. So she decides to make friends with the tree, giving it plenty of fertilizer, etc., putting up a bird feeder in it, and decorating it extravagantly at Christmas. Now it's her husband who can't get any shade.

Of the remaining short fiction (no Ballard in these issues), the best is probably Robert Silverberg's "Counterpart" (**41**), which suggests some of the directions he would take later in the 1960s. Jenner is a has-been actor. An old friend offers to renew his career through his invention, which will give Jenner the memories and personalities of someone else to draw on. The someone else proves to be an aspiring politician, who also gets Jenner's memories and personality. It works, they both succeed. They meet, hate each other's guts, but realize that they need each other. They smash the friend's equipment and vow never to meet again but to exchange advice by mail. The friend wonders how long they will let him live.

The other short items include a couple of amusing *Unknown*ish fantasies: "Too Bad" by E. C. Tubb (**40**), about a business that hires and lends people with bizarre talents, like those whose presence in a store makes people show up and buy (or the opposite), accident-prones, etc., and "Deities, Inc." by Leroy B. Haugsrud and Dale R. Smith (**42**), in which a man in a dark suit with briefcase and Homburg arrives by spaceship at the old gods' retirement home, hoping to coax the likes of Zeus,

Odin, Ishtar, Hermes, and a host of leprechauns, gnomes, etc., to take jobs on primitive planets where people will believe in them. Edward Mackin's "Trading Post" (**40**) is the obligatory Hek Belov story, less irritating than many of its predecessors though just as arbitrary and insubstantial, in which Belov is summoned to assist with an automated assembly line that seems to be taking his employers' stuff and replacing it with valuable items from another dimension, planet, or what have you.

Finally, there are two stories by Brian Aldiss which again serve to remind that he produced a lot of rubbish early in his career, though he had enough discernment to keep it out of his collections. "Faceless Card" (**40**) is a sour dystopia in which human complacency is challenged by sending psychopaths around to perpetrate cruel disruptions in the lives of the settled, told in a cynically showy style that reads like "Judas Danced" with a bad hangover. E.g.: "Mr. Nigel Alexander was prey. He had it stamped all over him. Ordinary citizen. Safety first. Ideas keep out. He came into the Dive at a slow trot, moving on his heels as if his toes had corns." Etc.

"Stage-Struck" (**41**) is a ponderously whimsical time-travel story in which the characters must get by stage-coach from London to Birmingham in 1835 in order to catch a ride back to the future. It, too, suffers from excessive showiness, for example beginning: "The Wells Memorial Wing of the library was a long grey room, while by coincidence the under-librarian was a long grey man." This kind of attention-demanding writing can work if it is suitably yoked to a story of sufficient substance, as Aldiss himself had already demonstrated in "Poor Little Warrior!" and "The New Father Christmas," both in *Fantasy & Science Fiction* in 1958, and in the aforementioned "Judas Danced." Here it just clangs and bumps.

15: *SCIENCE FANTASY*, VOLUME 15 (ISSUES 43- 45)

Science Fantasy, volume 15, for October and December 1960 and February 1961, rolls on as before, starting with a less than excellent Lewis cover on **43** (the more abstract and stylized the better with Lewis—this one is much too illustrative), a reasonably pleasing one by Jarr on **44** (as long as you don't look too closely and see that the bicycle is being repaired by the same silly-looking alien who rode the roller coaster on the cover of **39**), and a much better Lewis on **45** (again showing the more abstract the better—his strength is color and balance of form, not representation).[50]

The big news infrastructurally is that the International Correspondence Schools have full-back-cover ads on **43** and **44**. The Rosicrucians are back in **44** (appropriately, the Special Weird-Story Issue), and Pergamon Press has a full interior page in **43** for their edition of Konstantin Tsiolkovsky's *Beyond the Planet Earth*. The shift towards longer stories continues, with four stories in **43**, three in **44**, and two in **45**. There's an installment of Moskowitz's Studies in Science Fiction in each issue (Verne, Fitz-James O'Brien, and of course Lovecraft in the Special Weird-Story Issue).

There's also an article in **43** called "The First Decade" by

---

50. See these covers at http://www.sfcovers.net/mainnav.htm or http://www.philsp.com/mags/sciencefantasy.html.

Kenneth Johns, a pseudonym of Kenneth Bulmer and John Newman, who used it for science pieces in *New Worlds*. The article is what it sounds like, a brief account of the first ten years of the magazine. They were no doubt in a summing-up mood at Nova since *New Worlds* **100** came out about contemporaneously. It's superficial but with a few interesting nuggets.

For example, after E. C. Tubb's over-the-top post-nuclear *noir* novella "Tomorrow" in **8**, "Editor Carnell commented ruefully that he was snowed under with grim, tough, realistic yarns...for years." In **31**, the cover story was uncharacteristically a short story, Sturgeon's "The Graveyard Reader." The Lewis cover previously commissioned for Bulmer's "The Bones of Shosun" in that issue was "used on John Kippax's 'Destiny Incorporated' an issue earlier." (Well, that issue didn't *say* it illustrated the Kippax.) Bulmer and Newman mention that Reina Bull was "a cover artist whose loss is sadly missed in British science fiction circles" without saying what happened to her. Jose Rubios, who did covers for **22-25**, is revealed to be a pseudonym for Terry, who was doing *New Worlds* covers too. The artist who calls himself Jarr is revealed to be "a team"—but of whom, the authors do not reveal.[51] And they single out for special praise Edward Mackin's Hek Belov stories, "one of the better things about modern s-f and...one which, we can only fervently pray, will long be with us." I am reminded of James Blish's observation that on being notified of a certain Nebula Award result he stepped quietly into his kitchen and bit the cat.[52]

The notable items of fiction in these issues include two J. G. Ballard stories, "The Last World of Mr. Goddard" in **43** and "Studio 5, the Stars" in **45**, the second Vermilion Sands story, not counting "Mobile," which as previously noted was inducted into the Vermilion Sands canon some years later as "Venus Smiles." We will return to these.

---

51. As mentioned in Chapter 8, n. 33, the www.sfcovers.net site gives a different account of Jarr's identity.

52. William Atheling, Jr. [James Blish], *More Issues at Hand* (Advent: Publishers, 1970), p. 134.

§

Bulmer's "Beyond the Silver Sky" in **43**, while a step up from the dreary "Strange Highway," is a fairly lackluster and derivative story about an undersea breed of humanity beset with attacks from other life forms, a recurring mutation (the Hopeless Ones, children born with webbed hands and feet who must of course be killed), and a lowering sea level (from the characters' standpoint, the sky is falling, albeit slowly). The story is about a far-fetched but courageous scientific expedition onto land.

Apart from being a more diffuse and humdrum reiteration of James Blish's classic "Surface Tension," it is populated by stock characters (except for the women, who don't rise to the level of characters, stock or otherwise) and no surprises at all. This one became an Ace Double under the same title. The most interesting thing in it is a brief reference which I suppose is at least the equal of J. T. McIntosh's daring in matters of gender:

> His fingers were sure and steady as he strapped on the wide skin belt, adjusted the shoulder harness and the rank badges which, in covering his operculum over his gill slits also performed the necessary function of modesty. A girl might show anything—within reason—but to no man save her husband would she reveal her operculum. Most women, Keston heard, fiercely resisted showing their naked gill slits even to a husband of many seasons familiarity. This was just another of those unspoken-of mysteries stretching back into the womb of time.
>
> A man breathed in through his mouth, the ambient fluid entered his lungs where oxygen was extracted and was then, recharged with carbon dioxide, passed out again to be ejected through the gill slits which also, in their fashion, carried on a minor oxygen-carbon dioxide exchange. This was a mere physiological function.

But many a man had been stabbed to death for merely raising a girl's cloak over her operculum.

The short fiction in **43** is a very mixed bag: Ballard's splendidly perverse "The Last World of Mr. Goddard" is accompanied by Alan Lindsey's "Stardust," a four-page blank verse epic about a man who travels to another planet but doesn't inspire anyone else to follow him. It's neither conspicuously good nor conspicuously bad. "Expectations," by Richard Graham, is one of the more labored dystopian visions I've encountered. The first-person protagonist has summoned the Scientist, the Bank Manager, and the Parson to discuss his fascinating theory that relatives who resemble each other physically are likely to have a similar life expectancy. It is hinted that this theory might be contrary to the Orthodoxy, but the discussion goes on. At the end it's revealed that they're all on Candid Camera, the protagonist is a spy for the Orthodoxy, and the others will soon be picked up for reconditioning.

§

Things improve in the next issue (the Special Weird Story one), as usual when John Brunner supplies the lead story. In "All the Devils in Hell" a decent ordinary man for some reason attracts the attention of Deirdre, the canonical Evil-Hearted Woman, a person of almost preternatural allure, who is offended when, notwithstanding her toying with him, he decides to marry Fiona, his slightly frumpy but good-hearted woman friend of several years' standing. Lightning strikes a tree they are sheltering under and Fiona's mind is destroyed. He denounces this monster, and suddenly becomes a wreck: sick all the time, can't remember anything, etc.

Eventually he's in such an extreme state that he heads for Deirdre's house with a knife. When he gets there, it turns out she *is* preternatural. She's sold her soul to be irresistible, is eaten up with jealousy by being resisted, and generally is a burnt-out case (i.e., soulless). Her pentagram proves to be damaged, and "the power of darkness claimed Deirdre Slade"—and without the protagonist having to murder her. Once she's dead, his fiancée makes a miraculous recovery.

In summary it sounds pretty overripe, but Brunner the canny professional clearly knows how easy it would be to make a fool of himself with this hyper-melodramatic material. (I'll bet there were half a dozen stories using a similar device among *Weird Tales*, *Fantastic Adventures*, and the weird menace pulps, each more lurid than the next.) He tells the story in a flat and matter-of-fact first-person style that is more powerful for its under-statement, well anchored in visual and physical detail. The last portion of the story, in which he portrays Deirdre as more tragic and pathetic than terrifying, is particularly well done. Fiona, too, is well portrayed, presented as an unusually decent and perceptive person but not a saint, so the story never descends into the whore-vs.-Madonna style of misogynism that its plot might suggest.

Brunner is followed by John Rackham's novelette "The Black Cat's Paw," a sort of mage-procedural. A man rents an office (and lives in it) writing poetry, the fortune-teller upstairs gets murdered, the poet-protagonist is suspected, but he points out the trappings of black magic and refers the Inspector to his old service buddy, Egyptologist K.N. Wilson, to whom he is known as "Chappie" Jones. (Wilson is known to Chappie as "Pepper"—K.N.—get it?) Wilson shares his house with a myste-rious Egyptian and an overwhelmingly beautiful and innocent young woman named Yalna. Wilson is at first unwilling to get involved. There was a Solomonic seal left on the body, Belial has been invoked, and clearly there is one powerful magickal dude behind these events.

But anybody who has looked at the seal is now targeted, so Wilson relents, and they all try to figure out who they're dealing with and put a stop to it. At the climax it is revealed that Chappie himself has quite a bit of the power and he saves everyone's bacon. He's invited to stick around, and the prospect of getting next to Yalna is in the air. I suspect there's a strong element here of pastiche of British boys' books or thrillers from the 1920s and '30s, vide the nicknames. The Inspector, a hard-headed Scottish materialist ("You're verra cautious, Mr. Jones") is straight from Central Casting, as is the aristocratic and hyper-competent Wilson. Overall it's a slick and capable entertainment. By the way, I don't find a black cat, or the paw of one, in this story anywhere. The title must be metaphorical—for something.

This issue is completed by Thomas Burnett Swann's "The Painter," a variation on a familiar theme: "But by God, Eliot, *it was a photograph from life.*" Swann proposes that Hieronymus Bosch didn't make it up, he painted what he saw. Bosch and his young brother are sleeping off a drunk in a neighbor's barn when they are visited by extraterrestrial sleazebags, several varieties of them travelling in a giant blue fish (as it appears in the sixteenth century). They are evil and stupid and sadistic, and he buys his life and his brother's by drawing them on the spot. This story is a lot better than it sounds because it is very well and plainly written and Bosch and his social world and viewpoint are sketched in satisfying depth.

§

Bulmer is back in **45** with "The Map Country," which later became half of an Ace Double under the title *The Land Beyond the Map.* It's considerably livelier than his two recent SF novellas, though still pretty unsatisfying. Independently wealthy Roland Crane spends his time on archaeological digs during the season and his money on antique maps. One stormy night the glass in the frame of one of them bursts for no apparent reason. The phone rings and there's a Miss Harbottle on the line who wants to sell him a map *right now* despite the ghastly weather. When she arrives, it turns out her name is really Polly Gould. She's not selling maps but looking for one and thinks Crane might have it. This map is torn and is in the back of a tour book.

The connection: Crane's family, following the map when he was a child, drove into what looked like another world and was chased out by robot monsters. Gould's cousin went into the map country with his girl friend to seek his fortune and never came back. Crane and Gould team up to find the map, shortly find themselves tramping around County Tyrone in Ireland, are menaced by one McArdle who wants the map himself, watch a parking lot attendant swept up by a luminous cloud, find the man with the map, find themselves in the map country fleeing McArdle, encounter various bizarre phenomena (menacing tank/robots, for which hand grenades are just the thing; undulating roads; migrating vegetation. Etc.), and finally are caught by aliens.

The aliens maintain them in a sort of disembodied state and explain that creating order in the universe is a hard job but somebody has to do it, and they're elected, and the way they do it is by mapping the worlds (it's a bit like the joke about the postmodern baseball umpire: "They're nothing till I call them.") Now that the aliens have the map back, they can leave, and can return Crane and Gould, along with the other people they have collected, including the parking lot attendant, but not including Gould's cousin, who has asked to move on with the aliens. Oh, and that exploding glass on the first page? Fuhgeddaboutit, the author does, or at least he never explains or connects it.

The problem with this story is that Bulmer is really a pretty tone-deaf and unreflective writer. The story starts out as a sort of pastiche of early adventure and fantasy fiction, like something you might have found in *Famous Fantastic Mysteries*, with some pleasingly snappy lines ("Miss Harbottle had fair wavy hair, cut murderously short."), but he doesn't keep it up. The story turns into a pretty routine thriller. Bulmer seems on his way to portraying a pretty feisty female character, but he doesn't follow through with that either. She doesn't register clearly, and neither does Crane. The science fictional revelation at the end is an unsatisfying and incongruous resolution of the supernatural-seeming build-up of the plot. Perhaps Bulmer already had in mind his series of such yarns, published by Ace beginning in 1967, as his *Keys to the Dimensions* series, comprising *The Key to Irunium* and various sequels.

§

The Ballard stories in volume 15 of *Science Fantasy* are, as mentioned, "The Last World of Mr. Goddard" in **43** (October 1960) and "Studio 5, the Stars" in **45** (February 1961).

"The Last World of Mr. Goddard" is thoroughly uncharacteristic for Ballard, reminiscent in its solemnly crazy way of John Collier. It's a neat story, in both senses of the word. The elderly Mr. Goddard is ground floor supervisor in a department store, and all day there is an annoying sound of thunder, though it's a clear day. At the end of the day, he goes home, where all the windows are shuttered, and there are steel grilles inside them. He dines, in the company of a neighborhood cat, and then inspects the house, which is entirely empty, the fireplaces bricked up, except for the kitchen and a rear lounge, which contains a chair and a safe. He sits in the chair and opens the safe, which contains a metal box. He hears the sound of thunder again outside, and a moth flies out from the confined space above the box, where it has been beating its wings trying to escape. He opens the box.

It contains a finely worked scale model of an area of buildings including the department store where he works and the surrounding buildings. And there are little people, going to work and starting the day—the next day, it appears. Mr. Goddard leans over the box, wearing a green eyeshade under a bright ceiling light, and watches and listens. (Elsewhere Ballard alludes to Dali in some of his descriptions. I visualize Mr. Goddard as the Pharmacist of Ampurdan.) Then he notices some of the little people on a high balcony, trying to fasten a ladder so they can climb to what appears to be empty air. They're trying to escape from the box! Mr. Goddard hastily shuts the box and returns it to the safe. The next day, there's a commotion outside the store.

The top half of the ladder has fallen, the two people trying to climb it have fallen to their deaths. No one can figure out where they were trying to go; the ladder reached to nowhere.

Meanwhile, Mr. Goddard is quietly offering a loan (which is resentfully rebuffed) to someone who seems to be in financial trouble, based on his observations in the box, consistently with his practice of benign meddling based on inside information. In the ensuing evenings, Mr. Goddard continues to study developing events in the box. Things look suspicious. There seems to be some conspiracy in the air. On his 65th birthday, Mr. Goddard is informed that he is being retired as of that day, like it or not, and he realizes everybody is glad he is going. He goes home, where the cat is waiting for him, and straightway opens up the box, in hopes of learning what has happened. But he loses his balance and falls and passes out while opening the box, which lands on its side. Small figures begin to emerge. When Mr. Goddard wakes up, the cat is polishing off the last one. He steps outside, followed by the cat. "Together they walked out into an empty world."

To my taste this is a near-perfect exercise in imaginative perversity, told in exactly the right voice of dry detachment, and close to the perfect length. Apparently nobody much agrees with me, though. It appears never to have been anthologized. It is reprinted in Ballard's collections *The Terminal Beach* (US) and *The Day of Forever* (UK), and of course in the *Complete Stories*. It certainly seems there was some intent in the selection of "Goddard" (Ballard overlaid by God, or close) as the character's name. And I wonder if Ballard had read Shirley Jackson's "One Ordinary Day, with Peanuts" and maybe was a little annoyed with it.

Editor Carnell once more demonstrates his tone-deafness in the blurb for the story: "If you remember the taut suspensefulness of Merritt's 'Burn, Witch, Burn' (originally published in 1932 but still read as a classic of its kind and constantly being reprinted) you will find much in common with it in this short Ballard story of a manipulator of human destinies." It's amusing to imagine the reaction of a Merritt devotee to this dry, precise, and subtle artifact.

Our hypothetical Merritt devotee might well have felt more at home with Ballard's next *Science Fantasy* offering, "Studio 5, the Stars," which begins:

> Every evening during the summer at Vermilion Sands the insane poems of my beautiful neighbor drifted across the desert to me from Studio 5, The Stars, the broken skeins of coloured tape unravelling in the sand like the threads of a dismembered web. All night they would flutter around the buttresses below the terrace, entwining themselves through the balcony railings, and by morning, before I swept them away, they would hang across the south face of the villa like a vivid cerise bougainvilia (sic).

And there she is, as they say at the Miss America pageant:

> I had only once seen my neighbour, on the day she arrived, driving down the Stars in a huge El Dorado convertible, her long Nile-blue hair swept behind her like the heraldic head-dress of a dynastic goddess. She had vanished in a glimmer of speed, leaving me with a fleeting image of sudden eyes in an oval ice-white face, a profile like the death mask of an Assyrian princess.

She's not quite Abraham Merritt's Lur the witch-woman...but not totally unrelated, either.

Protagonist Paul Ransom edits an avant-garde poetry magazine, *Wave IX*. These days, poetry is all written by computers ("VT"—Verse-Transcriber—sets, made by IBM). Human authorship is limited to programming them. Aurora Day moves in, with her hunchbacked, club-footed, twisted-faced chauffeur, and intimidates Ransom into agreeing to let her control the contents of one issue of his magazine after, essentially, a campaign of magic: substituting her copy for his in the magazine at the printer, materializing a sand ray in his chair, raising a colossal boil on his face, and causing lines of poetry to be inscribed on his front step, the door lock, the door, the walls, the furniture, and his skin.

Meanwhile, all the Verse-Transcribers in Vermilion Sands have been mysteriously trashed. How to get material? The poets should write it themselves, says Aurora, but they all refuse except Tristram Caldwell, who becomes Aurora's main squeeze after a disquisition by Aurora about Melander, the spirit of poetry, and Corydon, the young man who died for her. (Indeed, she has a frieze on her wall representing it, with a likeness of the chauffeur as Pan.) During a sand ray-hunting expedition, they are beset by a swarm of rays and Caldwell is stung and seemingly killed under circumstances for which Aurora was responsible. She and her chauffeur depart immediately. But Caldwell reappears, having faked his death (he knew, but nobody else did, that the rays' stings are passive during the hunting season). Suddenly all the poets of Vermilion Sands have discovered that they can write without their VTs, so Ransom will be able to publish.

The careful observer will have noted that the plot of this second Vermilion Sands story is essentially the same as that of "Prima Belladonna": exotic spellbinding woman hits town, fascinates and dominates, blots her copybook big time in the course of acting out her obsessions, and flees. Of course there are big differences too. Jane Ciracylides, aside from having a few kinks in her head, was basically a sweet kid, as one might have said in 1956. No one would ever say that about Aurora Day.

Another similarity is the contrast between the florid imagery and vocabulary of parts of the story and the light satirical tone of other parts, such as the interaction between Ransom and his collaborators on the magazine. Says Raymond Mayo—who "looked even more dapper than usual, dark hair smoothed back, profile adjusted for maximum impact"—about Aurora: "There's something formless and unstated there, reminded me of Dali's 'Cosmogonic Venus.' Made me realise how absolutely terrifying all women really are. If I were you I'd do whatever I was told." But here the disjunction is a feature, not a bug: Ballard seems now to have a clearer idea of Vermilion Sands as a place that provides a sort of low-stakes backdrop against which the deranged, melodramatic, and self-absorbed can make major fools of themselves without doing too much harm. It's also now a place of near-total isolation. Jane in "Prima Belladonna" at least came from somewhere (Peru) and was later heard of "this side out of Pernambuco" (in Brazil), but Aurora Day comes from nowhere and flees there, and the only place names acknowledged are part of the greater imaginapolitan area of Vermilion Sands: Red Beach, Lagoon West, Ciraquito.

When Ransom needs copy in a hurry, the only people he solicits are the poets of Vermilion Sands. You'd think he'd have some international contacts. (He says "reimbursing a year's advance subscriptions would bankrupt me"—about a *poetry* magazine. Hard to believe it would sell that many copies locally.) Ballard does acknowledge the existence of IBM, but only as far away as the dealership in Red Beach. The ever helpful Carnell, in his blurb, describes Vermilion Sands as "a coastal paradise where the 'long-hairs' idled their time away." Seacoast of Bohemia, anyone?

This story, even more than "The Sound-Sweep," is deeply Ballardian, pervaded by what will later become recognizable as his characteristic mannerisms and preoccupations. The vocabulary is definitely there, illustrated by the quotations above from the story's beginning, and by his description of Aurora Day's own poetry, Ransom's rejection of which triggers her campaign against him: "All were written in the same strange hectoring tone, at once minatory and obscure, like the oracular deliriums of some insane witch." If the works of Ballard were to be considered as a Friday night Rotarian bowling tournament, that sentence would be a strike.

There is the theatrical and deranged female muse, and the

Caliban figure, the visual arts references—here the syllabus is Dali, as indicated by the "Cosmogonic Venus" reference above. Also: "Raymond Mayo saw her as one of Salvador Dali's exploding madonnas, an enigma serenely riding out the apocalypse." And later, as Aurora is pressing her demands: "We sat together in the luminescent dusk, the long shadows playing across the purple landscape of Dali's 'Persistence of Memory' on the wall behind Aurora...." There's the usual quota of passing ironic inventions, e.g.: "Most of us were suffering from various degrees of beach fatigue, that chronic malaise or tedium vitae which exiles the victim to a limbo of endless sun-bathing, dark glasses and afternoon terraces...."

Nonetheless the story doesn't quite work for me, for a couple of reasons. First, there's an overdone protesting-too-much quality about its language and imagery. Second, Aurora's witchcraft (like Jane's paranormal powers in "Prima Belladonna") doesn't fit well into the Vermilion Sands milieu, which, while not exactly a hyper-rationalistic setting, isn't a magic kingdom either. We may not expect perfect logic from Vermilion Sands, but this isn't quite the right sort of illogic.

16: *SCIENCE FANTASY*, VOLUME 16 (ISSUES 46-48)

Science Fantasy, volume 16, for April, June and August 1961, is Brian Lewis's last hurrah on *Science Fantasy*, with three covers by Lewis, two of them up to his usual standard and the third decidedly not. **49** will usher in the brief renascence of Quinn. The substandard Lewis cover is on **47** and illustrates the first of Michael Moorcock's Elric stories, but his cartoony rendering of that decadent and tortured figure looks like a robust Joe College at a fraternity costume party.[53]

There's one other big development on the cover: the price goes from 2/ to 2/6. Advertisers include the Science Fiction Book Club; the Psychology Publishing Company with something called *Realization* by Geoffrey A. Dudley, which seems like a diffident UK cross between *Dianetics* and *How to Win Friends And Influence People*; *Film User*, a magazine for aficionados of 16 mm., and the British Science Fiction Association. Sam Moskowitz's Studies in Science Fiction series continues with Karel Capek, Olaf Stapledon, and Stanley G. Weinbaum.

§

The three issues contain three, four, and five stories respec-

_____

53. See these covers at http://www.sfcovers.net/mainnav.htm or http://www.philsp.com/mags/sciencefantasy.html.

tively. The only US reprint is Theodore Sturgeon's "Need" in 46, a novella first published in Sturgeon's 1960 US paperback collection *Beyond*. The only other US author I can identity is Will Worthington, whose "The Food Goes in the Top" is not a reprint. Most likely it was a reject from the US magazines where Worthington published the rest of his stories.

"Need" is one of those Sturgeon stories that make you want to reach into the pages and grab him by the lapels and shake him, not because it's a bad story but because it could have been much better if he had only curbed his self-indulgent habits. Like bloviation. This one starts out "Some towns seem able to defy not only time, but change...." Not a bad line, but he goes on about these towns, and on, and it is not until the end of the second page of text that he discloses that this is North Nyack, New York he's talking about, and not until the third page of text that an actual character makes an appearance. It's good stuff, but not dumped in a lump at the very beginning.

The substance of the story is mainstream Sturgeon, with a cast of sensitive misfits plus a crass and insensitive slug in urgent need of an education about life, the whole about as didactic as Ayn Rand though considerably more readable. Sturgeon never did quite catch on to "show, don't tell." The main misfit is someone who perceives need and has to do something about it, though that doesn't make him particularly nice. He responds to a hitchhiking drug addict by running him out of town. The real hero is an eccentric but (of course) very wise junk shop owner who permits Sturgeon to indulge his preoccupation with tools and gadgets and how to use them. And if my comment sounds overly cranky, again: it's not a bad story, it's just a reminder of how much better Sturgeon *could* have been.

47 leads with the first Elric story, "The Dreaming City," which both shines and stinks. Or maybe I mean babbles and jangles.

Elric, the moody-eyed wanderer—a lonely man who fought a world, living by his wits and his runesword

Stormbringer. Elric, last Lord of Melnibone, last wor-
shipper of its grotesque and beautiful Gods—reckless
reaver and cynical slayer—torn by great griefs and
with a knowledge locked in his skull which would turn
lesser men into babbling idiots. Elric, moulder of mad-
nesses, dabbler in wild delights....

It's easy to see how this shameless floridity at least made
an impression. Even the most imaginative of *Science Fantasy*'s
prior material maintained a rigid decorum by comparison. After
this muted introduction, Moorcock dives headlong into the plot,
which, as I'm sure everyone knows, involves Elric's plan to
hire a fleet of pirates to invade and raze his home town of Im-
ryrr, saving only his cousin Yyrkoon and his sister Cymoril. He
expedites this plan through various debilitating magicks ("Elric
still crooned his hideous, mind-juddering song of sorcery as the
spirits of the air plucked at the sail and sent the boat flying over
the water faster than any mortal ship could speed.")

It's acceptable to raze this perfectly good city because cousin
Yyrkoon, who has usurped Elric's throne (not that he wants
it), allows only his drug-addled decadent class buddies to stay
there. Everybody else better be out by sundown every day. Not
that Elric himself is a model of mental health—"though he had
a lonely, obscure urge to wander and sample the less sophisticated pleasures of the outside world, ten thousand years of a
cruel, brilliant and malicious culture was behind him and the
pulse of his ancestry beat strongly in his deficient veins."

Elric sneaks into the city, and Old Tanglebones, who taught
Elric fencing and archery, lets him into the castle and cooper-
ates in the clumsy festival of bloodshed that ensues. Upstairs,
Elric gazes maudlinly upon his sister, who is comatose under
some spell of Yyrkoon's; Yrkoon shows up ("You offspring of a
festering worm, Yyrkoon. You'll have cause to repent this vile
spell before your time is run!"). It is revealed that Elric is in
love with his sister. More blood is shed. Elric escapes to bring
in the waiting fleet, more bloodshed ensues, and Elric goes

after his sister, who is now held in the Tower of B'aal'nezbett (Gesundheit!). He and Yyrkoon have a gaudy battle with their runeswords, and the dying Yyrkoon shoves Cymoril onto the point of Elric's sword. This last event serves two important plot points: stoking Elric's remorseful morbidity and avoiding having to ask the next question, incest, which would probably have been a bit more color than the *Science Fantasy* audience was prepared for in 1961.

So Elric and the fleet make their getaway after the razing and find themselves pursued by dragons. Everybody's doomed, except that Elric calls up the winds again and gets away while everybody in the other ships of the fleet gets left behind and crisped by the dragons. Elric broods, and realizes that it's his damnable sword that is calling the shots and maintaining his vitality at the cost of his peace of mind, so he throws it overboard. Being magical, it doesn't sink, but sticks upright in the surface of the sea. "It remained throbbing in the water, six inches of its blade immersed, and began to give off a weird devil-scream—a howl of horrible malevolence." So Elric does the only natural thing and jumps over the side to get it, as opposed to calling up the winds again and getting the hell out of there.

Re-bonding with the sword, he swears a mighty oath—in substance, "You and me, babe"; *in haec verba*, "Bound by hell-forged chains and fate-haunted circumstance." His proposition: "give this age *cause* to hate us as we wander its young lands and new-formed seas." Whew! Elric and sword are last seen swimming toward an island, much to the relief of his sailors, and the story ends like this...as if anybody needed to be told that there would be sequels as far as the eye could see. If one did not know that Moorcock's background was in comic books, it wouldn't be too hard to figure out.

§

Propriety is restored in the issue's other long story (longer than "The Dreaming City," in fact), "The Veil of Isis" by John

Rackham, a sequel to **44**'s "The Black Cat's Paw" and perfectly conventional in presentation. A lady journalist, as it might have been put in 1961, shows up at the house of Egyptologist K. N. Wilson. Chappie Jones is home alone and lets her in, contrary to instruction. Wilson comes home followed by Inspector Ferguson, champion of the mundane, who reports that 18 unidentified dead bodies have been found in the last two weeks. Meanwhile the journalist has been recruiting beautiful Yalna, Chappie's muse, for some sort of fashion display, which turns out to be a trap, and Chappie gets knocked on the head and Yalna is kidnapped.

The same evil mage as in the earlier story is at the bottom of it all, and he's got Yalna rigged up as a sort of battery for the Veil of Isis, a supernatural force field. The dead have been recycled from local graveyards, and the good guys have to storm an old house and defeat a couple of platoons of these undead to get it all put right. By the way, the lady journalist was actually a man, and a member in good standing of the undead himself. Good order is restored, with Sir Cyril of the Yard and Wilson the Egyptologist agreeing to keep each other informed of "anything unusual." Here, too, room is left for another sequel ("Think he'll bob up again?" "I'm absolutely certain he will, when he's ready.") Surely this is a conscious pastiche of some UK predecessor of the 1920s or '30s.

§

We proceed from propriety to sobriety in **48**, where the lead story is John Brunner's novelette "The Analysts," graced with a particularly well composed and strikingly colored Lewis cover. Joel Sackstone is a visualiser, with a sort of para-intuition about design that allows him to look at plans and models and their orientation to land and know immediately what's wrong with them and how to fix them. (Extravagant fiction today, Feng Shui tomorrow, or yesterday.) He consults for an architectural firm. Some clients want them to erect a building that Sackstone says doesn't make any sense. When he visualizes walking around in the hypothetical building, at one point the logical direction to walk runs him into a blank wall.

The clients, who represent something called the Foundation for Social Trends, seem pretty weird, and strange things keep happening related to them. Finally Sackstone crudely replicates the building design in his living room and follows the strange dead-end path, and when he fetches up against the blank wall, goes right through it into another world. This world's denizens remark on his speaking Ancient English and compliment him on understanding that he's in the far future, that the man who looks like a gray tree trunk is from another planet, and—almost—that the Foundation for Social Trends are conducting a "socio-analysis" of human history.

It seems when humanity first encountered extra-terrestrials, it panicked and attacked them, and now is trying to exorcise its guilt complex. Sackstone and his girlfriend (who along with one of the Foundation agents have followed him through his living room wall) are offered the chance to sign up, and of course they do. This is a pretty clever and entertaining story with a well-set-up mystery until Sackstone goes through the wall, at which point it becomes preachy and high-minded as Brunner was prone to do.

Of the short fiction, the most promising seems to be J. G. Ballard's "Mr. F Is Mr. F" (**48**), but it proves to be one of his less successful efforts, a sort of labored misogynist fable. The protagonist Freeman has married at age 40 to a woman a few years older and a few inches taller than he. Freeman had chosen her as "an ideal mother-substitute," seeing himself "as her child rather than as her parental partner." But now she has unexpectedly become pregnant—and Freeman starts growing younger, at first enjoying the renewal of his physical capabilities, but then finding the situation becoming awkward, for example at work (he stops going). His suggestions of consulting a doctor are brushed off by his wife, who has meanwhile been covertly taking up the seams in his clothing, and who starts bringing him comic books. All the while, as she makes and buys baby clothes, he is trying absurdly to conceal from her how small he has become. He tries to escape and she puts him in a playpen. After watching her interact with another man, one Hanson, he realizes:

> *She knew! . . .*
> *SHE KNEW!!!. . . .*
> *All along she had known what was happening, had deliberately pretended not to notice his metamorphosis! Carefully she had anticipated each stage of the transformation, the comprehensive wardrobe had been purchased well in advance, the succession of smaller and smaller garments, the play-pen and cot, had been ordered for him not for the baby!*

And matters progress until he re-enters the womb, with a phrase either telling or ironic:

> Gradually his memory of the house and his own identity began to fade, and his shrinking body clung helplessly to Elizabeth as she lay on her broad bed.
>
> Hating the naked hair that rasped across his face, he now felt clearly for the first time what he had for so long repressed, the ceaseless quest for his mother that had been the generating power behind his metamorphosis, and which had secretly prevented him from resisting her.
>
> Just before the end he cried out suddenly with joy and wonder, as he remembered the drowned world of his first childhood.

There's a little more—we follow Freeman to the moment of un-conception—but the picture is clear enough, having been telegraphed from nearly the beginning of the story. The whole thing is remarkably unsubtle for Ballard, and much too long for the flimsiness of its conceit. This invocation of "the drowned world" precedes by five months the publication of the first, shorter version of the novel of that title in the January 1962 *Science Fiction Adventures*.

Aside from Ballard, the short fiction in these issues is mostly pretty entertaining, though not at all above criticism. In **46**, there is yet another Hek Belov story by Edward Mackin, "Behind the Cloud." This one is actually quite clever. Belov is hired to fix a malfunctioning solido (3-D movie to you) projector and the characters all wind up precipitated into the fictional world of the scriptwriter. Too bad I've already read the preceding X number of these stories and am so tired of Mackin's schtick that it's hard to appreciate the fact that he's actually getting better. Next is "Displaced Person," said to be Australian Lee Harding's first story, which is also the issue's second Philip K. Dick companion piece, about a man who suddenly stops making much of an impression—people forget he's there, then don't notice him in the first place. Ultimately his hands pass right through them. It's well conceived and worked out but is a bit overwritten and overlong and suffers from a theological ending (non-denominational, at least—the protagonist realizes that Somebody, quote unquote sic, is in charge, and has lost track of him). Harding expanded it into the Young Adult novel of the same title (changed to *Misplaced Person* in the US), which won him the 1978 Alan Marshall Award and the Australian Children's Book of the Year Award in 1980.

Next, in **47**, John Kippax rotates the formulae in "Blood Offering." A stolid Aussie man runs a store on one of the Pacific islands, scoffs when the shark god is invoked, and learns his lesson, though it's actually his Chinese assistant who winds up as lunch. This one makes up for lack of originality by convincing detail, local color, and good writing—though it, like the Rackham novelette, reads like a pastiche of a 30-year-old model. W. T. Webb's "Valley of the Rainbirds" is a crude but effectively strange story about a woman who lives alone in a valley beset by huge flocks of starlings, which seem to bring the rain with them, and a man who shows up at her house claiming they aren't really birds, and we know who will have the last squawk.

Lee Harding's "Sacrificial" (**48**) features a man who is fascinated by an old house built by slave labor. The house has ideas of its own, though. This is another formulaic weird tale, but it isn't redeemed by handling. It's too long and heavy-handed for its overly familiar idea. "Parky," by another Australian, David Rome (pseudonym of David Boutland), is a slight but deft story about a man who runs a carnival and employs a mind-reader. Aliens decide that's just what's needed to help keep the peace on their world, and trade the carnie-wallah a new novelty act for him. Judith Merril picked it up for her annual anthology. Will Worthington's "The Food Goes in the Top" starts as a slightly heavy-handed satire of the life of quiet desperation of an urban nobody (a bit reminiscent in attitude of Sladek's later "Masterson and the Clerks" and in style of Avram Davidson) and then turns surreal and slouches—again Philip K. Dick-wise—toward a revelation suggested by the title.

I think these issues are a fair representation of what made this magazine worthwhile and keeps its memory alive. Most of the stories are capably done, most are pleasingly off-trail, and enough of them are both to give the magazine a distinctive personality. And, despite Carnell's repeated poor-mouthing about how you can't really have a fantasy magazine these days, it is in fact largely a fantasy magazine at this point.

17: *SCIENCE FANTASY,* VOLUME 17 (ISSUES 49-51)

Science Fantasy, vol. 17, for October and December 1961 and February 1962, marks the departure of Brian Lewis and the brief return of Gerard Quinn as cover artists. Quinn's cover on **49**, not illustrating a story but titled "Queen of the Wheel," is a pleasant-looking Richard Powers-y nebulosity which on closer scrutiny resolves into a sort of metaphysical cheesecake. The next two seem to be on the theme of Weird Women of the Universe (at least by 1961 standards). The cover of **50**, titled "A Present from Earth," portrays a completely bald woman admiring a wig which she is about to don. The untitled cover of **51** depicts a pretty pre-pubescent girl sitting completely naked, holding a doll. The doll very visibly has one eye in the middle of its forehead, but the girl's head is turned so her hair obscures the relevant part of her face. This one is interesting for two reasons: first, its perverse cleverness, and second, the fact that it is one of the few things in the world that could appear on a magazine cover in 1961 but not today, at least not without subjecting the publisher to likely prosecution and/or vigilante violence.[54]

The contents are in the now-established mode: longer and fewer stories (four, three, and four respectively) mostly by UK writers—this volume has *no* US reprints. The only US author as far as I know is the then sixty-one-year-old Wallace West, who sold to Farnsworth Wright at *Weird Tales* in 1927 and to

54. See these covers at http://www.sfcovers.net/mainnav.htm or http://www.philsp.com/mags/sciencefantasy.html.

Gernsback in 1929. West's "Heinrich," Carnell gently empha-sizes, is "a *new* humorous story dealing with a haunted castle." (Carnell describes West as "another popular American writer." At this point in his career, West was dusting off his old pulp material for the bottom-of-the-market Avalon Books, and had only a handful more magazine stories to come, though he did hit *Galaxy* and *Analog* with several of them. Around this time—my personal Golden Age of thirteen—I belonged to the National Fantasy Fan Federation; West was one of the handful of writers who remained in that agedly juvenile organization. He issued a bitter protest that no one was paying any atten-tion to him and his work. None of this, of course, speaks to the merits, and "Heinrich" is a pretty good humorous fantasy.) The Moskowitz "Studies in Science Fiction" series concludes, with Philip Wylie in **49** and Shiel and Heard in **50**. The advertising is per usual: house ads, British Science Fiction Association, *Film User* magazine, and the Rosicrucians, who demand to know: "Are You Conscious of Your Inner-Consciousness?" (Not when I can help it, thank you for asking.)

50 is labeled "Anniversary Issue," though not based on the calendar: it marks 11.5 years of publication. There's a celebra-tory editorial by Carnell, which first explains: "Although I was unable to build a 'special issue' for this mile-stone in the history of *Science Fantasy*—we do not use many short stories and it would have taken over a year to compile sufficient to make an issue similar to the 100ᵗʰ edition of *New Worlds Science Fiction*—this is nevertheless a rather proud moment for many of us." And, finally, he no longer denies that he is actually publishing a fantasy magazine!—though he does implicitly deny that his American colleague Cele Goldsmith is doing so at *Fantastic*: "At the moment, it is the *only* magazine of its type in the world and lends a sympathetic ear to any author who feels that he wants to write an off-trail story without the necessity of backing his plot with scientific concepts or theories." Well, he has at least part of a point: *Fantastic* was publishing a lot of fantasy by the likes of Leiber and Robert F. Young, but, e.g., the serials in the 1961 *Fantastic* included one pretty bad fantasy, "Magnanthropus" by Manly Banister, and three outright SF novels, James White's "Second Ending," Laumer's "Worlds of the Imperium," and the conclusion of one of Poul Anderson's Dominic Flandry stories.

§

The lead story in **49** is Moorcock's "While the Gods Laugh," the second Elric story. The first one, as noted above, was extraordinarily noisy and scenery-chewing, simultaneously hysterical and maudlin, and both at the top of its lungs. This one is more muted—relatively speaking, of course. We last saw Elric, having jumped overboard after his sword, swimming away from the boat towards an island and vowing memorably evil deeds. This one opens with Elric entirely dry, and nothing more is said about the island, how he got off it, etc. Drinking alone, he is approached by Shaarilla of the Dancing Mist, a "wingless woman of Myyrrhn" (sometimes one gets the impression that Moorcock's mythic muse is Scrabble) who offers him her comely person if he will go with her on a perilous journey to rescue the Dead Gods' Book, legendarily thrown into the Sun by the Old Gods (capitalized) but perhaps intercepted by the "dark ones" (no caps).

After a suitable consumer warning ("I should admit that I scream in my sleep sometimes and am often tortured by incommunicable self-loathing. Go while you can, lady, and forget Elric for he can bring only grief to your soul."), he goes with her. Why are they doing this? She wants to figure out how to grow wings so she can fit in better in her home town. Elric's needs are more abstract: he needs to know if there is a God. For some reason they think the answers will be found in the Book—perhaps a pre-Mosaic mosaic of *Summa Theologica* and an Audubon compendium—and that they can believe them.

To get to the alleged Book, they have to go through the Marshes of the Mist and the Silent Land. Elric inquires about the route, and Shaarilla discloses that she has lost the map. On they go nonetheless. They encounter and Elric dispatches a Mist Giant and a pack of devil-dogs. The latter are chasing one Moonglum, a sort of diminutive Falstaff figure who joins their parade. Shaarilla loses her nerve, wants to go back, reveals on cross-examination her father's warning that "He who guards the Book" will stop at nothing to keep them away. They are pursued by more devil-dogs, these accompanied by zombie-men a.k.a. the centuries-dead Lords of Dharzi. Elric remembers his magic just in time, and all of them are swallowed by the earth ("A deep unholy chuckle arose from the shattered pit. It was the mocking laughter of the Earth Kings taking their rightful prey back into their keeping.")

They come to a cave mouth bearing the sign of Chaos: "We are standing in territory presided over by the Lord of Entropy or one of his minions... This can mean only one thing—this book is of extreme importance to the order of all things on this planet—possibly the galaxy—or the entire universe!" After some ruminations on Law vs. Chaos, they go into the cave, which proves to be a tunnel, which leads to a peculiar underground sea which isn't really water and has a convenient intact boat on the beach.

Off they set to nowhere in particular, albeit with a strong tailwind, repel *en passant* an attack by flying apes, and fetch up at a castle—still underground, but with daylight filtering down from overhead. The castle is open, and its giant Keeper doesn't even try to stop them going in...and there's the Book, its covers encrusted with glowing gems. "'At last,' Elric breathed. 'At last—the Truth!'" But he opens the cover, and: "Beneath Elric's twitching hands lay nothing but a pile of yellowish dust." You have to hate it when that happens.

They clamber out of the Lord of Entropy's hole and Elric proclaims his unrelieved philosophical anguish. Shaarilla offers to comfort him, but he spurns her for having gotten his hopes up to no purpose, and stalks off. Moonglum chases after him, his pockets full of the jewels from the book cover, after giving Shaarilla one of them. She drops it on the ground and heads back underground, in search of God knows what.

The saga continues in **51** with "The Stealer of Souls," which is considerably more pedestrian and doesn't deserve such detailed mockery. Elric takes a commission from the local Chamber of Commerce to rid them of their competitor Nikorn, who hangs out in a castle protected by the sorcerer Theleb K'aarna, comforted in turn by his mistress Yishana, Queen of Jarkor, who is also one of Elric's old girlfriends. This time the bestiary comprises assorted Wind Giants, the Fire Lord Kakatal, and the malodorous and toad-like Quaolnargn, who eats souls at K'aarna's summoning and between meals reposes "in a smoking pit of Hell, somewhere beyond the limitations of space and time"—just catty-corner from Azathoth, I would think. As usual, Elric's schemes result in the deaths of the worthiest characters, though the remorse is a bit *pro forma* this time around; Moorcock already seems a bit bored with this series.

§

The other novelette in the issue **49** is "The Seventh Stair" by Frank Brandon, a pseudonym of Kenneth Bulmer. Bulmer is by now a well established contributor to the magazine under his own name, but not so prolific that he has to worry about multiple stories in an issue. So why a pseudonym? It's not as if he is trying to do anything particularly new, though this one is a bit jokier than most of Bulmer's.

A man's old Army buddy demands he come over right away. He can't go down the stairs without disappearing into another world full of dinosaurs and smaller reptiles. What to do? Call another old buddy in the Fire Department and get the victim down the ladder outside and to the protagonist's apartment. But then he can't get down those stairs either. Why? He's a mathematician and the work he's just done apparently has time- or dimension-traveling as a side effect. (You liked the syllogismobile? You'll love the equation wagon.) So the protagonist calls up all the other old Army buddies in the area and they arm themselves to the teeth to make an expedition to the reptiles' world, except that he has so little mathematical aptitude that when everybody else disappears going down the Tube stairs, he's left behind—he hasn't understood the equations. A sequel is clearly signaled.

49 is the Old Castle Issue of *Science Fantasy*. In addition to Moorcock's castle containing the disintegrated Book, John Kippax's "Reflection of the Truth" presents an old legend about an Eastern European king, his young and restless wife, and the sorcerer he hires to make him some gold, told by the man who shows visitors around the castle and who also has a young and restless wife. It's clever and well-turned. Wallace West's "Heinrich" is odder. The protagonist and his wife have befriended a poltergeist of German pedigree. They are dispatched to Munich to run a trade fair and Heinrich persuades them to rent the old family castle, which is haunted by his deceased brother Adolf, a Bismarck enthusiast for whom Hitler was the next best thing. Adolf holds in thrall the ghost of Heinrich's great love Trudy, who manifests with bloodstains and bullet holes, having died in 1937 fleeing the Gestapo. There ensues an *Unknown*ish war of haunts and a ludicrous scheme of exhuming Adolf and burying him at a crossroads in mid-Oktoberfest. This is a pretty good example of a kind of black humor not often seen in the SF/fantasy magazines that early (I'll bet Cele Goldsmith, then editor of the US *Fantastic*, saw it and had no idea what to make of it), and it's never been anthologized.

§

The lead novelette in **50** (57 pages, so it would have been a "short novel" earlier) is "Ankh," the last of John Rackham's three stories about Chappie Jones, sidekick of Egyptologist K. N. Wilson, and the struggle against the sinister necromancer Ram Ferras. It's entertaining enough, as were its predecessors, but toward the end it begins to read less like a pastiche of something from the 1920s and more like a not-bad Ace Double, with a final titanic mental battle that yanks the characters from one historical virtual world to another and winds up with humble Chappie proving the most psionically, er, magically, talented of them all.

The rest of the fiction is more of a mixed bag, but all quite readable with one exception. Most peculiar is "The Legend" by W. T. Webb (**51**), another "novelette" at fifty-plus pages, a sort of inverted Scooby Doo. The protagonist takes a job as headmaster of a remote school after the mysterious death of his predecessor. The eponymous legend is about Brown Robin, a sort of demon-figure who has been showing up at intervals of years since medieval times and performing various types of mischief, including fatal; clearly it's happening again. But there's really a mundane explanation: an extraterrestrial who crashed his spaceship into the lake about 60 years previously and hypnotized the inhabitants into believing he'd been around for centuries and faking the historical records.

Edward Mackin contributes "Still Centre" (**50**), another of the Hek Belov stories. Belov encounters a sort of Tesla-writ-small figure who has made great advances in the science of gyroscopy. After cranking out quite a procession of lead balloons over several years, Mackin is finally starting to become reasonably funny. Leroy B. Haugsrud's "A Cure for Mr. Kelsy" (**50**) is a pleasantly amusing if rambling story about a man who is becoming a vampire and goes to a doctor for it (referred by the gypsy woman, no less). John Brunner's "Ouef du Coq" (**51**) is an adroitly executed trifle about a mysterious statue and a restaurant menu, which comes about as close as possible to making something out of nothing. The worst of the lot is "The Big Sound" (**51**) by P. F. Woods (pseudonym of Barrington Bayley), a completely muddled story about a thoroughly uninteresting eccentric who assembles the world's largest orchestra, evokes a response from another galaxy, produces something that he declares to be solidified sound, confesses himself to be stone deaf and to hear with his mind, and goes to prison for financial shenanigans. Say what? And why?

18: *SCIENCE FANTASY,* VOLUME 18 (ISSUES 52-54)

Science Fantasy volume 18, for April through August 1962, presents itself as more of the same, but that's about to change. The three Gerard Quinn covers on these issues are the last painted covers on the Nova *Science Fantasy*. It's on to drawings and photos after this. These covers range from the pedestrian to the splendid. **52** is an agreeable picture of two male faces superimposed against each other over a starfield, **54** depicts a shirtless man either struggling or canoodling with a tentacled tree, but **53** is one of Quinn's best: against late-afternoon desert sands, a sea shell, a half-buried broken-stringed harp, a *TRES-PASSERS WILL BE PROSECUTED* sign also half-buried, and in the distance beyond a rock outcropping, a derelict electrical pylon. This is about as Ballardian as one can get, and indeed there is a Ballard story in the issue, "The Watch-Towers." But the cover doesn't seem to illustrate the story, which is one of Ballard's least landscape-obsessed (plenty of sky though).[55]

The ads are as usual—British Science Fiction Association, Easter Convention, *Film User*, house ads—except for the inside front cover of **52**, which advertises *Bloodhound Detective Story Magazine*, "The Crime Monthly with the Top American Authors" including Mickey Spillane, Evan Hunter, James M. Cain, Fredric Brown, John Ross Macdonald, and—excuse me?—Erskine Caldwell? I don't think I've seen him in this kind

---

55. See these covers at http://www.sfcovers.net/mainnav.htm or http://www.philsp.com/mags/sciencefantasy.html.

of criminously hard-boiled company before.

There is an innovation in these issues, a book review column, written by Carnell, in **53** and **54**. In **53**, it takes up only the last page of the magazine and isn't listed on the contents page, suggesting it was last-minute filler after a miscalculation on the way to the printer. Carnell briefly reviews Michael Sissons (ed.), *In the Dead of Night* ("a fine macabre collection"), Bradbury's *Timeless Stories For Today And Tomorrow* ("probably the most outstanding collection of its kind for many years"), August Derleth's *Not Long For This World* (no opinion), and Leo Margulies (ed.), *The Ghoul Keepers* ("a good assortment for the new reader"). In **54**, however, the column is on the contents page and takes up three pages, with one section of Fantasy and Macabre and one of SF. The reviews are mostly even more cursory than in the previous issue, in some cases merely listing contents. In the ensuing issues the column appears several more times, shorter and more focused on fantasy than in **54**.

In **52**, Carnell is back to his old tricks. The cover announces "Special Fantasy Issue." What did he think he had been publishing for the past several years? It's particularly ironic since one of the three stories in the issue, Claude and Rhoda Nunes' "The Problem," is unequivocally SF, albeit an especially inane specimen. The most notable of the stories is Thomas Burnett Swann's celebrated "Where Is the Bird of Fire?", his retelling of the Romulus and Remus story, discussed below. That story, incidentally, is blurbed in part: "Outstanding fantasy stories are all too rare these days—*Science Fantasy* is the sole outlet for authors who still love this medium," which is as off-base in its way as the "Special Fantasy Issue" designation, since *Fantasy and Science Fiction* and *Fantastic* were both appearing monthly in the US and publishing some fantasy, though with a heavy admixture of SF—not unlike *Science Fantasy*.

§

Lead story in **52** is John Brunner's "Father of Lies," another of his Fantasies Against Magic, in which *Le Morte d'Arthur* meets "It's a *Good* Life." Ex-college friends are investigating a seemingly empty area on the map of England. Go into it and you start to see strange things, like dragons. And cameras, car engines, and other newfangled gadgets stop working. Sound a bit familiar? Obviously it is a predecessor in some sense of Robert Holdstock's World Fantasy Award winner *Mythago Wood*.

Our hero leaves his car and presses on, on foot, finds a beautiful naked woman staked out for the dragon, and rescues her. She's from outside, terrified and bewildered. Soon (though not before our protagonist slays an ogre with his axe) they are captured by the primitive locals and taken before "he," a creature with underdeveloped child's body and bulging cranium, who holds court in a shabby castle and clearly maintains this tatty medieval diorama through some sort of paranormal mental power. The moderns prevail without too much difficulty, the king-monster is slain by his brother, all is explained. It's an agreeable story if not up to the standard of Brunner's previous work for this magazine, and it preaches the same sermon as its predecessors: magic (in this case, strictly speaking, psi) is a dead end and things go better with reason.

53 presents Moorcock's "The Eternal Champion," in which one John Daker wakes up to find he is Erekose, the deceased but resurrected hero of either a far-future or a long-past Earth (time is circular, in case you hadn't noticed) that is threatened by the Hounds of Evil, strange extra-dimensional near-humans. Erekose is the Champion because he has a poisoned sword that kills everybody it touches. Why everyone doesn't put poison on his or her sword, or maybe in a fire hose, is not explained.

Exactly what's so bad about these Hounds isn't so clear, either, and as the story progresses Erekose becomes less and less convinced, and finally sides with the Hounds and helps them wipe out humanity, which he has concluded is irredeemably warlike and vicious. This appears to be a Burroughs pastiche—the slightly stilted but flat style, and the arbitrary manner of Daker/Erekose's appearance on the scene, seem like a conscious homage to John Carter's impromptu flight to Mars.

Frankly, it all seems pretty boring and slapdash (absolutely nothing is done with the fact that the character seems to contain the personality of a contemporary English-speaker as well as that of Erekose), unlike the Elric stories which at least started out as floridly novel and slapdash.

Speaking of which, Moorcock appears again in **54** with "Kings in Darkness," another Elric novelette, in which he and his sidekick Moonglum are run out of town, viz. Nadsokor, City of Beggars, because Elric is known to be "a nigromancer of superlative powers" (so the locals go after them with knives, bows, and torches, as you would). They escape through the ill-rumored Forest of Troos, where they rescue Zarozinia of Karlaak, who has escaped an ambush. She and Elric hit it off, but their goods are taken in an ambush by the Orgians, so naturally they head for the kingdom of Org to retrieve them, first concocting a potion of invulnerability from the local vegetation.

Once there, they find a decaying regime and a decaying castle, and are treacherously cast in irons. Elric escapes to the barrow where the old King is buried, and where Zarozinia narrowly escapes being sacrificed. They head back to the castle to retrieve their stuff from amidst the drunken revelers, but are interrupted by the arrival of the dead King and his revenant posse, whom Elric and Moonglum dispatch by setting the castle on fire. Exit stage left to the next adventure.

While the atmosphere of the first stories is still invoked by periodic bursts of florid rhetoric ("It was Elric, Lord of the lost and sundered Empire of Melnibone, who rode like a fanged wolf from a trap—all slavering madness and mirth"), at this point they have settled down to a routine of fairly conventional picaresque storytelling, and the initial impulse to morbid inversion of Sword & Sorcery tropes seems largely to have spent itself. The result is less over the top but also considerably less entertaining, and at the end of this one Moorcock seems to have capitulated entirely to off-the-rack cliché. Referring to Elric's impending marriage to Zarozina:

> For it would be more than a marriage between the awful evil-bringer of legends and a senator's youthful daughter—it would be a marriage between the dark wisdom of the Ancient World and the bright hope of the New.
> And who could tell what such a combination would bring about?
> The Earth would soon know, for Elric of Melnibone was the maker of legends and there were legends yet to make!

Bah.

§

The lead story in **54** is pretty lackluster: "Perilous Portal" by Frank Brandon, i.e. Kenneth Bulmer. This is the thoroughly telegraphed sequel to "The Seventh Stair" from **49**, and my question about why Bulmer is using a pseudonym for these stories may be answered: it's pretty ripe.

The story so far: Phil and his old Army buddies were going into a parallel world full of prehistoric reptiles using the irresistible equations developed by one of them. But Phil is so lousy at maths that he got left behind on the Underground stairs. Now he is, so help me, taking a correspondence course in the hope that he, too, can comprehend the equations and vanish from the face of the Earth. But he accidentally sticks the fatal equations in the envelope along with his homework. Realizing his mistake, he rushes across England to try to intercept them. Too late of course, and he and his tutor—she's a babe! though initially termagantish—are translated to the reptile world, which actually turns out to be a world with its own several sentient species, the Dumps, the Smilers, and the thumblings (capitalization sic).

This world is under siege by the evil Porvone who enslave

everyone in sight, and who have designs on our world and know how to get here. But all the Army buddies show up with their artillery and set everything right. This is pulpy in the pejorative sense, reminiscent of *Thrilling Wonder Stories* circa 1941, just before Leigh Brackett and Henry Kuttner and Murray Leinster raised the taste and intelligence level just enough but not too much. I can't tell if it's an ironic pastiche or Bulmer is just cranking it out for the rent, and don't much care.

It's a relief to find something as good as "Where Is the Bird of Fire?" or Ballard's novelette "The Watch-Towers" (**53**). The latter is one of Ballard's stranger and more perverse pieces, to my taste one of the best of this very fruitful period for his short fiction. A nameless town is beset by observation towers hanging from the sky—dozens or hundreds of them, arrayed in precise rows and columns, ascending into a featureless haze that obscures the sky. Occasionally observation windows open or close and something appears to be happening inside them; the townspeople are intensely concerned with these hints of activity, and, it appears, pervasively anxious about what the unseen watchers may see. The town appears to be completely isolated; there is no reference to anything outside it; the only magazines and newspapers to be found are old. Nothing is said of a time before the watch-towers, or of their arrival. The town is governed by a Council which, it is hinted, is in some fashion in communication with the towers, but nothing is made explicit. The protagonist Renthall starts to make waves by proposing to hold a garden party—i.e., a conspicuous event outside, under the watch-towers' gaze—causing much nervousness among the townspeople and the Council. But as plans proceed, the Council backs down, and suddenly people are setting up sunbathing decks on tops of buildings. Now no one but Renthall can see the watch-towers, or even remember them any more. At the story's end, he is wandering the waste ground at the edge of the town, and looks up:

The haze had vanished and the shafts of the towers were defined with unprecedented clarity.

As far as he could see, all the observation windows were open. Silently, without moving, the watchers stared down at him.

This cryptic story might best be read as a sort of Freudian fable of the superego—those who struggle the hardest against repression have the hardest time accepting that they have won. Could it have been a prescient allusion to the general opening up of British culture, famously placed (part of it, anyway) by Philip Larkin in the following year?[56]

Swann's "Where Is the Bird of Fire?" (**52**)—later expanded into *Lady of the Bees* (Ace, 1976)—was a striking break for this author. It achieved the 1963 Hugo ballot—the only story from the Nova magazines to do so—in the company of, for example, Theodore Sturgeon's "When You Care, When You Love," and Jack Vance's "The Dragon Masters." This is an impressive feat for a story published in a magazine with limited US distribution, and did a lot to publicize the Nova magazines in the US. It is considerably longer and much more impressive than Swann's two earlier stories in the magazine, and first in the mode that Swann practiced for the next decade and a half, the fantasy-drenched retelling of ancient mythology and history.

In the familiar story, Romulus and Remus are the twin grandsons of Numitor, deposed king of Alba Longa, who are to be killed but instead are set off down the Tiber in a basket, found and suckled by the wolf Luperca, and then discovered and reared by shepherds. Much later, Remus is kidnapped and taken to Alba Longa and Romulus raises a band of shepherds to liberate him. They restore Numitor to the throne, plan to start their own city nearby, and Remus is killed in a dispute over which hill to build on—the Palatine or the Aventine?

---

56. As he put it, "Sexual intercourse began/In nineteen sixty-three." "The Watch-Towers" appeared in mid-1962 and was presumably written in early 1962 or late 1961.

In Swann's version the narrator is Sylvan the Faun, carried off after a mock raid by Romulus, who is already scheming to take Alba Longa. It is Remus, however, who takes Sylvan, rescuing him from the dangerous designs of Romulus. Sylvan stays, sharing Remus's household with the elderly Luperca, and becomes Remus's constant companion and admirer. Romulus is the dynamic and confident go-getter; Remus is the one in harmony with nature, the bird of fire as Faunus puts it. The fantasy plot that is interwoven with the pre-existing legend (which was already pretty fantastic) starts when Remus's bees start getting sick. Faunus points out that there are always other bees, and Remus says, "But I am fond of *these*. . . . They are my friends, Sylvan. Not once have they stung me, even when I took their honey." So they consult Sylvan's father Nemus, who advises that they need a Dryad, and gives directions. Mellonia the Dryad instructs Remus in bee physick, and becomes his lover. Later, when Remus is captive in Alba Longa, Mellonia tricks the guards into opening the gate and sends *her* bees into the city to help Romulus's shepherd army to victory. But victory turns sour: Alba Longa is looted by the disreputable types Romulus has recruited; Mellonia is raped and beaten and dies of her injuries; and Romulus kills Remus.

Swann's ancient Italy is a much more alien place than most of the other strange worlds the characters of *Science Fantasy* are thrust into, since we see it through the eyes of those who live there and partake of its thoroughly pagan and premodern world-view. His style is generally low-key and matter-of-fact, notwithstanding—and maybe accentuating—the otherwise deeply strange presentation. At times his in-passing lyricism can be startling. *E.g.*: in the battle for Alba Longa, Remus tells Sylvan to run to Romulus while he holds off the dictator Amulius: "Behind me a prince and a tyrant grappled in roses and thorns." At other times it is not startling at all, like the predictable set-piece crescendo at the conclusion, in Sylvan's voice near the end of his ten-year life:

Where is the bird of fire? In the tall green flame of the cypress, I see his shadow, flickering with the swallows. In the city that crowds the Palatine, where Fauns walk with men and wolves are fed in the temples, I hear the rush of his wings. But that is his shadow and sound. The bird himself is gone. Always his wings beat just beyond my hands, and the wind possesses his cry. Where is the bird of fire? Look up, he burns in the sky, with Saturn and the Golden Age. I will go to find him.

But even this is better controlled and less overdone than the usual in high fantasy. Swann, unlike many of his fellows, would be a hard fantasist to parody—an odd compliment, no doubt, but a real one.

§

The best of the shorter fiction is "Hat Trick" (**54**) by one Colin Denbigh, of whom I've never heard before and who seems to have had one other story in *Science Fiction Adventures* and that's it. (Later on, he reviewed some books for *Vector*, the journal of the British Science Fiction Association.) An actor rummaging in a costume store buys an old top hat which turns out to confer omniscience and omnipotence on its wearer. Power corrupts real fast. It's a nice sardonic farcical nightmare, seemingly never reprinted.

Also present are Theodore R. Cogswell's "The Man Who Knew Grodnick" (**53**), an amusing but slightly diffuse satire about a literary poseur thrust 100 years into the future. There is also the obligatory Hek Belov story by Edward Mackin, "Under the Lemonade Hat" (**53**), and "Beginner's Luck" by Steve Hall (**54**), in which a doctor tells a vampire story to a meeting of the Midnight Club, a bunch of fantasy writers. It's pretty lame and has Series written all over it.

19: *SCIENCE FANTASY*, VOLUME 19 (ISSUES 55-57)

Science Fantasy volume 19, for October and December 1962 and February 1963, is where the big change in presentation starts. Painted covers are gone. **55** features a black on yellow drawing by Jim Cawthorn of Elric and, one presumes, Moonglum (but if so, Cawthorn hasn't read very carefully—this guy *is* glum), which is technically acceptable but lifeless. **56** has a tatty-looking b&w still from the film *The Premature Burial*, which occupies only a little more than a quarter of the page. **57**, however, has a striking three-color drawing by Gerard Quinn which is well worth looking at.[57]

The familiar arrangement of picture and contents listing on the cover is gone. Now Carnell is improvising. I assumed that the abandonment of full-color covers and the embrace of movie PR—which also occurs on **58** in the next volume—were moves of economic desperation on Carnell's part, i.e., that Carnell was paid for putting movie PR on the cover, or at least got it free, rather than having to pay artists, and that two or three-color drawings were either cheaper to buy or cheaper to print than full-color paintings. But in connection with a similar change in *New Worlds*, Carnell claimed to believe that more people would buy

---

57. See these covers at http://www.sfcovers.net/mainnav.htm or http://www.philsp.com/mags/sciencefantasy.html.

the magazine if it had a "sedate non-pictorial cover."[58] Whether that reasoning applied to his fantasy magazine, he didn't say. Straight advertising is very limited in these issues. The British Science Fiction Association puts in a couple of appearances, and *The Industrial and Commercial Photographer* appears once. Otherwise it's house ads only.

The Carnell book reviews put in one more appearance in **55** (one page worth of short squibs on US fantasy reprints and anthologies), and **56** contains a "Film Review" of *The Premature Burial*, which consists of a few paragraphs of review, several more paragraphs from a letter from Ray Russell, and a three-and-a-half page scene from the script which wound up being cut from the film for length reasons. This is, in effect, the cover story; I find it hard to believe that either the cover or the review did much to attract readers.

Though overall these issues are shabbier in appearance than their immediate predecessors, the fiction is noticeably better, much of it quirky and off-trail and a reminder of why this magazine has the reputation it does.

§

Two long stories by Moorcock do much towards remedying the boredom and exasperation that were setting in after his last few epics. "The Flame Bringers" (**55**) is another Elric story, this one refreshingly straightforward and unmannered compared to its predecessors. Elric has married Zarozinia, settled down, and seems about ready to join the Rotarians. He has even broken his addiction to his sword and instead keeps up his strength by eating magical plants, in a sort of Sword & Sorcery version of methadone maintenance.

But a barbarian horde is approaching Kaarlak, led by an Attila figure who has managed to capture a major-league sorcerer *and* the black cat in which he has stashed his soul.

---

58. http://www.sfcovers.net/mainnav.htm (visited 10/19/11).

The sorcerer has to play ball or else. Elric blows the cobwebs off Stormbringer and he and Moonglum set off to infiltrate the barbarian horde and see if they can set the sorcerer free. This they do, after various entertaining misadventures in the enemy camp, and the dragon master of Melnibone rides to the rescue to boot, so Kaarlak is saved and the barbarians incinerated. Here Moorcock has de-emphasized the doomed and nihilistic attitude, which was beginning to pall, and given good weight in storytelling.

In **56** the Moorcock novelette is "To Rescue Tanelorn..." which is not an Elric story, though Elric is mentioned in passing (missing, presumed dead). It has been collected both in the Elric volumes and in an Eternal Champion omnibus. "Tanelorn had a peculiar nature in that it welcomed and held the wanderer." Tanelorn's inhabitants have mostly turned away from the Lords of Chaos, who are mightily peeved as a result. So they've raised their own barbarian army against Tanelorn, this one consisting of a horde of ragged beggars from Nadsokor. Rackhir, the Red Archer, goes off in search of the Grey Lords, who are neutral between Law and Chaos and might be inclined to help out a renegade city.

Rackhir proceeds to seek them out through a series of bizarre parallel worlds, one of Law, one of Chaos, and a few others, and to recruit the Boatmen of Xerlerenes, who actually fly, and who net and dispatch the beggars assailing Tanelorn. The story is told in a sort of faux fairy tale style, but one that is simpler and less overwrought than some of the Elric stories—

> In Tanelorn dwelt the Red Archer, Rackhir, from the Eastlands beyond the Sighing Desert, beyond the Weeping Waste. Rackhir had been born a Warrior Priest, a servant of the Lords of Chaos, but had forsaken this life for the quieter pursuits of thievery and learning.

—and the descriptions of the successive dimensions through

which Rackhir travels are vivid and effective. Here Moorcock actually starts to describe the scheme of Law vs. Chaos that he has only hinted at in the earlier stories, giving the impression, which may or may not be correct, that he is actually starting to think it through for the first time. Moorcock displayed enough professionalism and assurance from the start that it's easy to forget that at this point he's twenty-three years old and still has only been at it for a year or two. It's refreshing to see that he seems to be backing away and thinking a bit about what he's doing rather than just charging along in the same direction.

§

Among the other long stories is Brian Aldiss's "Matrix" (the lead story in **55**, a.k.a. "Danger—Religion!" in some reprintings), an odd and amusing parallel-worlds story in which Sheridan, resident of a dour and impoverished post-thermonuclear world in which Edinburgh has become Europe's capital, is snatched into a world in which the Christian church is dominant and the elite is maintained in stagnant luxury by a large slave population. To overthrow this odious system he seeks allies among the others who have been taken from their own worlds, and discovers to his dismay that to most of them, slavery is either not a problem at all or not a big deal. He escapes to his home continuum with a renewed appreciation of it with all its faults.

For anyone who doesn't get the point, there's a minor character named Candida.

This perversely mannered and cartoony story, which was well worth publishing though I wouldn't want to read a hundred like it, probably could not have been published anywhere else in the genre at the time (otherwise Aldiss would have sold it somewhere else for more money!) and exemplifies the generous eclectic openness of this magazine through most of its history.

John Brunner is back in **57** with the energetically clever and creepy "Some Lapse of Time" (at fifty-six pages a "long novelette," the "short novel" appellation having conclusively fallen out of favor). Dr. Max Harrow is having a bad dream of a group of starving people living in ruins, one of whom is holding a human finger bone in his hand. He wakes and there is someone at his door: the police, because a tramp has collapsed in his garage. The tramp proves to be suffering a rare disease (hetero-chylia, an inability to metabolize fats, which become lethal) that Harrow is uniquely qualified to recognize, his infant son having died of it only recently, and which should have made it impos-sible to survive to adulthood. He also has clamped in his hand a human finger bone—the same bone, the end of the left middle finger, as in Harrow's dream.

Unintelligible to the hospital staff, the tramp proves when examined by a philologist to speak a badly distorted version of English, like one might expect a primitive and isolated group to use. Meanwhile, Harrow's marriage is blowing up under the emotional stress caused by his son's death and his own preoccu-pation. When his wife slams the car door in his face, she catches his hand in the door and severs the end of his left middle finger, which falls down a gutter. Meanwhile, the tramp is sent for a head x-ray, but he turns out to be so radioactive that not only do the films turn out unusable but he has to be put in strict isola-tion.

Brunner brings all these elements to a thoroughly grotesque resolution—it doesn't quite work, but is a grimly ingenious nice try. This story has apparently been reprinted once, in Brunner's paperback collection *Now Then* from the mid-1960s, but not since. (It was also dramatized by the BBC in their "Out of the Unknown" series in the mid-1960s.[59]) An omnibus of Brunner's *Science Fantasy* novellas would be one of the more entertaining SF collections ever. Too bad nobody would buy it.

The least of the longer stories in this volume is John Rackham's "Fire and Ice" (**56**), another "long novelette," and an extension of the series about Egyptologist K. N. Wilson, which

---

59. http://www.imdb.com/title/tt0279432/ (visited 10/19/11).

had appeared to be resolved by the dispatch of the magical bad guys. But no, there are always more bad guys. In this story, American sociologist Cyril Cadman shows up at Dr. Wilson's door, having been referred by a colleague. Cadman, for his research, has infiltrated a hierarchical and secretive organization called the Seekers of Knowledge, with "lodges" all around the US and elsewhere (any resemblance to anything we've heard of is entirely coincidental, of course). He gets outed and threatened, and the places he's staying start bursting into flame, one after another.

Trailing suspicion of arson, he's come to Dr. Wilson, is introduced to the preternaturally beautiful Yalna, who declares him to be "one of us," and then Dr. Wilson's house bursts into flame. They all flee to Scandinavia, where "Chappie" Jones has moved to a fjord and lives in nudist harmony with Nature and with the also preternaturally beautiful Anna. How they make a living is not discussed. Now their house bursts into flames too, and in broad daylight.

By this time Dr. Wilson is pretty annoyed. They return to England, to the boarding house run by the daughter of Chappie's Scandinavian friend who delivers their food—herself a sociologist, who is running the boarding house for her research. She's preternaturally beautiful, too, or close to it, and also seems to be "one of us." When things start warming up in her place, Dr. Wilson whips up a sort of séance in which the flames get rerouted to their source. It gets very cold in the boarding house, and it transpires that all of the Seekers' lodges everywhere have burst into flame. This is all accomplished through the power of Love, we are told at length, and the story ends "I have the feeling that we haven't heard the last of the Seekers."

Fortunately, we have. There are more Rackham stories in *Science Fantasy* but they are not part of this series, and I don't find any indication of such in other venues. Either Rackham thought better of further extension—the series by now has entirely lost its initial charm and is assuming the extruded-product, running-the-changes form we have become all too familiar with in recent years—or he wrote them but they had become too tedious to sell.

§

There are several gems among the short fiction, precious and semi-precious. The best of them is Thomas Burnett Swann's "The Sudden Wings" (**55**), which features Mark and his sister Phoebe, refugees from Pompeii, aged twenty and nineteen and long marriageable but completely absorbed in each other. They fetch up on the island of Petra where they encounter the Dragonfly, a winged boy who calls himself Eros and seduces both of them, metaphysically speaking. (Well, actually, he induces them both to jump off a cliff, but of course that is a mere vulgarization.)

This story, like the earlier "Where Is the Bird of Fire?" makes it clear enough that Swann's reputation is deserved—beautifully written and visualized and pervasively strange, in a very different way from the rest of this magazine's often strange contents. Except for a fugitive publication in *Fantastic Universe* in 1959, Swann (1928-76) didn't get his fiction published in the US until 1966, when *Fantasy & Science Fiction* published his novella "The Manor of Roses" and Ace reprinted one of his later *Science Fantasy* serials as *Day of the Minotaur*. I assume that he, like Ballard, was submitting his stories to the higher-paying American markets all along and getting nowhere, and for example that *Fantasy & Science Fiction* and *Fantastic* rejected both this story and "Where Is the Bird of Fire?" Interestingly, this fine story went entirely unreprinted for over three decades until Tom Shippey's *Oxford Book Of Fantasy Stories* in the mid-1990s.

There are a couple of very readable variants on the "what is reality" theme that is cropping up with some frequency in *Science Fantasy*. Philip E. High's "Dead End" (**56**) is a hokey but vigorous and entertaining van Vogt or Philip K. Dick homage. Sherwell has a disturbing knack for predicting the future, such as his co-worker's fatal auto accident. He goes out on the moor to test his talent by shooting a rabbit, a connection that is not too well explained. The rabbit proves to be mechanical, the grass is plastic, the path back has disappeared, and a blank-faced man appears and warns Sherwell not to let Mother classify him. There follows a rapid sequence of bizarre and arbitrary events, at the end of which Sherwell is a million years in the future, brought there to help revitalize humanity by the rulers of time, who also present him with the love of his life—whom he has foreseen. She in turn informs him that it looks like the universe is coming to an end in about twenty years so they'd better make the most of it while they can. None of this makes much sense on close examination (revitalize humanity? in twenty years?), but the scenes are vivid and the sense of displacement well conveyed. High packs material into fifteen pages that most writers would have stretched to many times that, so there's little temptation to stop and think about it.

In a similar but more leisurely vein is Steve Hall's "Out of Character" (**57**). Harding, a photographer, sees a young woman killed by a hit-and-run driver. On inspection, her corpse turns out to be mechanical, and not even entirely anatomically correct. After he has watched the police salvage her head and disintegrate the rest, he is sitting in his car with his own head spinning when another young woman taps on his window and asks for a ride—her scooter's broken. But this one is real (she's cut her hand and is bleeding), so he shows her his photos of the defunct robot and enlists her as an ally.

But nobody sees or hears them until they resume their normal routines the next day. The only logical course is to kidnap the disintegrated robot woman, who has by now resumed her daily routine, presumably with the old head on a new body. They do just that, in front of oblivious passers-by, and drive her to an isolated location. She continues walking and talking just as if she had met her friend for a movie and not been snatched off the street and stuffed in a car trunk.

When Harding pulls out his gun to shoot her, the sky goes

dark and he and girlfriend are transported into the presence of the Director, who bemoans the delay to the production ("our sponsor is not to be trifled with"), explains the mistakes that led to the present pass, and sends them back into the production, this time with the appropriate knowledge of their own natures and of the Mechanoids'.

Hall is not a polished writer: "To say that [events] had bordered on the fantastic was to understate the case to a degree which itself was fantastic.... The boiling upsurge of questions and ideas whirled around in Harding's head like particles being accelerated in a cyclotron, until he felt like a man both blind and deaf searching for a needle in a lightless, soundless chamber, and forced to wear feather pillows for gloves." But these sins of enthusiasm are entirely forgivable in a story as well paced and visualized as this.

Hall (Stephen Peter Hall, b. 1941) is a quintessential Little Known Writer,[60] having published a double handful of stories under his name and a couple of pseudonyms in 1962-64 in Carnell's magazines and one shortly thereafter in Carnell's *New Writings in SF*, and then nothing. None of his magazine stories seem to have been anthologized.

Neither Hall's nor High's stories have ever been reprinted. "Dead End" is probably not serviceable for an age that didn't grow up on van Vogt, but "Out of Character" remains an agreeable read even without the gloss of nostalgia.

§

It's downhill from here, though not too steeply, with "Möbius Trip" (**57**), the obligatory Hek Belov story by Edward Mackin, this one involving a machine that duplicates people (they're really just unstuck in time, and giving them pep pills re-consol-

---

60. "Little Known Writer" reflects the view of members of the listserv on which this material was first aired that Attention Must Be Paid to the obscure and forgotten producers of decades-old magazine fiction, a preoccupation in which I enthusiastically joined.

idates them) (no questions please). Again, it's amusing enough, but less so for my having read all its predecessors. David Rome's "Inside" (**57**) features Snuggie, a cute little kid who never gets to go Outside, and his menagerie of talking stuffed animals (like Jiffie) and equally chatty furniture (like Bed). It's a period piece reminiscent of David R. Bunch with the edges filed down.

Steve Hall reappears with "Weekend Trip" (**55**), another of his innocuous Midnight Club stories (after-dinner speakers at a fantasy writers' group), this one about a benign alien encounter. Under the name Russ Markham, Hall has "Discontinuity" in **56**, a deal-with-the-devil story, also very well-written and set up but ruined by an ending that is too gimmicky even for this gimmicky subgenre.

A new Australian writer, Stephen Cook, contributes "Love Is a Relative Thing" (**55**), an unpleasant if well-written story about an alien serial killer who victimizes homely women by being nice to them and then eating the resulting emotions. Cook is the other Little Known Writer here; he published a couple more stories, then killed himself in 1967 at age twenty-five.

20: *SCIENCE FANTASY,* VOLUME 20 (ISSUES 58-60)

Science Fantasy, volume 20, for April, June and August 1963, has much the same drab look as the previous volume, with two covers consisting of three-color drawings and the third of a movie still. The arrangement of pictorial and printed matter remains ad hoc. **58** advertises "*Captain Sinbad*. Metro-Goldwyn-Mayer's spectacular fantasy based on 'The Arabian Nights,'" and the cover photo, black and white and pretty tatty-looking, is captioned "Anna Luise Schubert and John Schapar perform their startling *Spider Dance* in 'Captain Sinbad.'" The inside front cover is devoted to a rather fawning description of the film, unsigned but presumably written by Carnell.

59 features a pretty hokey black/white/yellow drawing by Quinn of a seemingly dead or unconscious man being magicked by a scantily clad woman kneeling next to him, and **60** a black/blue/white Quinn drawing illustrating Mervyn Peake's "Same Time, Same Place." Neither is impressive, to my taste.[61] The only other notable feature of these covers is the appearance on **59** of Steve Hall's name although he does not actually appear in the magazine, not even under a pseudonym (he is in the other two issues).

Outside advertising remains minimal (nothing in **58** except for the *Captain Sinbad* puff piece; British Science Fiction

---

61. See these covers at http://www.sfcovers.net/mainnav.htm..

Association and *Industrial and Commercial Photographer* on the back cover of **59** and a full page from the UK SF Book Club. Nothing in **60**).

§

There is more nonfiction than usual in these issues. In addition to the *Captain Sinbad* item, Carnell has more book reviews in **58**, praising Ray Russell's *The Case Against Satan* at unusual length for this column, noting the paperback reprint of Leiber's *Gather, Darkness!*, and bemoaning the lack of newer material in the US anthologies *Ghosts And Things* (uncredited) and *The Frankenstein Reader* (ed. Calvin Beck).

59 has "The Wall Game," a report by Carnell on the Easter convention, much of which took place unofficially at the Great Wall Chinese restaurant. Highlights of the report include Ted Tubb's on-the-spot authorship of "The Birth of Elric" for Michael Moorcock. (So Harlan Ellison didn't invent writing as a performing art.) At least five other writers added to it and it was eventually bought for one penny by Tom Boardman, Jr. Did it ever see print? Not to my knowledge. And here's Carnell pioneering new clunky territory: "As the convention closed in the usual dismal manner on the final day, with the staff wearily wending their working hours through the jaundiced premises...."

60 contains an editorial by Carnell, the first in quite some time, celebrating *Science Fantasy*'s appearance on the Hugo ballot along with Swann's "Where Is the Bird of Fire?" as well as the appearance in this issue of Swann and Mervyn Peake, not to mention the fourteen-year-old Terry Pratchett. (Carnell refers to Swann as "an American, although unhonoured and unsung in his own country!") Finally, he says he's going to make the magazine monthly just as soon as he can get enough good material. In the real world, of course, Carnell managed only four more issues. In addition, the issue contains a four-page appreciation of Peake by Michael Moorcock.

Speaking of Americans, Swann is the only one in this

volume, and the same was true in the previous volume, and (peeking ahead) in the remaining four Carnell issues. Otherwise this has become, if not an all-British magazine, at least an all-Commonwealth one, allowing for an Australian here and there.

§

Moorcock continues his dominant presence. In addition to the Peake appreciation, he contributes "The Greater Conqueror" (**58**), a "long novelette" at forty-one pages, and "Dead God's Homecoming" (**59**), merely a novelette at forty-five pages. "The Greater Conqueror" is Moorcock's rendition of Alexander the Great. The real deal, it proposes, is that Alexander was possessed by Ahriman and, to save the world from his evil designs, was assassinated by the protagonist, one Simon of Byzantium who allied himself with the local resistance movement. The fatal fever was just a cover story. It's unpretentiously entertaining, notwithstanding the bibliography at the end.

"Dead God's Homecoming," an Elric story, is a bit of a letdown by comparison both with "The Greater Conqueror" and the previous Elric story, "The Flame Bringers." This one has distinct overtones of "the rent's due, got to crank out a story, make it a long one" both from the contrived plot and the seemingly hasty and careless writing. ("Elric had long-since pulled his thoughts together and was capable of thinking and acting coherently, but he could spare none of this for Dyvim Slorm while intratemporally asking nothing of his cousin who rode at his side, frustrated in that he was not called upon to give help.")

Elric's wife is kidnapped. He extracts from one of the culprits a cryptic rhyme that tells him he has to go to the ends of the earth, which are about to be consumed in war, to get her back. The Lords of Chaos are stirring up war and trying to take over, and doing pretty well. Turns out they are trying to get hold of the sword Stormbringer and its littermate, Mournblade, which is in the possession of Elric's relative Dyvim Slorm. But Elric remembers just in time the obscure property of these blades when they are together: they will do their masters' bidding even at a distance. So they hand over the blades, get Elric's wife back, and the blades then make mince-ectoplasm of the Dead God Darnizhaan, who has wound up this elaborate set-piece in the first place. There's a lecture that the likes of Elric are doomed either way. If Chaos wins, everybody will be miserable, and if Law wins, a new breed of folk will shortly be taking over. This is undoubtedly a major brick in the Moorcock façade, but for the non-devotee the perfunctory execution renders it rather uninteresting.

Swann's "The Dolphin and the Deep" (**60**), a novelette (but not "long") at fifty-one pages, is the other major item in this volume, about a footloose Etruscan dandy. In the company of a Triton (merman) and a dolphin, along with several other sailors, he's looking for love in all the wrong places, notably the hideout of Circe, whom he tracks down the African coast. Like Swann's earlier stories, this one is convincingly strange, conveying a sense of a world where people think differently to us. It's longer and more wandering than the others and suffers from it, and the theme of the beautiful boy (admittedly, this one is a fish from the waist down) leading the long-unmarried protagonist into danger is less well integrated into the story than in "The Sudden Wings." However, the story survives and is ultimately impressive and satisfying. It smacks a bit of what one might get if Tennessee Williams had ghost-written *Peter Pan*.

John Rackham contributes two novelettes, fortunately not continuations of the by-now-insufferable series about Dr. Wilson the Egyptologist. "What You Don't Know" (**59**) is of some academic interest and reinforces the notion that you never quite knew what you'd find in *Science Fantasy*: it's a failed *Analog* story. That is, a failed version of the *Analog* magical fantasy of the early 1960s, which was rationalized by psionic blather or warmed-over Forteanism—New Age before its time.

The mainspring, supposedly, is the protagonist's theory that people bias the laws of nature and probability. Class A people get the right results regardless of natural law—like Ben

Franklin's kite demo, which should have killed him. Class B people's guesses are always wrong. Class C people's actions always turn out wrong. And class D consists of "people who make a thing come out in some way it just can't, by design, but with successful results." The protagonist gives the specs for a supposed rain-making machine to a character who is famous for gadgets that don't work, except that they do work if he doesn't believe they will work. He doesn't believe in this one, so the device generates so much rain the dam bursts, and the protagonist hastily gets him to use the rain-making machine to turn back the resulting flood—but he has to keep the subject from believing that it will work, or it won't. This man is supposedly a class D, but the story doesn't exactly fit the class D description, and where all the embroidery about belief and disbelief fits in is more than a little murky. Rackham is a reasonably lively writer or this silly story would be as tedious as a late Campbell editorial.

More or less the same is true of Rackham's "With Clean Hands" (**60**), which starts out as a story of human colonial domination of an inhabited planet, then starts looking suspiciously like the run-up to the Crucifixion, with the colonial administrator cast as Pontius Pilate. Indeed, the administrator deliberately turns things into a re-enactment, complete with ritual handwashing, and contrives to have the alien Messiah figure's body disappear—but the body disappears without his assistance.

The point escapes me. If it's supposed to be an affirmation of religious values, it's a bit odd that there's a subplot in which the administrator has about decided to send his tiresome wife and their kids back to Earth and strike up a relationship with another woman who has come on to the scene. (He doesn't quite say "My wife doesn't understand me," but that seems to be the idea.) Though readable enough, these two Rackham stories are fairly disappointing. I have much more favorable recollections of the ones I read in the US magazines around this time ("Ethical Quotient" in *Analog*, under his real name John T.

Phillifent, sticks in the mind).

One K. W. Bennett is represented by the long novelette "The Seventeenth Summer" (**58**), which proposes that after World War III, the flower of the survivors' youth is selected for a rite of passage: a quest, conducted by bicycle (greased with beeswax and bear fat)—and for what? For the end of the road, which runs from somewhere in the eastern US to the West Coast. "I don't know what you'll find, but you must go and you will die if you fail," the village elder says in sending him off.

So off pedals our hero Loki and has various picaresque and life-threatening road adventures, killing or driving away a series of colorful assailants and picking up a girlfriend along the way, traveling with her (entirely chastely as far as one can tell) until he does indeed come to the end of the road, where he finds the people who are rebuilding civilization and who have been watching over him the whole time. It's quite a readable story as long as you don't stop to ask whether there might not have been a simpler recruitment program.

This K. W. Bennett is certainly a Little Known Writer, or maybe several of them. The byline appears on "Who Builds Maos Traps?" in the sole issue of *Ten Story Fantasy* from 1951—the one with "Tyrant and Slave Girl on the Planet Venus" on the cover—and "In Hoc Signum Vincit" in *Fantastic Universe*, May 1957, but whether all these Bennetts are actually the same person, I have no idea.

§

Among the shorter fiction, the outstanding item is Mervyn Peake's nightmarishly perfect "Same Time, Same Place" (**60**). Moorcock says this is one of only two fantasy short stories in Peake's entire oeuvre (the other is in the next *Science Fantasy*, and there were also a couple of appearances in *New Worlds* in 1969 after Peake's death.) J. G. Ballard contributes one of his more minor efforts, "Minus One" (**59**), a heavy-handed satire about a mental institution from which one of the patients has inexplicably disappeared. By the end of the story, the pompous director, through a line of blarney much assisted by destroying the patient's file ("I am now concerned with the phenomenology of Hinton, with his absolute metaphysical essence"), has convinced the staff that the patient never existed and was a collective delusion. It's amusing enough, but it reads more like a bizarre collaboration between Eric Frank Russell and Stanislaw Lem than like the other stories Ballard was publishing by this time.

Terry Pratchett's first story, "The Hades Business" (**60**), published when he was fourteen or so, is a reasonably amusing account of a different kind of deal with the Devil: making Hell a commercially successful proposition, a sort of theme park.

Lee Harding's overlong and overwrought "All My Yesterdays" (**59**) is about a man whose wife has died, who finds a carnival operation that can bring his memories of her alive, and then finds out he's become a content provider for voyeurs. There are two more of Steve Hall's mildly clever Midnight Club stories, "Hole in the Dyke" (**58**) (who leaked the budget when nobody but the Minister and two aides knew about it? *Cherchez le* stage magician) and "Party Piece" (**60**) (another stage magician—this one literally handwaves a Klein bottle into existence, and his assistant disappears into it).

Bringing up the rear, decidedly, is Hugh Christopher's "The Mind of Young Crandle" (**58**), about a pair of twins who share one mind (they're never awake at the same time). Then one commits a murder; can he be executed given the consequences to the other twin? This one has a Gernsbackian clunkiness to it—it's been a long time since we saw *that* in *Science Fantasy*. This story is apparently the only appearance in the SF magazines by this Little Known Writer.

21: *SCIENCE FANTASY,* VOLUME 21 (ISSUES 61-63), PLUS VOLUME 22 (64)

Science Fantasy, volume 21, for October and December 1963 and February 1964, and the final Carnell issue, volume 22, **64** (April 1964), continue the amble towards the bottom visually.

Two of the issues (**62** and **64**) have no cover illustration, just titles, authors, and blurbs, against red-orange and violet backgrounds respectively. Of the others, **61** has another b&w movie still, this one (from *Jason and the Argonauts*) very small and murky, not helped by the orange background, and **63** has a Jim Cawthorn black and white drawing that might have looked good on a fanzine.[62] Otherwise the magazine is physically the same as it has been for several years, except that **64** is 124 pages rather than 112. Also, as of **61**, the price has gone up to 3/- from 2/6.

Advertising actually increases a bit in these issues. In all of them, the British Science Fiction Association has half a page and the back cover is divided between *Industrial and Commercial Photographer* and *Film User.* **62** and **64** have half a page for Cockcroft's *Index to The Weird Fiction Magazines,* available from Ken Slater. **64** has an inside front cover half-page ad for *Science Fiction Review* (not the Richard Geis magazine of that

---

62. See these covers at http://www.sfcovers.net/mainnav.htm or http://www.philsp.com/mags/sciencefantasy.html.

title, a much earlier one), also available from Slater. There are also the usual house ads, plus this unusual one in **64**: "The Editor Regrets...to announce to all readers that this issue of *Science Fantasy* is the last to be published by Nova Publications Ltd., after thirteen years of continuous appearance. Arrangements have been made, however, for its continued publication by Roberts & Vinter, Ltd., 44 Milkwood Road, London, S.E. 24, from which an announcement will be forthcoming. Your Editor regrets that owing to other commitments he will not be connected with the new enterprise. John Carnell."

§

These issues, like the previous volume, are heavier on nonfiction than usual. An installment of Moorcock's essay series "Aspects of Fantasy" appears in each issue. In **61** there is Carnell's puff-piece review of *Jason and the Argonauts*. In **62**, there is a Readers' Letters section, the first in years. It contains a three-page letter by one David Busby and nothing else.

The "Aspects of Fantasy" series starts appropriately enough with the seven-page "Introduction" in **61**, in which Moorcock argues that the primary function of fantasy is the expression of subconscious symbolism. Corollary: "The typical *Unknown Worlds* story is a kind of rational ghost-laying substitute for the child's fairy story—it diminishes that which is described to the level of whimsey and makes it appear harmless—but it avoids the essential nature of the horror story/supernatural romance and is in many ways a corrupt and unproductive form." Well, he's not *completely* wrong, though that's far from the whole story.

Moorcock traces fantasy from hero legends through romances to the Gothic novel. In **62**'s installment, "The Floodgates of the Unconscious," Moorcock notes the vision-inducing qualities of mescaline, LSD, and opium, but declares that he gets high on the real thing: Gothic novels. He discusses Anne Radcliffe's *The Mysteries of Udolpho* and Poe's "Usher" and the connection of landscape and architecture to the characters' mental states, then grudgingly admits Lovecraft to their company ("I find most of his stories hard going").

Part 3 in **63** is "Figures of Faust," which suggests that Christian ideas of good and evil have lost their moxie, but there's still a kick in the Faust theme: "the curious and brilliant man destroyed by his own curiosity and brilliance." Moorcock pursues this notion from the original Faust through Mrs. Radcliffe again, *The Monk, Frankenstein, Melmoth the Wanderer, Dr. Jekyll, Dorian Gray, Dracula*, and Byron, touches base at William Burroughs, and fetches up at Ballard's *The Drowned World*, comparing the character Strangman to a Byronic hero-villain. Well, he said he was defining the Faust theme broadly.

The final part, "Conclusion" in **64**, begins: "For reasons that are now obvious to you, I am forced to wind this series up faster than I should have liked." He says: "I should like to have shown that whereas the form which I've loosely called Fantasy is a creative and dynamic form (if not as important as I sometimes like to think) its more recent off-shoot Science Fiction is on the whole a self-defeating, self-limiting form—that where it is good is usually in the elements which it has borrowed from Fantasy or mainstream fiction." That's a revealing manifesto from the man who was about to take over *New Worlds* rather than *Science Fantasy.*

But going back to fantasy, he talks about two modern branches: Sword and Sorcery, a descendant of Gothic historical romance, and the story of "the haunted palace of the mind," derived from the Gothic haunted castle story. Their respective exemplars are of course *The Lord of the Rings* and *Titus Groan*, of which he much prefers the latter. He traces Sword and Sorcery from historical romances through Lord Dunsany, Clark Ashton Smith, and Robert Howard to Fritz Leiber's Fafhrd/Mouser stories, which he thinks combine the best of their predecessors and are an exception to his judgment that the subgenre is, overall, emotionally unconvincing and immature. "What good it achieves, if any, is that it forms a useful bridge between childhood sense of wonder and adult sense of surrealism. However, that bridge seems to be infrequently crossed."

Few fantasy writers learn to use the dream landscapes and structures they create for their own artistic purposes. "It is what I have tried to do in the Elric tales—evidently without much success since the less escapist themes I tried to carry on the Sword and Sorcery vehicle have escaped a great many readers. I shall have to try again with a fresh or altered vehicle." (Jerry Cornelius, perhaps?) He lists "the best current developments of fantasy's various streams": *Titus Groan, Two Sought Adventure* (the first Fafhrd/Gray Mouser book), Ballard's *The Drowned World* ("representing S-F") and Burroughs' *Naked Lunch* trilogy ("representing how the elements of Fantasy can be developed to push forward the progress of the novel").

Moorcock thinks fantasy will have to be absorbed back into the mainstream if it is to progress, and to the extent it doesn't it will "wither, die, and be forgotten." He also goes on about SF at too great length to quote much. Executive summary: "The fact is clear that S-F is a vein of Fantasy which has been more or less worked out." Talk of sociological or satirical SF is "a load of old codswallop." A decent writer "doesn't need a gimmicky vehicle to carry his ideas." Ballard's term "speculative fantasy" is preferable for the best of what is called SF, which includes the work of Ballard and Aldiss. "A reaction away from S-F towards fantasy may already be taking place—but I could be thinking wishfully." (Be careful what you wish for.)

He concludes with a sensible tribute to *Science Fantasy*: it "has published a proportionately higher number of good stories than any other magazine to date. The comparative freedom allowed to the writer for this magazine has been greater than anywhere else. I only wish I could have written better stories for it while I had the chance."

Generally, Moorcock's presence moves from dominant to overbearing in these issues. He's in every one of them, more than once in most. In addition to the four installments of "Aspects of Fantasy," there are three Elric novelettes ("Black Sword's

Brothers" in **61**, "Sad Giant's Shield" in **63**, and "Doomed Lord's Passing"—"Dead Lord's Passing" on the contents page, and "Doomed Lord's Prayer" in a note in the previous issue—in **64**), plus "The Deep Fix" under the James Colvin pseudonym in **64**. In that final issue, 107 of 124 pages (all but two short stories and the contents page) consist of Moorcock copy.

It's interesting in this regard that not one but two Moorcock series—Elric and "Aspects of Fantasy"—come to an end in the last issue (or so it appeared in the case of Elric, killed off in "Doomed Lord's Passing"). Moorcock says he trimmed "Aspects of Fantasy" because the magazine was shutting down. One wonders if there was any interaction between that fact and the Elric series—if the magazine was kept going long enough to finish it, or if Moorcock wound it up knowing how quickly the magazine would fold. Though the last issue is dated April 1964, the decision to pull the plug was made at a meeting in September 1963, according to Mike Ashley in Tymn/Ashley, and I get the impression that Carnell maintained a smaller inventory, with the time between acceptance and publication probably shorter than the six months or so that was apparently characteristic of US magazines.

§

Again the contents of these issues are all-British Empire except for that prophet without honor Thomas Burnett Swann, present in **63** with "The Murex." Also notable is what I believe is the longest story ever published in *Science Fantasy*, Brian W. Aldiss's 94-page "Skeleton Crew" (**62**). The "Short Novel" designation has been dusted off for the occasion.

"Skeleton Crew" is an earlier and shorter version of Aldiss's novel *Earthworks* (Doubleday 1966), which made a considerable impression on me (if no one else) at the time with its nightmarish picture of a future England in a grossly overpopulated world, bulldozed flat so all the land can be farmed by machines, the whole poisoned by insecticides. This magazine version is considerably sketchier (not surprisingly, since the book looks to be about half again as long), and its future England is not as well developed.

Knowland—brain-damaged, schizophrenic, haunted by a hallucinatory apparition he calls the Figure—has escaped the life of an agricultural near-slave and become captain (for what that's worth) of a highly automated cargo ship. When the ship runs aground off the coast of Africa, he gets caught up in a plot to assassinate the president of Africa, thereby to plunge the world into war that will relieve the overburdened Earth of the better part of its human civilization. At the end, he's weighing whether to do it. This misanthropic theme is underscored by the damaged and repellent characters and a lot of extreme imagery, like that at the very beginning:

> The dead man drifted along in the breeze. He walked upright on his hind legs like a performing nanny goat, as he had in life. A few flies stayed with him, big and ripe and blue as a Bordeaux grape. Perhaps they were regretting it, for the man was far from land, moving steadily above the surface of the South Atlantic, his feet occasionally catching a splash from the slumbering water.
>
> He was coming out from Africa, moving steadily towards me.[63]

§

Moorcock's "Black Sword's Brothers" (**61**) continues the saga of the war between Law and Chaos in a fairly uninteresting and cartoony fashion, marked by sloppy if still vivid writing, hokey dialogue, gimmicks, and idiot plot. As to the latter, Elric falls, swordless and therefore debilitated, into the hands of the main bad guy, who decides that rather than just disposing of this

---

63. We later learn that he's drifting in the breeze because he is strapped to an antigravity unit.

dangerous character out of hand, he will first defeat the forces of Law and then torture Elric at his leisure. So instead of leaving him chained in a nice safe dungeon, he takes him along with the war fleet and feeds him a magical substance that brings back his strength, with entirely predictable results.

In **63**, "Sad Giant's Shield" posits that since Elric is fighting Chaos, what he needs is the Chaos Shield, which is invulnerable because it is made out of Chaos itself. This item is conveniently in the possession of the Sad Giant, who, once Elric and pals hack their way past a stand of homicidal trees (tasty souls they have, though), is happy to hand it over. Moonglum kills him anyway, though. Why? To fulfill the prophecy. In other developments, Elric's sword is back to killing his own companions, and his wife has been kidnapped, her body transformed into a worm by exposure to Chaos. She impales herself on Stormbringer when Elric finds her. In the main action, the Ships of Hell are defeated.

That brings us to the grand climax, "Doomed Lord's Passing" (**64**). Moorcock seems to slow down and pay more attention, as befits the end of the world as his characters know it. The writing seems much more careful than in the previous stories and the pace is more even. The metaphysics of Elric's world are set out in greater detail. Elric's mentor Sepiriz takes him off for a rendezvous with the radiant and perfect Lords of Law, who say they'd like to help in the war against Chaos, but they need to get a summons from the battlefield on Earth, which requires a blast from the Horn of Fate. Actually, three blasts—one to wake the sleeping dragons, one to get the Lords of Law past the doorman, and one to bring the old world to an end.

They instruct Elric to climb a tall building and step off into space, whereupon he finds himself in another world (his future, I believe), where a dwarf directs him to the tomb of Roland, who has the Horn and is prepared to defend his possession of it despite being the inconvenience of being dead. Elric renders him even more dead and heads home with the Horn, wakes up the dragons with it, leads the dragons to the scene of battle, kills a Dark Lord, blows the Horn again and summons the Lords of Law, who proceed in their majestic and overlit splendor to kick ass. Elric takes out the chief bad guy, the Theocrat Jagreen Lern, but borrows a sword to finish him off so he won't have to drink the guy's crufty soul through Stormbringer. The world transforms. By this time Elric is too exhausted to blow the horn a third time and finish the job, so Moonglum volunteers for Stormbringer's point, reviving Elric long enough for him to do the deed. Then Stormbringer kills Elric and slithers off into the cosmos.

Well, this is totally ridiculous, though reasonably amusing in places and full of vivid imagery and over-the-top language. One problem is that as the series' cosmic gravitas grows, its cartoony aspects become more and more incongruous, as does its thrown-together, made-up-as-it-goes along quality. Moorcock may have been trying to be the anti-Tolkien, but unfavorable comparisons to Tolkien in terms of background and detail multiply more inescapably as the series progresses. On the other hand, work that demands comparison with Tolkien (and not because it's just a knock-off, as with certain other profitable series), even an unfavorable one, is certainly an accomplishment of sorts, even if not the sort that appeals deeply to me.

§

Moorcock's "The Deep Fix" (**64**), as by James Colvin, makes a virtue, of sorts, of a thin, thrown-together world. Seward is the perpetrator of hallucinomats, which have almost brought down civilization. Now, assisted by drugs to keep him going, he's struggling to perfect the tranquilomat, which will straighten things out. His current fix, Mescalin-Andronen Nineteen, precipitates him into another world. There's a castle inhabited by various loonies who want his help in destroying the rest of Earth's population, and are ready to torture him to that end. He escapes with the help of a black man named Farlowe who addresses him as "son," drives him through a depopulated land-scape, and drops him off in a park. There he is greeted by a teenaged girl who acts as if she knows him and takes him home to her mother, whom he sleeps with.

It is hypothesized that this world is a sort of mock-up, with the population brought from Earth and conditioned to believe that they were born there. Meanwhile Seward is popping back and forth between this world, as his dose wears off, and that one, as he fixes again. Eventually he returns to the castle to have it out with the bad guys and is precipitated back into our world—and then he woke up! No, it wasn't exactly a dream, just an experimental procedure, and the other world was all in his head, so it's okay that it doesn't quite add up. Moorcock has said this story "was about as close to [William S.] Burroughs as I've ever written and...was intended as a kind of bridge for a reader between the fantasy they were reading in the magazine and what I was enjoying in the Olympia Press Burroughs books."[64] Thus it is not surprising that he also reports that Carnell had to be persuaded to publish this story by J. G. Ballard.[65]

§

The best item of fiction in this volume is probably Swann's "The Murex" (**63**), another displaced variation on dangerous love for young boys. Here the protagonist, Daphne, is a member of a troop of Amazons, who have nothing but scorn for men, for good reason in many cases. (Daphne was rescued after having been left newborn on a hillside to die.) They encounter the Myrmidons, who in Swann's rendition have vestigial wings and antennae, live in an underground nest, and eat mushrooms. All are male, since their queen has been kidnapped by pirates. Daphne and friends raid the nest, Daphne is captured and released but falls for one of the Myrmidons, Tychon, who later

---

64. Interview conducted by Nick Owchar, http://www.latimes.com/entertainment/news/arts/la-caw-sirens-call9-2009aug09,0,398012.story (visited 11/6/11).

65. http://www.ballardian.com/angry-old-men-michael-moorcock-on-jg-ballard (visited 11/6/11).

gives her a murex shell: "with delicate coilings and a mouth of purple shading into rose."

Much inter-cultural misunderstanding ensues. The Amazons are contriving a bloody execution for Daphne and Tychon, the Myrmidons rescue them, and Daphne is awarded their treasure, which belonged to their mother, i.e., the kidnapped queen. The treasure is reached by descending through a tunnel whose "smooth walls flickered a roseate purple" and reminds her of the murex shell. At the end of the tunnel is a chest containing a gown, a mirror, a headdress, and other items suitable for a royal wedding. She addresses Tychon and the other Myrmidons as "My beloved husbands." Once more, Peter Pan out of Tennessee Williams suggests itself, with Daphne playing Wendy (and that's the best construction—it forestalls the thought of a queen ant). But as usual with Swann, unobtrusively fine writing keeps the story on the right side of risibility.

§

Overall, the short fiction is lackluster compared to the standard of the last few years, even that by the most respected contributors. Mervyn Peake's "Danse Macabre" (**61**) is far inferior to "Same Time, Same Place" in the previous issue. It's about people whose clothes seem to be haunted, a plot device so giggle-worthy that all Peake's resources of fine writing and sensibility aren't enough to save it. Think *Weird Tales* meets *The New Yorker* and they beat each other to a pulp rolling in the gutter.

J. G. Ballard's "Time of Passage" (**63**) has time running backwards, and follows the protagonist from death to birth. It's well enough done, but it seems a waste of writerly talent on an irredeemably inane theme.

From there it's downhill pretty fast. John Baxter's "The New Country" (**64**) is another one about the last of the old gods. It's mildly clever filler. Sydney J. Bounds' "Scissors" (**63**), about a psychiatrist assigned to treat a Miss Atropos who decides it's essential to get those shears away from her to make any progress, is also clever but gimmicky. Steve Hall's "Three of a Kind" (**61**) courageously ventures into...astrology, with a private eye who is looking for a vanished scientist and winds up getting help from a learned astrologer. All three of them have the same birthdate and are therefore much alike. And from there it becomes less interesting, if that is possible.

W. T. Webb's "The Face of Mark Fenton" (**64**) manages to be even less interesting than Hall's story: a man buys a rubber mask hanging on a barroom wall, is warned that the mask really doesn't want to leave, the mask finds its way home, there's a tiresome supernatural semi-explanation. Another Hek Belov story by Edward Mackin, "The Jung at Heart" (**61**), is...another Hek Belov story. Are they over yet? Well, not quite; there's another one after 29 more issues, in *SF Impulse* **9**, the first issue edited by Harry Harrison. Gweneth Penn-Bull contributes the silly "Dial SCH 1828" (**62**), a sort of deracinated Weird Menace story, in which the protagonist visits a pompous psychiatrist with a story about using fake telephone numbers as mnemonics for dead composers, and then using those numbers to dial them up from beyond the grave. The explanation is drearily mundane.

§

As mentioned, the letter column in **62** consists of one long letter, and the author is not entirely pleased, lamenting the lost heyday of Brunner and Bulmer and Aldiss and Ballard, who have been relatively scarce in the magazine of late, and noting that *New Worlds* seems to have been publishing more science fantasy (like Lee Harding) while *Science Fantasy* has been publishing more straight fantasy—that is, not science-flavored—especially by Moorcock, whom the correspondent doesn't much care for. "I don't know where things will end," he says, "with heavy leanings towards the 'myth' story[,] weird and psychological chillers [sic], but I know I'll always dream of those Otherworlds of *Science Fantasy*, those long stories of magic." The man's got a point.

Over the last couple of years or so, a bit of a pall has crept over *Science Fantasy*. Part of the problem is Moorcock fatigue. The weary and doom-laden attitude is sometimes stronger and sometimes weaker in his stories, but it's always there. I've already mentioned his dominance in these four issues. In the preceding three volumes (18 through 20, nine issues) he had six novelettes. There's not much here to stand up against a flavor that strong. Aldiss's two stories, "Matrix" and "Skeleton Crew," are both pretty sardonic and oppressive in their different ways. The other major contributor during this period, Thomas Burnett Swann, is in his superficially sunnier way just as doom-laden as Moorcock, at best a brighter shade of fey. Even Brunner's last contribution, "Some Lapse of Time" in 57, is uncharacteristically downbeat.

In theory there is other material to provide variety and counterpoint, but mostly it isn't very good, like the lame and dreary stories of John Rackham and the trivial Midnight Club series by Steve Hall. When almost all of the strongest material in a long stretch of a magazine shares variations of the same attitude, it gets old fast.

So after a stretch of pretty good years, this magazine ends with a bit of a whimper, both in content and in appearance, to my taste, and it seems to others' as well, since apparently its circulation was declining.

§

After reading through sixty-four issues of the pre-Compact *Science Fantasy*, I'm left with two strong impressions: the magazine published a fair amount of rubbish, but it also published quite a bit of good material, much of which has been completely or nearly forgotten. There's much more than a hefty book's worth of material worth preserving there. In the spirit of a bored child drawing maps of imaginary kingdoms, here is how one might proceed if one had a mind (and a publisher).

First, here's a list—a book's worth in itself—of pretty worthy stories that seem never to have been reprinted, selected partly for pure merit and partly for reflecting one or another aspect of the magazine's eccentric spirit:

Lan Wright, "Insurance Policy" (**6**)
A. Bertram Chandler, "The Wrong Track" (**12**)
Alan Barclay, "The Dragon" (**12**)
Wanless Gardner, "Auto-Fiction Ltd." (**12**)
Jonathan Burke, "The Adjusters" (**13**)
Howard Lee McCarey, "Double Act" (**14**)
Duncan Lamont, "The Editor Regrets" (**16**)
Peter Hawkins, "The Daymakers" (**23**)
Kenneth Bulmer, "Castle of Vengeance" (**37**)
Leroy B. Haugsrud and Dale R. Smith, "Deities, Inc." (**42**)
E. C. Tubb, "Too Bad" (**40**)
John Rackham, "The Black Cat's Paw" (**44**)
John Kippax, "Reflection of the Truth" (**49**)
Wallace West, "Heinrich" (**49**)
Colin Denbigh, "Hat Trick" (**54**)
Steve Hall, "Out of Character" (**57**)

And here are some more never-reprinted stories that might make the cut for a large enough book:

John Kippax, "Me, Myself, and I" (**27**)
Julian Frey, "Life Size" (**30**)
John Kippax, "Destiny, Incorporated" (**30**)
Clifford C. Reed, "The Misfit" (**31**)
Philip E. High, "Dead End" (**56**)

Some other stories, similarly selected, have been reprinted, but not recently or prominently, and are as deserving as (in some cases more so than) those on the first list:

Jonathan F. Burke, "Once Upon a Time" (**8**)

E. C. Tubb, "The Last Day of Summer" (**12**)
A. Bertram Chandler, "Late" (**13**)
John Brunner, "Death Do Us Part" (**16**)
E. C. Tubb, "The Wager" (**16**)
Richard Wilson, "The Ubiquitous You" (**24**)
Robert Presslie, "Dial O for Operator" (**27**)
E. C. Tubb, "Return Visit" (**28**)
E. C. Tubb, "Fresh Guy" (**29**)
E. C. Tubb, "Enchanter's Encounter" (**38**)
J. G. Ballard, "The Last World of Mr. Goddard" (**43**)
Will Worthington, "The Food Goes in the Top" (**48**)
Thomas Burnett Swann, "The Sudden Wings" (**55**)
Swann, "The Murex" (**63**)

And here are some more well-known stories that ought to be included because they are at the heart of what the magazine was about, though even in a big book there wouldn't be room for all of them:

Brian W. Aldiss, "The Failed Men" (**18**)
Brian W. Aldiss, "Let's Be Frank" (**23**)
Brian W. Aldiss, "Judas Danced" (**27**)
J. G. Ballard, "The Sound-Sweep" (**39**)
Thomas Burnett Swann, "Where Is the Bird of Fire?" (**52**)
J. G. Ballard, "The Watch-Towers" (**53**)
Moorcock, "To Rescue Tanelorn..." (**56**)
Mervyn Peake, "Same Time, Same Place" (**60**)

An essential feature of any *Science Fantasy* anthology would be at least one of John Brunner's novellas. Since some of them have been expanded and published as novels or included in his collections, a judgment would have to be made balancing familiarity against merit. To my taste the best of them are "This Rough Magic" (**18**), expanded into *Black is the Color*, and "Echo in the Skull" (**36**), published by Ace under that title and later revised as *Give Warning to the World*. The best of the unreprinted ones is "All the Devils in Hell" (**44**). Also worthy of consideration are "A Time to Rend" (**20**) (somewhat rewritten in Brunner's DAW collection *Entry to Elsewhen*), "Earth Is But a Star" (**29**) (later *The 100th Millennium* and *Catch a Falling Star*, and as the title exhibit in Damien Broderick's Dying Earth anthology *Earth Is But a Star*), and "Some Lapse of Time" (**57**) (only in the 1965 collection *Now Then*, and outstanding for sheer ingenuity and weirdness).

Regrettably, no *Science Fantasy* anthology could possibly be complete without one of Edward Mackin's Hek Belov stories, of which the most tolerable are "Chaotics" (**32**), "Time Trap" (**37**), and "Behind the Cloud" (**46**).

And, if one were inclined or compelled, the following might be included to get a prominent name on the contents page:

Arthur C. Clarke, "Time's Arrow" (**1**)
John Wyndham, "Pawley's Peepholes" (**3**)
Terry Pratchett, "The Hades Business" (**60**)

§

Onward, now, to the Bonfiglioli issues.

22: *SCIENCE FANTASY,* VOLUME 22 (ISSUES 65-66)

Science Fantasy, vol. 22, **65-66**, comprise the first two Compact issues edited (in a manner of speaking) by Kyril Bonfiglio-li.[66]

The volume numbering has gotten a bit flaky. Previously, each volume had three issues. The final Carnell issue was the first of volume 22. These two issues, plus **67** and **68**, complete volume 22; volume 23 has four issues; volume 24 has nine. **65** is dated June-July 1964, **66** is July and August 1964. After **65**, the date disappears from the cover, though it remains on the contents page. These issues have the Compact name and logo (an eye) on the spines, but the colophon says only that they are published by Roberts & Vinter Ltd. on Milkwood Road in London. The copyright attribution, however, is to Science Fantasy. The magazine is printed by Rugby Advertiser, same as the Nova magazines. The colophon declares: "All terrestrial characters and places are fictitious."

---

66. SF historian Mike Ashley comments: "By all accounts, Bonfiglioli pretty much drank himself to death. Several people told me how lazy Bon was and that he wouldn't lift a finger to do anything if he could get someone else to do it for him (which is why I can barely come to think of him as the editor of *Science Fantasy*, because Keith Roberts did all the work—and before him, James Parkhill-Rathbone). It's probably also why he ended up writing so little—though what he did complete was very good" (personal communication).

Given the inconsistent volume numbering, I will discuss these issues in units that make sense in terms of content, which will be defined to some degree by the fact that *Science Fantasy* starts running serials for the first time in issue **67**. In the same issue, editor Bonfiglioli says that **67** is "the first with which I am fully satisfied." So the first two make a sensible package.

§

Compact changed the magazine physically to neat little mass-market-paperback-sized volumes with simple and colorful cover designs, definitely over to the side of Graphic Design rather than Illustration, though an editorial note says the **66** cover is a "free interpretation" of David Beech's "Building Blocks." To my taste they are unpretentiously attractive and a considerable improvement over the previous year-plus under Carnell after the abandonment of painted covers. The covers are unattributed but (based on signature) are by Roger Harris.[67] In **66**, a filler squib announces that the next cover will be by one Haro of the *Evening Standard*, but later Bonfiglioli apologizes for Haro's non-appearance. The price is back down to 2/6, and the page count is up to 128, though the word count per page appears smaller than in the digest size.

There's advertising on the inside covers: the Postal Paperback Book Club (inside front of **65-66**). The inside back covers of **65** and **66** are house ads for *New Worlds*. There's no advertising inside the magazine except for a squib in **66** from somebody who wants to buy old SF magazines. The back covers have partial contents lists.

Each of these issues has an editorial by Bonfiglioli. The first one is refreshingly brisk, exhorting the readership to *buy* the magazine: "Every time you miss buying an issue, every time you borrow a number or liberate it from a friend's bookshelf, you strike a half-crown blow at a living organ of s-f in this

67. See these covers at at http://www.sfcovers.net/mainnav.htm or http://www.philsp.com/mags/sciencefantasy.html.

country." An increase of three or four thousand readers would let the magazine pay as much as the US magazines and encourage young writers to try SF. He bemoans the quality of submissions: "I have just read through a quarter of a million words of MS and half of it was so bad it made me blush."

And there are the beginnings of an editorial credo: "I don't believe that there is any such genre as science-fantasy. It is either, at its best, off-beat science-fiction with a touch of poetry or, at its worst, degraded science-fiction, in which the author wriggles out of his plot-difficulties by introducing 'mystic' or 'transcendental' elements.... My editorial watchword, then, is 'Science Fiction for Grown-Ups!'"

In **66**, he reports that circulation has gone up by about 15%, so "I am sticking my neck out and raising the basic rate for this magazine by—to be exact—19.047%." He continues: "Science fiction's task is to abolish itself." In ten years, he predicts, either it will have abolished itself as a separate category (well, actually he says "as a separate disease") or will be "as extinct as the old-style whodunit...." This, he says, may well save not just SF but the novel, "which is running down as the dominant literary form: people are beginning to tire of the endless intricacies of other people's adultery." (Oh, I don't know. John Updike was still doing okay back then, and lasted a bit afterwards.) He segues into instructions on manuscript preparation that betray a bit of impatience with detail ("If there is a division in the story it is unwise just to leave an extra space: put in a row of stars or something."), but he doesn't forget the S.A.E.: "One doesn't like to be mean over tenpence, but there are only a couple of dozen of them in a pound note."

Aside from the editorials, there is little non-fiction in these issues. In **65**, a competition is announced for the best SF story by a professional scientist (and there's a squib in **66** indicating that doctors and engineers are eligible), but it is not mentioned again in the magazine and Mike Ashley says in Tymn/Ashley that nothing further was heard of it. The rationale for the contest, of course, is to bring respectability to the field, which is said to be suffering three disadvantages, the second and third of which are "sloppy science content" and "ignorance of s-f's merits." But the first is: "Lurid covers. Serious, well-planned, thoughtful writings by major writers in this field are still being published with coloured jackets displaying strumpets being stripped by ghouls...." Obviously Bonfiglioli never got over *The Mating Cry*.[68]

There is also a not-bad poem leading off **65** called "Science Fantasy" which could be read to suggest that fantasy fans are a bunch of reasonably nice anoraks ("I sit through Shakespeare mostly for the scenes/where I am Caliban and love myself"), by one Peter Levi, further identified in another filler squib as Fr. Peter Levi, S.J. Bonfiglioli says "It is probably the first time that a new poem by a leading poet has been printed in an s-f magazine." Perhaps not so; the Miller/Contento magazine index lists for *Fantasy & Science Fiction* poems by C. Day Lewis in the February 1957 issue and by C.S. Lewis in June 1959, neither with any indication of earlier publication. Other poets listed, though maybe not "leading," are Winona McClintic, Doris Pitkin Buck, P.M. Hubbard, Lewis Turco, Walter H. Kerr, and Starr Nelson.

§

Bonfiglioli's statement that half the submissions were so bad as to make him blush is supplemented by Brian Aldiss's account, as retold by Mike Ashley in his essay in Tymn/Ashley. Bonfiglioli was desperate for good material and asked Aldiss if he had any spare stories. He did, but they were old and (his words) "no damned good"; Bonfiglioli said they couldn't be worse than what he had. So Aldiss agreed to submit them as long as Bonfiglioli made up some pseudonyms. Hence John Runciman and Jael Cracken, used only for a couple of stories

---

68. This appalling cover, for a sexed-up and retitled version of A. E. van Vogt's *The House that Stood Still*, can be seen at http://www.isfdb.org/wiki/images/0/0f/THMTNGCRBK1960.jpg (visited 10/19/11).

each in *Science Fantasy.* Thus, **65** has three Aldiss stories, "Pink Plastic Gods" under his own name, "Lazarus" by Cracken, and "Unauthorized Persons" by Runciman, together comprising a little over half the wordage of the issue. None seems ever to have been reprinted.

"Pink Plastic Gods" does not read like an old bad story. It reads like an interesting experimental story of the time and of that point in Aldiss's career. A bitter man scratches out a living by farming after his family has been ruined through his father's financial misadventures. He encounters the squire living up the hill who is quite affluent as a result of the same events that impoverished the farmer, but equally miserable because of his lost love and his indifference to his present family. The farmer says the toff has the better of it because at least he has something good to remember, but the story suggests the farmer is better off because he sort of loves his neosimian farmhands. It doesn't quite work, and the obvious question is why did this need to be told as an SF story? But it's a lot better than "no damned good."

That phrase does apply to "Unauthorized Persons," bylined Runciman, a turgidly plotty but dull and overlong story about time travel and a ruined outpost of another civilization. The third Aldiss story, "Lazarus" as by Cracken, is middling. Space travel has been abandoned for war, the protagonist wants to get back to the space station and does, only to find a supposedly lost moon explorer who doesn't really seem to be quite human but who alarmingly insists on being taken to Earth. It's all used furniture, but the story moves along well and Aldiss hits the right jauntily satirical note to distance himself from the clichés he is manipulating with considerable deftness.

The same can't be said for Kenneth Bulmer's "The Contraption," an astonishingly mind-numbing and airless by-the-numbers exercise. We're losing a future interstellar war against an implacable alien enemy. Intrepid military types try to figure out the function of a strange device they find on captured alien ships, and it keeps blowing them up. Eventually, they conclude that it has no function and is a piece of psychological warfare designed to keep them busy and off balance. But one particularly intrepid man doesn't believe this, and indeed it turns out to be a means of finding one's way through the impenetrable clouds of meteoric debris that completely surround certain planets (or, to be precise, "the hellish porridge of rocks and metallic fragments").[69] Another sample of the prose: "They vectored up on the alien, their radar baffles going at full blast, their Stellengers idling, matching velocities in this queer other-universe that extended in some impossibly distorted dimension." At the end, the protagonist speculates that one day maybe they can make friends with the aliens—"after we have beaten them to a jelly, of course."

An odd item titled "Blast Off," subtitled "Astronaut's thoughts" and allegedly translated from the Finnish, has no author credited. It's a sort of not-too-bad stream of consciousness of an astronaut getting ready for launch, like something you might get from a reasonably talented but inexperienced writer who had just read Sturgeon's "The Man Who Lost the Sea," but then it turns into the Crucifixion. Only later did the truth come out: in Judith Merril's New Wave anthology *England Swings SF* (Ace 1967) a.k.a *The Space-Time Journal* in the UK, it is attributed to Bonfiglioli himself.

The remaining contents include Peter Bradley's innocuous "Match Box," about a housewife who has devised a matchbox that will hold more than its inside dimensions would seem to allow. Of course it takes us to the stars. Archie Potts' "The Great Chan" presents an accomplished stage magician who at the end confesses that his real name is Cagliostro. This one's only virtue is brevity. Bradley and Potts are both certified Little Known Writers, unless they too are pseudonyms. This is the only story published under Bradley's name in the genre; Potts had one story two years earlier in *New Worlds*.

---

69. I'm no expert, but this notion of an impenetrable shell of debris around a planet has no relationship I can see to actual physics; the stuff would clump and coalesce pretty fast.

§

So the first issue of the new regime is pretty lackluster. The second, **66**, starts off on a similar note, with Kenneth Bulmer's "A Case of Identity," a rural police procedural in which sheep and people are being killed and mutilated, and something is leaving tracks like an agricultural machine of some sort, and the cops track it to a house where it is destroyed by fire, and the narrator gets a glimpse and sees that it resembles...a refrigerator door. Though this is more tolerably written than last issue's Bulmer story, it's pretty much pointless, and one suspects that Bonfiglioli had a conversation with Bulmer similar to the one with Aldiss.

This is followed by the equally uncompelling but talkier "God Killer" by John Rackham, in which a pastor who has lost his faith is approached by some guys who want to do away with God—who of course is maintained by collective belief—by taking a recording of his concept of God so they can add it to others' and, in effect, figure out how to jam God. The pastor declines on the ground that lots of people are comforted by belief even if he's stopped believing, and as his interlocutors leave he starts praying. This paragraph's worth of idea takes up ten pretty boring pages.

James Rathbone's "The Poachers" is more agreeable, a sort of underwater Western in which miners' operations start messing up the seaweed farms, the farmers fight back, and the range war is on, except that the protagonist's wife has developed ways of controlling fish behavior by transmitted brain stimulation. Why shouldn't it work on the miners? They, too, have a shoal mentality, unlike the citizen farmers. So the miners are dosed with a homesickness projection and they all run away. This is fatuous if you think about it, but you don't have to, since the story is well written and paced and not too long. It reads like a not-bad YA novel. James Rathbone is the clever disguise of James Parkhill-Rathbone, who became Associate Editor of *Science Fantasy* from issue **70** to **80**, but has no other s-f magazine publications except for a 1992 story in *Picatrix*, a short-lived small press fantasy/horror magazine.

"Building Blocks" by David Beech—the cover story, no less—is a rather twee piece in which kids who read newspapers or magazines are drawn into the pages and turned into small beings like yellow building blocks with legs. A kid is assigned work as a border guard and quickly finds himself human again and back in his living room, where he grabs a drink and a cigarette. Beech has no other credits in the SF magazines.

"Dear Aunty," by Daphne Castell, is a piece of arch slapstick. An advice columnist turns out to be moonlighting—her real gig is with the *Intergalactic*. It's like Evelyn E. Smith with a little more edge, not assisted by Bonfiglioli's blurb, which is not only arch but ponderously so: "This is a highly frivolous story and the authoress is strongly suspected of not taking s-f seriously. Readers are invited to treat it with grave disapproval." Castell (1930-83) is a slightly less Little Known Writer than Rathbone and Beech, having published 13 stories and an article from this one, her first, to 1984, mostly in the post-Carnell *Science Fantasy* and *New Worlds*, a few more in assorted other outlets. This is followed by "A Dish of Devils" by James Goddard, of whom Bonfiglioli says: "Mr. Goddard is probably the youngest writer in the science-fiction field. On the present showing, he may one day be the best." Mr. Goddard's first story, however, was also his last, though he did have a few articles and interviews in *SF Monthly* a decade later and was David Pringle's collaborator on *J. G. Ballard: The First Twenty Years* (1976). The story is a capably written piece of trivia about some aliens who drop in on a sixteenth-century peasant.

Next up is "No Moon Tonight!" (or "To-Night," on the story's title page) by John Runciman a.k.a. Aldiss, for which "no damn good" is *le mot juste*. The Earth passes into a region of complete darkness, where all light is completely suppressed. First, the protagonist drives two miles to pick up his wife at home and bring her back to the military base where he is stationed, and then the characters drive twenty miles in an experimental surface/underwater vehicle, submerge, and cross the English channel, fetching up pretty near the man they are looking for, who knows what's going on and what to do about it—all, as indicated, with no light *whatsoever*. Right. This one is too ridiculous for words, and its other virtues (if it had any) would not be sufficient to redeem it.

The issue ends with "Unto All Generations" by Paul Jents (who published half a dozen stories, 1964-67, all in this magazine or *New Worlds*, then nothing more[70]), another case of big wind-up and minimal delivery. Humanity is developing more and more sophisticated computers, but really the computers are in charge, and the ultimate computer will be installed in a human brain, at which point the rest of humanity can be disposed of. After this mildly interesting development, the chosen human becomes radiant, beholds "all wisdom unto the uttermost ends of the universe," starts praying and falls to her knees.

The bottom line: for these first two issues, the new *Science Fantasy* was overall a quite bad magazine with bright spots that barely transcended mediocrity. And the contents do not display the vices, or the virtues, of the not-yet-risen New Wave. Most of them could have gone unnoticed in the lower-echelon SF digests of the 1950s.

---

70. Jents is also reputed to have been a frequent flier in the short-story slot in the *London Evening News* in the 1960s, and was sighted in *Wine Magazine* in 1969.

23: *SCIENCE FANTASY*, VOLUMES 22 AND 23 (ISSUES 67-69)

Science Fantasy, volume 22, **67-68**, and volume 23, **69**—the issues containing Thomas Burnett Swann's serialized novel "The Blue Monkeys"—are respectively dated September and October 1964, December 1964 and January 1965, and January and February 1965. The lurch in dating is not explained. Maybe it has to do with the announcement in **69** that the magazine has "taken the plunge and gone monthly." In fact, the next issue is dated March and the magazine stays monthly for the rest of its existence. These issues also stay at 2/6 and 128 pages, but there are some physical changes.

The advertising disappears from the inside covers in **68**, and in **69** the magazine changes printers, dumping the faithful Rugby Advertiser for the ingénue Richmond Hill Printing Works. One hopes this was an economy move, since the result looks cheesier and more cluttered than previous issues without appearing to add any wordage. The cover stock is now glossy rather than matte. In addition to losing the advertising, the magazine is losing the editorial blurbs preceding each story, which under Bonfiglioli never carried much conviction anyway. By **69** only one of the stories has a blurb. In fact, this has become a pretty stripped-down magazine: there's nothing between the covers but editorial, stories, and table of contents. Even the Compact logo becomes smaller and more schematic in **69**.

The covers are also pretty schematic (though archaically so, presumably in honor of Swann's novel) on **67** and **68**, and unattributed. **69** represents the important debut of Keith Roberts as cover artist, and also an innovation in the relationship of text and illustration: it represents ("heralds") Roberts' first Anita story in the *next* issue, according to Bonfiglioli's editorial. (This doesn't appear to be entirely planned. The back cover says there is an Anita story by Roberts in *this* issue.) I continue to find these covers unpretentiously agreeable, though there's not as much to say about them as there was about the Carnell-era covers.[71]

There's not much evidence of any proofreading. This is the chief axis of continuity with the Carnell *Science Fantasy.*

In **67**, Bonfiglioli's editorial declares that this third issue is "the first with which I am fully satisfied." He notes the reprint of Kipling's "Easy as A.B.C." and says Kipling could have left Wells standing had he chosen to pursue SF. He was warned not to print Thom Keyes' "Period of Gestation" "since it deals with matters more familiar in the pages of *Seven Pillars of Wisdom* than in the curiously chaste and prudish ambience of science fiction... [But] to record unnatural crime is not to endorse it." He expresses pleasure at the presence of Keith Roberts and Thomas Burnett Swann, and prints and cruelly mocks a disapproving (and quite mock-worthy) letter from an American reader.

In **68**, he extravagantly praises Brian Aldiss's then-new novel *Greybeard,* and says he will start a letter column if the magazine goes monthly. The **69** editorial presents the (borrowed) distinction between "putters-in" like Swann, who build up their stories around key words and phrases, and "takers-out" like Kipling who dump it all on the page and then cut out the inessential. Keith Roberts, he allows, seems to be one of the latter, and by the way he's the cover artist too. Bonfiglioli praises the other contributors briefly, says the magazine is going monthly, and promises new stories by Harry Harrison, John Rackham, Brian Aldiss, and Robert Wells.

71. See these covers at http://www.sfcovers.net/mainnav.htm or http://www.philsp.com/mags/sciencefantasy.html.

There's only one piece of non-fiction in these three issues: "E. J. Carnell—A Brief Look" in **68** is a sort of personality puff piece by Harry Harrison that contains virtually nothing describable as information. Carnell is very busy, continuing to work as an agent, and editing the forthcoming *New Writings in SF.*

§

The major item of fiction is Swann's "The Blue Monkeys," serialized in all three issues and taking up about 124 pages, an enjoyable but curiously detached short novel. Again we have the devoted brother and sister who only have eyes (very asexual ones) for each other. These are Icarus and Thea, who live on Knossos and are the children of the Cretan noble Aeacus and a Dryad. The Dryads live in a forest with various other fabulous Beasts, like the Minotaur.

When the savage Achaeans invade Knossos, Thea and Icarus escape by means of a glider launched from a catapult. Steering isn't too good, so they wind up in the fearsome forest, which they quickly flee, seeking refuge in a cave where they encounter the even more fearsome Minotaur. But Eunostos, the Minotaur, is really an old sweetie, regardless of what you may hear from other sources, and sort of adopts the kids, though he'd like to do considerably more to Thea.

So they live for a while in the peaceable and civilized kingdom of the Beasts, who include Centaurs, Dryads, the bee-like and seductive Thriae, and the Bears of Artemis, who are mainly preoccupied with meals and naps and seem to have been recruited down the street at *Winnie-the-Pooh.* But the Achaeans move into the forest, assisted by the treacherous Thriae, and all hell breaks loose. The Beasts defend themselves, in scenes of extreme violence bloodlessly written, but the Achaeans wreak havoc with them. However, Thea, Icarus, and Eunostos, accompanied by Icarus's pet snake, figure out how to do in the Achaeans, finally giving the blue monkeys of the title something to do. But the Beasts have had enough and want to return to the Old Country, i.e., the Isles of the Blest. And Thea, now quite grown up, offers herself to Eunostos. This is all enjoyable enough but, as noted a bit distant, and Swann seems to be becoming more self-consciously arty in his writing. "The Blue Monkeys" was later published as *Day of the Minotaur* (Ace, 1966).

§

Aside from "The Blue Monkeys," the most substantial piece of fiction here is Kipling's familiar, very well done, and thoroughly reactionary "Easy as A.B.C." Aside from Kipling, these issues are striking for the large number of new writers—not just new to the magazine, but new to the genre. These three issues contain seven first appearances according to the Miller/Contento magazine index. Apart from Swann, the only usual suspect to be found is John Rackham, and the only other known SF name is Harry Harrison, who had two prior appearances in *Science Fantasy* (both reprints), and is here with a story and the above mentioned profile of Carnell.

By contrast, Kenneth Bulmer, a Carnell *Science Fantasy* regular who also had stories in the first two Bonfiglioli issues, is permanently gone except for a collaboration with Richard Wilson in *SF Impulse* a couple of years later. The bad news about these new writers, though, is that most of them seem to have been flashes in the pan, with few or no genre publications outside the Bonfiglioli *Science Fantasy* and the Moorcock *New Worlds*. It would be interesting to know exactly how Bonfiglioli managed to recruit these writers, and whether any of them went on to writing careers outside the genre.

The most notable exception among the new arrivals is Keith Roberts, who went on to a substantial SF career, and has no fewer than six stories in these three issues under his own name and his pseudonym Alistair Bevan. Roberts would be as dominant a writer in the Bonfiglioli *Science Fantasy* as Moorcock was in Carnell's waning days. But these early stories are not especially impressive. **67** contains "Anita," the first in Roberts' series about the sexy and naive witch reared in isolation by her grandmother. There are two episodes here, veering from the comical to the Guignolish, as Anita makes a friend who is then driven to suicide by her family, resulting in *Carrie*esque retribution. Next is "The Charm" in **68**, in which Anita is captured by a scholar of witchery, initially to her fury. But she's happy to make a deal in which she moves in, shares his bed, and assists him in a magical time-traveling scheme that ends in the revelation that there was another world before this one. The point of it all escapes me. Roberts doesn't seem to be sure whether he is writing screwball comedy, horror, or straight narrative, and he doesn't seem to be consciously playing one off against the other. If Anita is supposed to be some sort of iconic figure to be viewed from all perspectives and illuminating them all, she's not too interesting an icon, at least to my taste—maybe on the level of Little Annie Fannie or Daisy Mae.

67 also contains "Escapism," an earnest and overlong story about two men running a movie theatre and some time-traveling filmmakers who need a place to view the rushes of their historical epics. One of the characters, who hates the present, gets them to drop him off in the distant past, where he is killed in a battle. This distaste for the present gets a livelier workout in "The Madman" (**68**), as by Bevan, about a Senior Citizen who goes berserk and batters his great-grandchildren's plastic wishing well, and flees by bus to the now virtually non-existent countryside, finding that Stonehenge has been reduced to a display in a visitors' center. Apprehended, he is committed to the Sector Asylum, where they keep the few remaining books, wooden furniture, and patches of real grass—a derivative piece, but less boring than "Escapism."

69 has "Flight of Fancy," a post-nuclear-war vignette in which the conversation proceeds from bows and arrows to space flight in a page and a half, and (under the Alistair Bevan pseudonym, misspelled on the contents page) "The Typewriter," about a hack writer, author of the Flush Hardman epics, whose typewriter comes alive and starts dragging the author into the story. It's *Unknown*-ish and a bit formulaic but reasonably well done.

§

Other than Roberts, **67** features Thom Keyes' "Period of Gestation," which Bonfiglioli said he was counseled not to publish. It enthusiastically proposes that all-male spacefaring crews will go nuts and, among other deranged behavior, engage in homosexual acts. One of them is then observed by his fellows to be pregnant and obviously requires a Caesarian. This is about the first hard-core New Wavey story to appear in the magazine, other than some of Ballard's. Moorcock liked it enough to reprint it in one of his *Best of New Worlds* anthologies even though it's not from *New Worlds*. Keyes (1943-95) appears to have been a New Wave flash in the pan, with two stories in *Science Fantasy* and another in *New Worlds*, all 1964-65, but was a poet of minor note and author of the equally transgressive 1969 rock novel *All Night Stand*.

In Colin Hume's "Dummy Run" (**67**), yet again, aliens bent on invasion encounter a perfectly ordinary human being and are frightened away. This version involves a not-too-bright ventriloquist and his dummy. It's Hume's first story, and he published only one more, in *New Worlds* in 1965. George Rigg's "Symbiote" (**67**) is about some strange creatures who turn out to be a drunkard's pink elephants. Bonfiglioli's blurb says: "A very short story by an Oxford don whose special field is medieval literature. Its quality makes me hope that he will soon offer us something longer." In fact, it is Rigg's only story in the genre magazines. Johnny Byrne's (1935-2008) "Love Feast" (**67**) is blurbed: "Here is one of a series of strange little fragments called 'Shots from the Looking Glass,' sent to me by a friend of the author. This one is dedicated to Elias Canetti." It's a grotesque vignette about what seem to be nuclear war survivors, one feeding pieces of himself to the other. This is Byrne's first genre appearance. He had five more in *Science Fantasy*, then nothing—at least in the SF magazines. Having been a touring manager for rock bands, he published a novel titled *Groupie* in collaboration with one Jenny Fabian in 1969, scripted such films as *Adolf Hitler, My Part In His Downfall* (1972), wrote episodes of *Doctor Who* and *Space: 1999*, then moved up to *All Creatures Great and Small* and *Heartbeat*.[72]

§

68 is the veterans' issue. John Rackham's "Room with a Skew" is a formulaic gadget fantasy. A man needs the spare room cleaned up, and luckily his roommate has devised a "coil with a negative inductance" which makes things disappear, which is convenient. But they start getting strange TV programs and some of their stuff is returned in battered condition. The coil proves to be a doorway to another world populated by some weird characters. But nothing much actually happens. Harry Harrison's "Not Me, Not Amos Cabot!" is a *Galaxy* story gone over the top. A retired man starts receiving unsolicited copies of *Hereafter: The Magazine of Preparedness*, and learns he has been given a subscription based on the publisher's estimate of his life expectancy. He finds this annoying, and vows to beat the actuaries. He wins, the subscription runs out, but then he starts receiving *Senility: The Magazine of Geri-Art-Rics*, with articles like "Happy Though Bedridden and Immobile for Twenty-Five Years." Most likely this was rejected by all the US SF magazines, which generally weren't ready for comedy quite this black.

Now for the ingénues in **68**. "Joik" by Ernest Hill is his third published story. The first two were in *New Worlds*, and there are five more in *New Worlds*, *Science Fantasy*, and *Impulse* in 1964-66, several more in *New Writings in SF*, five in *Galaxy* and *If* in 1966-71, and a final one in *SF Monthly* in 1975. He was also responsible for half of an Ace Double, *Pity About Earth*,

72.   http://www.space1999.net/catacombs/main/crguide/vcwjb.html (visited 10/19/11).

reputed to be dire. "Joik" is a thoroughly bad story—that is, one whose badness reflects not simple ineptitude, but hard work and dedication, exercised in a framework of logic so peculiar as to suggest a New Age J. T. McIntosh, and to defy brief summarization. Attention must be paid.

Ngula, Chief Investigator of Scientific Security, contemplates the charms of Dadulina, a Curator of Antiquities in a future world dominated by Africans in which whites are injected with melanin to darken their skins and "Jomo!" is a common exclamation. "Ain't" is also a common, indeed inescapable, usage. This is the world of the Rationale, in which belief in beauty has been banished. Whether the Rationale is a philosophy, a technique, or an attachment is not entirely clear ("Ngula concentrated his Rationale"). Ngula is investigating the disappearance of Dadulina's significant other, Tantor, who was not heard from again after setting off in his spaceship and activating the Joik. Any doubt as to the referent of "Joik" is dispelled by the description of women as "boids" and reference to Professor Tantor's "woik." This particular vowel shift is entirely unexplained (there is no claim that Africa has been colonized from Brooklyn). So, a joik is an abrupt movement of several light-years by a spaceship.

Dadulina was in "inter-sensory perception" with Tantor when he disappeared, but professes to know nothing about his fate. So Ngula orders her to the Center for Questions, to which she is escorted by "Cardu the one-eyed and Rhoder the two-headed dwarf." Ngula listens to Dadulina's copy of Schubert's 8th Symphony (Unfinished), smoking a long black cigar from the narcotics dispenser, then heads for the interrogation room, where Dadulina is strapped naked to a chair and hooked up to various monitors, and is giving nonsensical and contradictory answers to questions about Tantor (she's in contact with him, she has no way to reach him, etc.)

Vordunga, who is running the show, says there's one way to get to the bottom of this: torture. So Ngula leaves the room. He hears a scream, runs back in, and Dadulina has weals across her back and there's a fly-whisk on the floor. Vordunga has disappeared, even though there's no way out. Ngula, who has just consented to her being tortured, says, "Boid, we gotta talk!" and "Dadulina, you gotta help me!" Sure, she'll help him, her torturer's accomplice, as much as she can. They go back to her apartment, he says he's sorry, she tells him he's a good man. They light up Marijuana cheroots (sic) ("she was a smoker not an addict") and she reveals the secrets of Joik, explaining that the universe is like a coiled spring and Joik allows one to go straight through rather than following around the coils. "Tantor and I are one," she says, but Tantor is now outside the coils, where the real All is.

Outside the coils, there's only one person, referred to as the Person. God? Tantor calls it the Dreamer, and everything and everybody here inside the coil is a loose splinter of its (his) personality emitted during dreams. Tantor is now one with the Dreamer, but his dreams are separate, and Vorunga the torturer is history because Tantor found his behavior unpleasant and just stopped dreaming about him. After these revelations, Dadulina and Ngula take the only logical next step: they engage in sexual intercourse.

Afterward, Ngula is worried the Dreamer might stop dreaming of him, too, since Tantor might not have approved. Dadulina's response: "Tantor is real—sex is real—like beauty—music." And also: "'Narcotics,' she said slowly, 'are the only real thing in a world of dreams. They bring us nearer to the Dreamer. Beauty, music are the gateways to reality but reality is hard for us dream-symbols to fathom.' He looked at her thoughtfully but accepted a second cheroot."

A bit later, Ngula is agitated, beginning to perceive "an awareness of entity for its own sake," Rationale to the contrary notwithstanding. So: "'Amphetamine!' She handed him a tablet. He swallowed it, feeling the luxurious sense of well-being return, coupled with a lucidity of thought impossible without the aid of the drug." He listens to Schubert's 8th with new appreciation. Dadulina offers to substantiate her account of the universe: get her a spacecraft, she will go the same route as Tantor and will return to the Dreamer. "You will all be happier when you know that the quest for knowledge is futile and that nothing ultimately matters in a world that is fundamentally unreal."

This plan of action requires Ngula to give up Dadulina, of course, "but where the choice lay between a boid and the quest for truth, Rationality necessarily predominated." They shoot Dadulina off ("Hovering for a moment on caryatids of fire the craft nosed forward"). She approaches the fatal point in space—"Joik!" She's gone. Proving what? Telepathically, she says "Thank you." Ngula is pleased that she thanked him. "He was no longer a Rationale, not even a Trash element. He was a primitive, an archaism, a savage," etc.

So they come and take him away, and inquire into just what he's been smoking. It's something new: "A compound of morphia, hallucinogenic, non-habit forming." Impound all stocks! The Bwana gives this order and sits doodling. "His doodles, indicators to the subliminal and possibly also to a conjectural universal subliminal, pointed often to a solution of much that was otherwise insoluble." He seems to be drawing the Dreamer with eyes half open. Implication: the end is near!

Whew! This is followed (and the issue closed) by "One of Those Days," the first published story by Charles Platt, whose subsequent career encompasses many items of fiction and non-fiction in *New Worlds* and original anthologies, a number of novels and non-fiction books, work on cryonics, etc. Fortunately this story doesn't demand quite the weight of synopsis required by "Joik": a man is driven nuts by the heat, the noise, the traffic fumes, his wife, his children, it keeps getting worse, he cuts himself on a broken flowerpot, and bleeds to death. The New Wave in a nutshell! By the criteria of its foes, anyway.

§

As mentioned, Bonfiglioli said that issue **67** was "the first with which I am fully satisfied." For me, **69** is the first Bonfiglioli issue that hits that mark—that is, in which my enjoyment exceeded my irritation for every item in the magazine (though just barely in a couple of cases). The two Keith Roberts stories, "Flight of Fancy" and "The Typewriter," are described above. The issue starts with "Present from the Past," the first and apparently only SF story by Douglas Davis, a well turned short thriller about a paleontologist who travels back to the Triassic to observe dinosaurs from the time machine, and feels compelled to take a walk and get a closer look. Langdon Jones' "The Empathy Machine," is his third story of about seventeen magazine items, all the rest of which were in *New Worlds*, with one later in *Orbit* and one or two more in Jerry Cornelius artifacts. In this one, our protagonist—who is pretty close to the edge, driven there at least in part by the pressures of a *Space Merchants*-like advertising-dominated culture, but also just a pretty nasty and self-absorbed man—takes his wife on a Martian vacation intending to dispose of her.

Arrived, they're immediately allowed to rent a vehicle and head out by themselves into the Martian wilderness, and find the previously undiscovered remains of a Martian civilization literally just over the first hill from the base. And of course they get out of their vehicle, climb down a steep ravine, and explore it, rather than going back and telling somebody about it. They find a strange headpiece, he puts it on, and his wife idly touches a switch in the next room, precipitating a sort of psychedelic interlude ("Awareness. Identity. Something something falling enclosed. I. The concept: the idea, hold that idea! I. Me." Etc.) in which he experiences his wife's psyche and realizes what an abusive jerk he has been.

Johnny Byrne is present with "Harvest," the second in his half-dozen *Science Fantasy* stories, a surreal account of people living (or failing to live) near a war zone, grotesque, vivid, and effective. "Petros" is by Philip Wordley, whom Bonfiglioli describes (in the only blurb in the magazine) as "another newcomer—one from whom we will be hearing a great deal." In fact, he published three more stories in *Science Fantasy* and then was heard from no more in the SF magazines, or anywhere else that I can find. An ordinary guy, post-nuclear war, has been delegated to build a church by the last remaining functionary of the Catholic Church. He is nearly killed by the scruffy local survivors but fights them off. Some of them then show up at the church believing he's a pastor, and our protagonist fakes it as best he can. After the service he runs into another scruffy little guy just outside the door, who says "On this rock I will build my church." (Boom boom.)

Patricia Hocknell's "Only the Best" is a "Twonky" reprise: this time it's a washing machine with attitude and ambition. Hockney would have one more story in *Science Fantasy* and nothing more in the SF mags. Roger Jones (who also had one more story, in *SF Impulse*, and then vanished from the genre) has "The Island," about three men who for no reason the author mentions are living on a beach hut on an island, observing a strict hierarchy in which only one of them ever goes to the House at the top of the Hill. In a blind taste test one might guess this was an early Barry Malzberg story.

There are things one can criticize about these stories—the logic, or lack of it, of "The Empathy Machine," and the clichéd *deus ex* hat end of "Petros"—but they are all capably enough written to cover at least a few sins. Reading them as period pieces and making the appropriate allowances, they're pretty enjoyable. This magazine is starting to develop a personality, very different from that of the Carnell era, but at least as interesting in its own way.

24: *SCIENCE FANTASY,* VOLUME 23 (ISSUES 70-71)

Science Fantasy, volume 23, **70** and **71**, March and April 1965, are linked by a serialized short story—installments of six and nine pages respectively. There is no editorial comment on why such a short item is serialized (most likely improvisation). Interestingly, the second installment does not indicate there was a first installment, which probably confused a few readers. J(ames) Parkhill-Rathbone, who as previously noted had a story in **66**, is now listed as Associate Editor. There is no editorial comment on the change.

The magazine is otherwise the same in presentation as the previous few issues, with trivial differences. There's a page of small ads at the end of **71**, mostly books for sale, but here's an interesting one: "CREATE the World of the Future today. Social Engineering sessions every Wednesday 7-9 p.m. 13, Prince of Wales Terrace, London, W.8. Admission 5/-. For better living: fraternal communities, urban, rural, overseas. Send unmarked 2/6 for information. Box 114, Roberts & Vinter." The last gasp of Technocracy? Scientologists? Rosicrucians? The only other innovation is that **70** has an interior illustration, by Keith Roberts for an Anita story. (Roberts has three stories in these two issues, one as by Alistair Bevan.)

70 has one of the Compact *Science Fantasy*'s most striking covers, one of three by Agosta Morol. **71** has one of the least striking.[73] It looks to me like a blurrily processed photo of a late

---

73. As usual, Broderick finds this cover design quite arresting, See these

night street scene with a traffic light in the upper right corner; I find no attribution for it.

Bonfiglioli's editorial in **70** takes half a page to say he doesn't have much to say, retails some gossip about forthcoming books, and mentions the next issue's highlight, Brian Aldiss's "Man in His Time"—"a long story (I'm afraid I cannot bring myself to use the word 'novelette')." **71**'s editorial is more substantial. It includes the promised letter column, but prefaced by a hypothetical composite uncomplimentary letter of the sort Bonfiglioli claims, not very credibly, to like ("It is hard to say which is the more pleasant—the free and unfettered rudeness of the few or the generous warm-hearted friendship of the many.") He goes on to say that what saddens him is letters that ask why the magazine can't be just like *Galaxy* twenty years ago ("The answer is easy: bring back the writers who were young twenty years ago, bring back the excitement about the exploding post-war technologies, give us an American-size circulation and we could produce something even better.")

Current British SF is "neither moribund nor second-rate," as shown by recent issues of *Science Fantasy* and *New Worlds*. He carps about the unfairness of comparing the contents of current magazines to those of anthologies, which leave behind the dregs of the older magazines. This takes not quite two pages, and the rest of the three-page spread comprises "Points from Letters." David J. Orme of East Dulwich allows that the magazine is getting better, but he doesn't like the name, and also doesn't want "science fact" articles of the ilk of "Is There Life on Mars?" and "The Problems Our Spacemen Face." Peter Winchurch of Solihull praises Swann and Roberts ("Anita is delicious") and says the magazine rivals *Fantasy & Science Fiction* at its best. Harry Harrison says (based on **68**) that it's "the most beautifully produced SF magazine that I have ever seen." That seems a stretch.

---

covers at http://www.sfcovers.net/mainnav.htm or http://www.philsp.com/mags/sciencefantasy.html.

Finally, a Mrs. Judith Mugliston says that she always buys the magazine because of the lovely covers and because two pages' worth is enough to put her to sleep, which is better for her than sleeping pills (and if she needs something stronger she reads the editorial). I would suspect that this one is a ringer, in part because of the address ("Speen, Bucks."), except that I have learned that seemingly parodic UK addresses are generally all too real.[74]

§

The best piece of fiction in these issues is the novelette that dared not speak its category, Aldiss's much-reprinted "Man in His Time." Westermark the astronaut returns from Mars experiencing time three minutes ahead of everybody else. His wife must come to grips with this grotesque distortion of life and with the fact that he is permanently lost to her. The psychologist character is looking to see what he can milk from the situation. It still stands up, despite the utterly implausible premise: beautifully written and characterized, a model of Bonfiglioli's slogan "Science fiction for grown-ups."

In this story, Aldiss (for the only time I'm aware of) used the device—probably prompted by Ballard's "The Terminal Beach"—of heading each brief section of the story with an italicized phrase, usually taken or adapted from the text in that section or the preceding one, and ending the story with one as well, taken from the wife's earlier description of Westermark's isolation: "All events, all children, all seasons." In another story this device would probably be unbearably pretentious. Here it fits the elegiac mood and also highlights the theme of temporal displacement subtly and effectively. Bravo. Aldiss was on a pretty remarkable roll during the early and middle 1960s and this is one of the high points.

---

74. It is, in fact, a village in the parish of Princes Risborough, in *Buckinghamshire*, England.

§

Of the rest of the fiction, some of it is pretty good and some of it isn't, but what is striking is how little outright fantasy there is—maybe not surprising in light of Bonfiglioli's first-issue declaration that his goal was "Science Fiction for Grown-Ups!" The exceptions include two more Anita stories by Keith Roberts: "The Jennifer" (**70**), in which she fobs off a sand replica of herself on her grandmother while hitching a ride with the Great Sea Serpent to the city of the mermaids (this is the one that was illustrated on the cover of the previous issue), and "The War at Foxhanger" (**71**) about a magic war between Anita's grandmother and another local witch. Bonfiglioli gives "The War at Foxhanger" one of his now-infrequent blurbs, suggesting that anybody who has missed the earlier Anita stories should get the back numbers immediately, without saying how to order them.

The serialized short story is "Hunt a Wild Dream" by D. R. Heywood, who has no other appearances in the SF magazines. The protagonist is a white hunter in Kenya who has always dreamed of capturing the legendary Chemosit, a sort of African Big Foot. He does, and the plot then turns to the Mau Mau and metempsychosis, with translations of the Swahili and Nandi dialogue at the end. This claim to authenticity is the main thing the story has going for it.

§

The rest of the stories are SF, not by any purist definition but as they present themselves. **70** leads off with Harry Harrison's "The Outcast," a competent but contrived, conventional story about a doctor, scapegoated and stripped of his license, who has to perform emergency surgery illegally to save the life of an unappreciative spaceship passenger, and how he is cleverly saved from arrest and prosecution on landing. It could have appeared unremarked in any of the second-line US magazines of the 1950s. This is followed by the promised Robert Wells story, "Song of the Syren," *Science Fantasy*'s second contribution to the subgenre of SF about singing flowers (the first one, of course, being Ballard's "Prima Belladonna"). The story is a clever and diverting if inconsequential mystery that takes place in an extraterrestrial botanical research station, with the singing flowers as murder victims. Wells published a modest number of other stories in the SF magazines, including a serial, "Inheritance," in *If* a few years later, as well as several novels, mostly with Berkley. The Miller/Contento index also lists "The Mine," from *London Mystery* 35 (1957), which—combined with his assured running of the investigative numbers—makes me wonder if he didn't also have more of a background in suspense and crime fiction.

Speaking of contrived, Philip Wordley's "Moriarty" involves an aspiring young safecracker whose attempts are always thwarted in advance by a large blonde telepathic and teleporting policewoman who wants him to lead a law-abiding life. She recruits him for a scheme to trap the local criminal gang by teleporting him into a bank so he can finally consummate a safecracking, removing the money before the robbers arrive and returning it after they are captured, all in what is eventually revealed as the name of love.

Also in **70**, John Rackham is back and considerably improved with "Bring Back a Life," in which the protagonist's consciousness is projected back in time through the ancestry of an important political figure, looking for the origin of a genetically transmitted illness in order to cure it, only to find that somebody else seems to be traveling down the heredity-line with him and trying to help him out. The idea is clever and original and the story is executed with commendable brevity. This is the liveliest piece of fiction in the issue.

R. W. Mackelworth (1930-2000), insurance salesman by profession if Wikipedia is to be trusted, was a late and apparently adaptable Carnell regular, with half a dozen stories in *New Worlds* in 1963-64, then another seven in the Moorcock and Bonfiglioli magazines through 1966, and then five more in

Carnell's *New Writings in SF* series. In addition he published several novels (*Tiltangle, The Diabols* a.k.a. *Firemantle, Starflight 3000, Shakehole, The Year of the Painted World*) before hanging it up in the early '80s. His "A Cave in the Hills" is a stylized suburban dystopia about a woman who lives in isolation in a house with Vision (virtual reality), supported by her husband's Credit Card (sic), except he winds up in Debtors so she gets a visit from the Arbitrator. It's better written and less heavy-handed than my description and the author's capitalization suggests.

In **71**, after Aldiss and Anita, there is "The Chicken Switch" by Elleston Trevor, who also gets a blurb: "Every day a few more readers—we devoutly believe—are converted to science-fiction. But it is not every day that an established professional writer like Mr. Trevor takes the plunge and we welcome him cordially." It was a short plunge. He didn't appear again in the SF/fantasy magazines. Trevor (1920-95) started out writing for the Gerald Swan magazines, wrote the Quiller suspense novels as Adam Hall, racked up eighty or so books under various names including his birth name Trevor Dudley-Smith, a number of them close enough to SF to get him an entry in the *Encyclopedia of Science Fiction*. This is a polished but inconsequential story about a journalist who gets a bit too wrapped up with an aspiring astronaut undergoing a week-long isolation test, with a weak paranormal twist at the end.

Here's Keith Roberts again under the Bevan pseudonym with "Susan," capably turned but a bit leaden and earnest and definitely overlong, about a student who isn't quite what she seems (mutant or alien, it isn't clear). Judith Merril selected it for her annual anthology. "Over and Out" by George Hay is a very brief vignette about a computer running amok. George Hay (1922-97) had a scattering of stories and articles ranging from a novel, "Man, Woman—and Android," in *Science Fiction Monthly* (one of the early guises of *Authentic*) in 1951, to a few stories in *Ghosts and Scholars* from 1979 to 1985, to articles in *Ad Astra* and *New Libertarian Notes* from 1973 to 1980, plus half a dozen anthologies from 1963 to 1979.

The longest item in the issue is B(rian) N. Ball's "The Excursion," in which a conventionally assorted group of tourists (the military man, the academic, the young couple, the older woman who comes along because she doesn't want to finish her knitting too soon) enact a conventional but entertainingly rendered there-and-back-again plot. On a robot-directed tour of a fort left over from an old interstellar war, they push the wrong button and find themselves transported into the *really* secret part of the fort, presided over by an AI who thinks the war is still going on and they are spies ripe for execution. They must discover how to outwit it and escape, revealing all their personal secrets in this crucible before getting back to their robot tour guide, who scolds them for getting off the authorized route. This story was later expanded into *Night of the Robots* a.k.a. *Regiments of Night* (1972). Ball (1932-) had a couple of earlier stories in *New Worlds*, and a few later in *Visions of Tomorrow* and *New Writings in SF*, as well as numerous other novels, mostly from DAW; one was enticingly translated into German as *Zeitpunkt Null*. And there's at least one *Space: 1999* novelization.

And Ball's versatility is proven by *The Quest For Queenie*, as summarized in its book rendition by a Kirkus review: "Jill and Harry find a talking sword (Sigismund, or 'Siggy') who says they've have been chosen for a quest involving an ogre and a dragon guarding a rescuee who—in the absence of a more suitable damsel (Jill is one of the rescuers, and Mom certainly isn't eligible)—proves to be Queenie, the family pooch. Off they go to 'Mandragora'; Harry carries Siggy, but Jill has the best ideas. The ogre isn't hard to divert with bubble gum.... (Fiction/Young reader. 7-1)."

§

After seven issues of the Bonfiglioli *Science Fantasy*, its differences from the Carnell version are beginning to gel.

There's little declared fantasy, though Thomas Burnett Swann is a notable exception. Most of the SF is surprisingly conventional, though (with some exceptions) capably done or better.

In general, there are more and shorter stories. Each of these issues contains seven items of fiction, compared to four or five, occasionally fewer, during the last few Carnell years. And most of them are pretty polished artifacts, which I suppose befits a magazine edited by an art dealer. There's very little of the pulpy, over-the-top strain that was one of the Carnell magazine's persistent flavors (Moorcock's "The Deep Fix," Steve Hall's "Out of Character," and Philip High's "Dead End" are late examples).

The wilder frontiers of the Bonfiglioli regime are represented by Johnny Byrne's very much calculated surreal fantasies of a few issues ago. Even a story as out to lunch as Ernest Hill's "Joik" (**68**) represents a carefully premeditated sort of bad judgment; you can't blame its upbringing or the kids it hung out with.

At the other end of the quality graph, Aldiss's "Man in His Time" is about as controlled a story as he ever wrote, a very different sort of presentation from "Matrix" and "Skeleton Crew," the last two stories he wrote for Carnell, which are altogether more scruffy and disorderly. So: the magazine is significantly more literate and disciplined under the new management.

25: *SCIENCE FANTASY*, VOLUMES 23 and 24 (ISSUES 72-73)

Science Fantasy, vol. 23, **72** and vol. 24, **73**, May and June 1965, contain the two installments of Jael Cracken's (i.e. Aldiss's) "The Impossible Smile." The magazine remains physically and visually the same as the preceding issues. Both covers are by Keith Roberts, neither particularly pleasing to my eye. **72** depicts a broadly smiling visage which may possibly be related to "The Impossible Smile" but reminds me entirely too much of Alfred E. Neuman. **73** presents a couple of very stylized trees that look like crude drawings of germs or dendrites.[75]

72 lacks the back page of small ads that appeared in **71**, but they are back in **73**, which strikes me as odd. Don't you have to run ads consistently in order to sell the space? Apparently not. Represented are the Postal Paperback Book Service, Fantast (Medway) Ltd., a couple of house ads, the British Science Fiction Association, and a couple of wild cards. "BECOME CO-OWNER large yacht, join private syndicate converting D.I.Y., meet sf fen, etc. Devon coast: details from Box 115, Roberts & Vinter." And this: "'*The Messenger*': a genuine communication. (Is this from a higher intelligence?) Send 2/6 (blank P.O.) Box 116, Roberts & Vinter."

Interestingly, though the ad page has a subscription ad for

---

75. See these covers at http://www.sfcovers.net/mainnav.htm or http://www.philsp.com/mags/sciencefantasy.html.

Science Fantasy and a house ad for the Compact SF paperback line, there is no ad for *New Worlds*. In three contemporaneous *New Worlds*, *Science Fantasy* is prominently advertised in two of them.

In general, this is a magazine without fillers. If an item ends a third of the way down the page, the other two-thirds remain blank. In the Compact *New Worlds*, by contrast, dead space was eschewed, mostly by way of house ads. *Science Fantasy* is also virtually without editorial blurbs. Only a couple of the stories have blurbs. One of these is a reprint, Brian Aldiss's "A Pleasure Shared" from the December 1962 *Rogue*, for which Bonfiglioli says it's taken him a year to get British rights.

These issues definitely show the development of a Bonfiglioli stable of writers: in addition to Aldiss, with the Jael Cracken serial and "A Pleasure Shared," Keith Roberts, with one Anita story and another under the Alistair Bevan pseudonym, and a new T.B. Swann story, there are appearances by Philip Wordley, Paul Jents, Patricia Hocknell, and Thom Keyes, all of whom have appeared before in the Bonfiglioli *Science Fantasy* and nowhere or almost nowhere else (Jents and Keyes also appeared once each in *New Worlds*). Wordley, in addition to his story in **72**, is listed on the cover of **73** (front and back) for "Goodnight Sweet Prince," a story that does not actually appear until **77**. Also listed on the cover, but absent from the contents, is Roberts' "Idiot's Lantern," which does not actually appear until **75**.

This matter of names on covers is one that Bonfiglioli does not seem quite to have figured out. **72**'s cover lists Jael Cracken, Keith Roberts, Alan Burns, and Philip Wordley, but not the most prominent writer in the issue, Thomas Burnett Swann. Similarly, **73** lists Cracken and the absent Roberts and Wordley, but not Brian Aldiss, the biggest name on the contents page.

§

Bonfiglioli's editorial in **72** starts out with public service announcements for the British Science Fiction Association and the 23rd Worldcon, to be held in London, and then offers the publishers of "fanzines" (as he repeatedly renders it) publicity in the form of "a page of 'fanzine' facts" if they want more subscribers. He is "continually tempted to embark...on one of those long dreary discussions about what Science Fiction really is, whether there is such a *genre* etc." He's resisted, but now he wonders why the temptation? The only literary parallel is with the detective novel,

> which also had its fixed conventions and rules, its fanatical enthusiasts, its pseudonymous part-time writers and its lovers of the pure and early vintages. But there the resemblance ceases: no 'tec story reader would have thought of running an amateur magazine for other enthusiasts, no editor would have bothered to discuss the nature of the medium in his magazine, certainly no World Congress of detective writers and readers would have been held every year for twenty three years.

Times do change, don't they? Bonfiglioli invites letters explaining this now vanished anomaly. He concludes by saying there's no letter column this month because of "lack of interesting material"—take that, readers—and that he is not going to run story ratings because so few people write that they would not be representative. "If two hundred readers each month commented on each story this would still not be a fair sample: it would be some 80 per cent of the letter-writers but only 1.4 per cent or thereabout of the whole readership...." So he's claiming a circulation of roughly 14,300.

In **73**, it appears there are still no interesting letters, so Bonfiglioli takes up the cudgels against Brian Aldiss's statement "The job of a critic consists of knowing when he is being bored, and why." Bonfiglioli wants to distinguish between stories that are well written and those that are well told—to what end is not exactly clear, though he promises to continue the discussion. In passing, concerning the James Bond books: "They describe with implicit approval the base actions of an amoral thug engaged in an unsavoury trade. They are implausible in content, undistinguished in style, palpably deleterious in their effect upon the young and clearly written within the terms of a cynically-devised formula intended to appeal to the most despicable elements in our characters. I read them avidly and so (statistically speaking) do you...." These are examples of the well-told rather than well-written.

§

Overall, these are a pretty decent couple of issues, with only one near-memorable story (Swann's), but a general quality and readability level probably somewhere between the contemporaneous *Fantasy & Science Fiction* and *Fantastic*. There are too many gimmick stories, but there are always too many gimmick stories everywhere. There is still very little outright fantasy.

As previously mentioned, when Bonfiglioli took over the magazine there was no inventory and he had to scramble for material, extracting from Brian Aldiss some old stories that Aldiss said were "no damned good" and he could only publish them under pseudonyms. It's not clear whether "The Impossible Smile," published a year later under the Jael Cracken name, is one of that batch, but I suspect so: it does read like something from which Aldiss would have wanted to distance himself, and it's reminiscent in tone of some of the lesser material he was producing five years previously.

The main character is a telepath in a tatty dictatorial UK of the near future. The regime is looking for a telepath to hook up to its master computer by means of vivisection, so he tries to get away to the Moon, where he knows there is a female telepath. More hugger-mugger ensues (he's framed for a murder he didn't commit, there are shootouts, helicopter chases, and a spacesuited escape, he's threatened with torture and/or death repeatedly, and is briefly hooked up to the master computer, but gets away) until all ends happily. It's a paradigm of a silly story written by an intelligent author who seems embarrassed by the proceedings and tries unsuccessfully to redeem them, or to put them at arms-length, by satirical tone and attitude. It's readable enough, as is usual with Aldiss, but annoying, not least because one knows he is capable of much better.

Having perpetrated "The Impossible Smile," Aldiss was unable to leave it alone. It is incorporated into what he describes as a "portmanteau novel," *The Year Before Yesterday* (1987), UK title *Cracken At Critical*, which begins with that book's Scandinavian protagonist finding the body of a woman named Cracken in a ditch and a book called *The Impossible Smile* by Jael Cracken in her effects. "Jael Cracken, the back cover informed me, also wrote under the names of Kyril Bonfiglini and Malcolm Edmunds." The book concerns a possible past Britain, and a previous Cracken novel, *Cyphers of the Bulldog Planet*, had won a Frederik Award. The protagonist reads the book, which (in heavily revised form, set in an alternative 1949) takes up the next 90+ pages of the book. It is followed by another Scandinavian interlude (seemingly an alternate Scandinavia) and then the next book from Ms. Cracken's bag, *Equator*, by an author whose name is unknown to the character, dedicated to the spirit of Hugo Gernsback, whom he's also never heard of. *Equator*, of course, is an early novel by Aldiss—a *New Worlds* serial that became one of Aldiss's earliest novels in book form, and certainly his first in the US, Ace Doubled as *Vanguard From Alpha*. When I read *The Year Before Yesterday*, I groaned, thinking that Aldiss had started down the same road of narcissistic preoccupation with his old work that blighted the late careers of Heinlein and Asimov. Fortunately he turned back from it. Or maybe that wasn't really what was going on. On his web site, Aldiss says of the book: "A novel put together to please a friend in America (Charles Platt)—never a very practical aim."[76]

---

76.   http://brianaldiss.co.uk/writing/novels/novels-s-z/the-year-before/ (visited 10/15/11).

§

The best item of fiction in these two issues is Swann's novelette "Vashti" (**72**), which like most of Swann's work so far centers around a charismatically beautiful boy, except this one, Ianiskos, is really a dwarf, and the homoerotic overtones are muted, since he is chasing a woman, literally—she's fleeing across Persia and Mesopotamia, having been divorced by Xerxes for refusing to show him and his retinue her lower back so they can see whether she has a scar indicating the amputation of a tail. That would reveal her as Jinn rather than woman. The truth is more bizarre and transcendent. This story, which appears to be based on Zoroastrian myth, is another effectively strange tale evoking a lost world of magic unlike anybody else's.

The other fiction in **72** includes Keith Roberts' "The Middle Earth," in which Anita the witch endeavors to help a ghost stuck in the waiting room of the afterlife. Getting no satisfaction from the Controller (analogous to an air traffic controller), Anita takes care of business herself. It turns into an exercise in posthumous matchmaking, agreeably enough. But Roberts still doesn't seem to have decided what he is doing—these stories have the substance of farce (oxymoron alert) without the requisite light touch.

Alan Burns, a very occasional writer (two stories in *Authentic*, three in Carnell's magazines in the early 1960s, two more in the post-Carnell *Science Fantasy*), contributes "Housel," another agreeably amusing story that would have fit well in the Carnell version of the magazine. A housel is a telepathic computer that makes your house look like what you'd like to have, not what you do have. The protagonist, who repairs them, gets a new client, whose housel turns out to present a case of extraterrestrial possession.

Philip Wordley is back with "Timmy and the Angel," about a child with extraordinary psi powers who is recruited by extraterrestrials to turn humanity's nuclear swords into ploughshares (refrigerator factories and the like) for the safety of the rest of the universe. The extraterrestrial is in fact on a mission from God, consistently with the theological bent of Wordley's other stories, and Timmy is revealed to be his son (the extraterrestrial angel's, not God's). Wordley is a capable enough writer that this actually works on the level of middle-of-the-road genre fiction.

§

73 contains eight pieces of short fiction in addition to the conclusion of "The Impossible Smile." The most interesting, if not the best, is the longest, "In Reason's Ear" by Pippin Graham, listed by Miller/Contento as a pseudonym of Hilary Bailey, used for this story only. (The title is quoted from Addison.) Her other work was mostly in *New Worlds*.

This one rides off vigorously in several directions and fetches up at the canonical conventional sentiment of SF. Wetherall, who has been in West Africa for some years doing international do-good work, returns to the UK to find that it is approaching social collapse, the currency drastically devalued, gangs of unemployed youth hanging out and intimidating the law-abiding. Women are unnaturally in charge because their men are unemployed. In Africa, Wetherall's old friend Pardoe, who had been in the US, showed up completely unexpectedly needing fare back to the UK and a passport, and returned with Wetherall. He'd been sent to the Moon as an astronaut, crash-landed in Senegal and disappeared, and everybody's looking for him. Somebody's been to Wetherall's parents' house trying to rummage through his papers. The two Russians who have been on the Moon have also disappeared. It is revealed that the experience of space flight is transforming: Pardoe is afraid that humanity will despoil the rest of space. Wetherall says the prospect of space will revitalize society. The astronauts agree to turn themselves in. The story ends with Wetherall walking home and—of course—looking up at the stars.

Aldiss's "A Pleasure Shared" is a different kind of period piece: it's a jolly first-person story about a sexually repressed guy who does his bit for morality by killing loose women and burying them in the basement of his rooming house. He encounters a female tenant who needs assistance in similarly disposing of an importunate suitor. Bonfiglioli blurbs: "This story may not be science-fiction in the accepted sense of the word but it is in our view a triumph of empathetic fiction." It's well enough done but probably seemed much more cutting edge (as it were) then, before we got quite so familiar with the real thing in the news media. Certainly the state of the art in first-person psychopathology has moved on considerably.

G. L. Lack, who has no other credits in the SF magazines, contributes "Great and Small," which recapitulates the beginning of *The Day of the Triffids*. A man wakes up in hospital, there's nobody around except an irritating fly. He looks around, and everybody's dead for no apparent reason. Wait a minute, aren't flies extinct since World Insecticide Year? He changes his mind about the fly, since it appears that it may be his only remaining companion, finds some jam to feed it as he works up his survivalist routine, then falls asleep on the beach. And the fly buzzes off and is joined by another. "And another. Many others." Environmental morality tale? Hallucinatory afterlife? It's well written and entertaining—enough of interest happens on the way that the dodgy ending does not seem a cheat.

§

From there it's downhill. Keith Roberts as Alistair Bevan has "Deterrent," a story about warring tribes, one of which finds what is quite obviously a missile silo and strips a missile to make spears. It has the same labored quality of most of his other non-Anita stories. The author of the brilliant *Pavane* has not taken shape yet.

The rest of the stories are pretty gimmicky. Ron Pritchett, another writer with no other SF magazine appearances, has "Ploop," a sort of housebroken version of van Vogt's "Black Destroyer," in which the dog-like alien is really hungry, the space explorers find it dangerously radioactive, so they shoot it with their blasters—food at last!

The last three are from Bonfiglioli's new stable of regulars. In Paul Jents' "Peace on Earth," astronauts from an unidentified nation occupy the Moon and declare their country destined to rule and enforce world peace. Then they find some ancient ruins with an inscription about how somebody else a long time ago was destined to rule and enforce world peace. Patricia Hocknell has the completely trivial "Prisoner," in which the bars are revealed to be those of a baby's crib. And Thom Keyes, of the supposed shocker "Period of Gestation," is back with "Xenophilia," about a gigolo who preys on extraterrestrial females and fails to research their amatory habits with sufficient prudence.

26: *SCIENCE FANTASY,* VOLUME 24 (ISSUES 74-76)

Science Fantasy, vol. 24, **74-76**, July through September 1965, contains the three installments of Keith Roberts' first novel, "The Furies." Presentation is as before, with two covers by Roberts and one by "unknown." Roberts' cover for **74** illustrates "The Furies," rather unsubtly portraying a giant wasp sitting on an I-beam. **75**'s, a landscape with domes, also illustrates a scene in "The Furies." It's about the first of Roberts' covers that I have actually liked. He is accomplished enough at what he does but so far it's rarely been to my taste. The **76** cover, a face lost in the murk, is much more to my liking.[77] The cover format remains the same, except that instead of listing several authors, the front cover now lists a single story, which simplifies the apparently fraught process of getting the cover to conform to the magazine's actual contents. But the back covers remain a minefield; **74** lists Harry Harrison and Philip Wordley, who aren't in the magazine. They get it right in the next two issues. J. Parkhill-Rathbone remains Associate Editor.

The small ads are back in **74** and **75** but are replaced by a page of house ads in **76**—Compact SF paperbacks and *Science Fantasy* subscriptions, but still no acknowledgment of *New Worlds* since the first couple of issues. In the small ads for **75**, here's another lost story: "MUTUAL adult adoption groups ('intentional' families, based on caring, sharing, sincerity) 2/-

---

77. See these covers at http://www.sfcovers.net/mainnav.htm or http://www.philsp.com/mags/sciencefantasy.html.

(blank P.O.) for details. Box 117." Story blurbs remain scarce.

Each of these issues has an editorial, but **76** contains a bibliographical ringer. Turning to the promised editorial, one discovers the heading "Instead of an Editorial": it's a review by Brian Aldiss of the new paperback edition of his own novel *Non-Stop*. Aldiss notes that there are no qualifications for reviewers. "With my latest novel, one eager young fan managed to pan it in three different places." (Referring no doubt to *The Dark Light-Years*, which reaped a great harvest of scorn in fandom. *Earthworks*, by popular reckoning (not mine) his other lead balloon of the period, wasn't out yet.) Aldiss notes the short version's publication in *Science Fantasy* "with vile illustrations," and the US publisher's removal of "a few entirely innocuous passages about Vyann's breasts and so on." (If memory serves, the publisher Criterion's only other SF ventures of the time were Hugh Walters' YA books, which may account for the attitude.)

Aldiss notes that he was labeled "a maniac Beatrix Potter" because of his thought-sensitive rats, rabbits, and moths, and tried unsuccessfully to get the publishers to adopt that phrase for publicity purposes. (Years later, when Iain Banks' first book was described as "a work of unparalleled depravity," publishers were more sensitive to their opportunities.) He says he might do things differently nowadays, but he'd probably muck it up, getting too interested in the writing and the characters. "It may not have netted me the praise that 'Greybeard' did, the cash that 'Hothouse' did, the opprobrium that 'Dark Light-Years'—my best-written book—did, but at least it encouraged me, whatever it did to its readers."

In **74**'s editorial, Bonfiglioli continues his discussion of readability and quality, identifying those writers who have both or only one, and stating that SF with its roots in the pulps has until recently emphasized readability alone because of its dependence on the casual reader rather than the devotee. "Even today, when the battle for SF's respectability is in some measure won, a magazine takes its life in its hands each time it prints a 'difficult' story." SF has its own special rules of readability, such as internal consistency (citing "Dr. Azimov").

And here's his point: the demand that every story must have a new plot or a new idea is absurd. "A good plot is susceptible to an infinite number of rescencions"—citing variations on Tristram as an example. The well of science has about run dry (!) and "fiction will have to pause while science catches up... [N]ew writers are either filling up the chinks or, like Aldiss, Miller and Ballard, turning their curiosity inwards, away from space, away from what man may next achieve." The finest recent SF novels are *A Canticle For Leibowitz* and *Greybeard*, which "celebrate defeated mankind." There's no hope for SF "as we have known it...unless this insistence on novelty relaxes."

75's editorial is a bit more interesting because it is less abstract. Bonfiglioli talks about his own background as an SF fan and attitudes about the field:

> American s.f. of the 30s bridged the gulf that many of us could feel was widening between our muddle-minded selves and the science world. We read Sir James Jeans and Sir Arthur Eddington. But this was not enough: we had to feel we were part of the new universe we could feel was being discovered. Cajoled or beaten about the brain by H.G. Wells, we were convinced of the possibility of a rational society....
>
> The charm of the 30s—to those s.f. fans who were teenagers at the time—was that we knew enough about science to appreciate the new possibilities, and too little to realise what a bore most real scientific research was....
>
> But the s.f. of the 30s was not an inferior form of the art so much as something different altogether. No one took seriously the cardboard masks of the heroes and heroines of the space sagas. They were the masks behind which we became, in imagination, what we thought we should be....

[Now] we have substituted illusions about ideals for illusions about ourselves being disillusioned, and get the kind of s.f. we deserve. Those brilliant images, those characters you can walk around and talk to, are all the result of taking a straight look into a mirror and having cold images of ourselves reflected back, our surfaces at this instant of time.

§

The major item of fiction in these issues is of course Roberts' novel "The Furies." Bonfiglioli's editorial condemnation of the demand for novelty was probably written with it in mind, since it stays well within the territory staked out by *The War of the Worlds*, *The Day of the Triffids*, and *No Blade of Grass*. All of a sudden the world is beset with giant wasps bent first on killing people and then on enslaving them, and there's a worldwide earthquake to boot, and the characters first have to survive and then figure out how to fight back, and that's a novel's worth of plot all by itself, except for the rather arbitrary and mildly anti-climactic end.

If you can swallow not just the idea of giant insects, but giant *flying* insects, without a passing nod to the square-cube law, it's by far Roberts' best piece of fiction to date. Part of the problem with his earlier stories (twelve of them, all but one in *Science Fantasy*, the other in *New Worlds*) was that their relatively inconsequential substance didn't quite live up to the portentous writing. The substance does live up to the writing in this grim adventure story. Roberts is extremely good at conveying place and its dislocations and at describing physical action, which is exactly what's called for here. There are a few too many and too long scenes of fighting the wasps—parts of it reminded me of the battle scenes in Eric Frank Russell's *Sinister Barrier*—but overall it's a very readable story with unusually well drawn characters.

Roberts' remarkable domination of the magazine during this

period is worthy of comment. In the ten issues from his first story in **67** through the end of "The Furies" in **76**, he contributed fourteen pieces of short fiction, one novel, and five covers. Bonfiglioli gives over 97 of 128 pages of **74** to the first installment of "The Furies." After **76**, Roberts vanishes from the pages of *Science Fantasy* for the remaining five issues (but remains on the covers, three of them), but then reappears in the first *Impulse* in March 1966, contributing eleven more stories and an article (not to mention seven covers) in a year's time to the remaining twelve issues, including five of the six *Pavane* stories (the sixth appearing in *New Worlds* during the same time period).

§

Of the rest of the fiction in these issues, there are no long stories—not surprisingly, given the amount of space given to *The Furies*. There are a fair number of short ones, from an eclectic mix of veterans, ingénues, and the magazine's developing crowd of usual suspects. There's also more outright fantasy than usual.

The best-known of the short stories is A. K. Jorgensson's "Coming-of-Age Day" (**76**). Everyone is fitted at puberty with a "consex," a sort of symbiotic appliance that saves them from temptation and frustration by administering sexual satisfaction on demand. But the story is told in the time-honored dystopian mode. The protagonist is not really comfortable with the idea, and overhears a conversation at the clinic with another boy who refuses the consex on grounds of principle, not very clearly stated. So maybe he won't accept it either. Amusingly, the author says that all the churches are on board with this device. Extravagant fiction yesterday, Joycelyn Elders and the Xandria catalog today![78]

---

78. For those with short memories, Joycelyn Elders was the Surgeon General under President Clinton who was instantly fired, amid a deluge of obloquy from the religious right, for suggesting it might be better for kids to masturbate than to get pregnant or contract AIDS.

This story made the Merril annual anthology and was anthologized several more times before it was forgotten. Bonfiglioli blurbs: "My first reactions to this story were—'Great stuff, but of course I can't print it'...my next reaction was 'Why on earth not?' It is not the sort of thing usually discussed in science fiction—or anywhere else, for that matter—but if SF is going to grow up perhaps it's time we stopped talking about what is proper for the genre." Rousing manifesto, eh? But it points up the fact that despite its corporate association with *New Worlds* and its association in memory with the New Wave, for the most part *Science Fantasy* by its content was a pretty conservative magazine, at least to this point. One final irony: the author of this then-daring story published it under a pseudonym. His real name was Robert W. A. Roach, and he seems never to have appeared again in the genre in any guise.

Almost as good, remarkably, is "Chemotopia" (**75**) by Ernest Hill, author of the egregious "Joik" of a few issues previously. This time Hill actually has a coherent idea rather than a pile of mismatched pieces and mannerisms. It's a free-swinging black satire, sort of gonzo *Galaxy* with *A Clockwork Orange* lurking offstage, of a better-living-through-chemistry future in which juvenile delinquents are titrated into acceptable behavior with mentatone, tolerantol, personadine, etc. etc., rather than being punished. At the end of the story the psychiatrist is trying to make time with his nurse. She's not attracted, but that's OK, she takes some amordine. It's quite entertaining if badly dated.

Keith Roberts has another Anita story, "Idiot's Lantern" (**75**), which Bonfiglioli says is the last for a while, and which is also the best of the lot so far. TV comes to the witches' household, to Granny Thompson's initial dismay, followed by fascination, followed by her application to become a contestant on a quiz show, with predictably catastrophic results. Roberts is beginning to develop a clue about being funny ("Many evenings the witches sat in silence, lips compressed, while in front of them the channel switch clicked backward and forward as their will contested possession of the set.") His "The Door," as by Alistair

Bevan (**74**), is another where he chews more than he bites off: underground civilization, repression, a man has a vision of escape, finds the way out against great odds, opens the door, and dies: he's been underground on Mars.

The other better known authors in these issues include the adaptable E. C. Tubb, who has not appeared in *Science Fantasy* since 1960 but is about to become a regular again, with four stories in the remaining five issues plus one in the successor *Impulse*, and who hit Moorcock's *New Worlds* a couple of times too. In "Boomerang" (**76**), the protagonist hates his enemy Granger so much that he burns his house, poisons his friends, mutilates his pets and does things to his family that makes the jury vomit. So he is sentenced to exile for life on a planet populated by giant spiders, insects who lay their eggs in whoever they can sting and paralyze, etc. He's determined to spite everyone and survive, but Granger follows him for a final confrontation. This is utter pulp hokum but enjoyable because it is done so professionally and so tersely—especially admirable for someone who is paid by the word. Harry Harrison contributes the amusing "At Last, the True Story of Frankenstein" (**76**), in which a journalist finds Victor Frankenstein's son displaying the monster at a carnival in Florida, and soon regrets it.

Clifford C. Reed, a frequent Carnell contributor from 1958 on, has "Paradise for a Punter" (**75**), which moralizes ponderously about the race track after death. It seems to be Reed's last story in the genre. In John Rackham's considerably sprightlier "A Way with Animals" (**75**), a soft-hearted man finds a rather confused dragon while hiking and takes her in at his London flat.

R. W. Mackelworth, who as previously noted was a late-developing Carnell writer who became a Bonfiglioli/Moorcock writer, has two stories. "A Distorting Mirror" (**74**) comprises an interview between a young couple seeking better housing and the Manager, who is trying to get them to stop rocking the boat. "Temptation for the Leader" (**76**) is a negotiation between the President, with his sage advisor close at hand, and an alien leader who isn't what he seems to be. Unfortunately Mackelworth is not a capable enough writer at this point to bring off these equivalents of dialogue-driven single-set stage plays. "A Distorting Mirror" is too long by about 100%, and the denouement of "Temptation for the Leader" is too silly for words. Bonfiglioli blurbs: "...The central idea in this story *has* been used before although in a completely different way. There is no suggestion of plagiarism and this story is, in my opinion, an important one. I await the storms of criticism." It appears that the earlier story he is referring to is Clarke's "Guardian Angel," which became the first part of *Childhood's End*.

Eric C. Williams (1918-2010)—who seems remarkably to be the same man who was publishing in *Amateur Science Stories* in 1937 and *Fantasy Adventures* in 2002—contributes the rather confusing "The Desolators" (**75**), which proposes an impoverished future in which everyone is trying to sneak out and build time machines, which only work backwards. They leapfrog back in time, stealing valuables, sending them way back, and then sending themselves not quite so far back to take advantage of their ill-gotten gains. That seems to be what has impoverished the far future. Williams published 10 novels after this, with titles like *Monkman Comes Down* (1968) and *Homo Telekins* (1981).

Science Fantasy now-regular Johnny Byrne also has two vignettes, both lame. "The Criminal" (**74**) turns out to be named Adam. "The Jobbers" (**76**) is back to his surreal vein. The protagonist's head is invaded by a couple of little men who are talking about remodeling it. Then we learn this is all occurring in a mental institution.

§

From here we hit the really unfamiliar names. Dikk (sic) Richardson contributes an inane and pointless vignette, "Grinnel" (**75**). His only other genre credit is another vignette published nearly simultaneously in *New Worlds*. Rob Sproat's

"Sule Skerry" (**76**) is about some folklore-hunters who unearth an old ballad, and the story underneath it. (The last of the silkies sires a child remotely with a human woman. Everybody comes to a bad end. Sounds pretty authentic to me). It's capably done if not very interesting. A year later Sproat had one more story in *Impulse*, then nothing more. Finally, there is "Omega and Alpha" by Robert Cheetham, about the deteriorating lives of some post-nuclear war survivors in the Seychelles, *On the Beach* writ small but intense. It's horrific, well written, and could be a poster child for what the run of SF fans hated about the New Wave, ending with the narrator losing his mind and two forgotten infant children eating rotten fish on the beach. It's never been reprinted, but if I were doing a retrospective New Wave collection I'd use this instead of some of the more familiar items. Cheetham was another Moorcock/Bonfiglioli short career: one story in *Science Fantasy*, three in *New Worlds*, one in *London Mystery*, 1965-1967, over and out.

Incidentally, several issues hence, Bonfiglioli will bow to popular pressure and begin to publish story ratings (though only the high end), and "Omega and Alpha" will come in second to *The Furies* ("an easy winner"), beating out Tubb and Harrison.

27: *SCIENCE FANTASY*, VOLUME 24 (ISSUES 77-78)

Science Fantasy **77** and **78**, October and November 1965, contain Thomas Burnett Swann's "fantastic new mythic novel," as the cover blurb puts it, "The Weirwoods." The first install-ment runs 72 pages; I don't think I have seen serial installments as long as this and two of "The Furies" installments, relative to the magazine's page count, in any other SF magazine.

The magazine remains the same as before in format and presentation, with one notable deviation. Until now, it has been virtually filler-free, with half or two-thirds of a page of white space common at the ends of stories. In **78**, however, every hole is filled with a house ad, four of them, for Compact SF novels—but still not for the post-Carnell *New Worlds*. The covers are pleasant, a fake fresco by Morol on **77** for the Swann novel, and Keith Roberts' most attractive cover yet for **78**, presum-ably representing if not illustrating Aldiss's "The Day of the Doomed King," the only story listed on the cover.[79]

The editorials are notable, first, for the brief flowering of J. Parkhill-Rathbone: the Associate Editor writes the editorial in **77**, commencing: "Mr. Bonfiglioli is in Venice observing heav-enly bodies from a little observatory on the Lido." He goes on to note that modern furniture design has again given way to Victorian bric-a-brac, that form doesn't really follow function

---

79. See these covers at http://www.sfcovers.net/mainnav.htm or http://www.philsp.com/mags/sciencefantasy.html. Unfortunately the scans of the **78** cover do not do it justice. The original is much more subtle.

because people don't like it that way, and that people's being illogical makes accurate prediction of the future pretty hard but also makes writing science fiction more fun. Thank you, back in the box please.

The editorial in **78** is actually headed "SF or Not SF?...a Letter from a Reader," which defines SF, breaks it up into categories, argues with its own definition, says it's all a matter of the writer's intent, takes on the sense of wonder, declares that SF has no limits, and is signed Brian M. Stableford. Not mentioned is the fact that this magazine also contains Stableford's first professional SF magazine publication, "Beyond Time's Aegis," a collaboration with a school friend, Craig MacKintosh (never heard from again), under the pseudonym Brian Craig.

At the end of the magazine there is another "Letter from a Reader," not listed on the contents page at all, signed Kenneth F. Slater (a notable UK fan and bookseller, 1917-2008), who disagrees with Bonfiglioli's earlier point that hack writing killed the pulps—hack writing, he says, is still with us, in the paperbacks and comics, and the pulps were killed by economics: paper costs and competition from comics, TV, and paperbacks. He warns against putting the "flag of literary excellence...too darn far up the flag pole," since that may drive the readership to the comics. There's not a word from Bonfiglioli in response. Maybe he's still in Venice.

Thomas Burnett Swann's "The Weirwoods" is about the best of his stories yet for *Science Fantasy* (and the last one), and as enjoyable as anything I've read in the magazine. Set in ancient Etruria, it has not one but two beautiful boys. Vel is a Water Sprite, stolen from his lake home in the Weirwoods by Lars Velcha as a slave for his daughter Tanaquil, who is conflicted and guilt-ridden about it and about him. Arnth is a red-haired minstrel who travels in a bear-drawn wagon. Arnth and Vel hit it off, Arnth heads off to the Weirwoods to get some help to free Vel from Vel's old ally Vegoia, the Water Sprite sorceress, with disastrous consequences, though not before some episodes of sex comedy between them.

We have definitely left the Age of Carnell and entered the Age of Carnal. "The Weirwoods" is by far the most sexually explicit story to have appeared in this magazine, though in 1965 that's still not too explicit (on the other hand, it's inexplicit at some length). As always Swann conveys a strong sense of displacement into a world where people, and not-quite-people, like the Water Sprites, think differently from us. His world is vividly realized through a wealth of sensory and social detail conveyed economically and unobtrusively. This is fantasy that is High without being Jumped-Up. If one were going to try to write fantasy, it might be better to study Swann as a model rather than, say, Tolkien—not because he's better than Tolkien, but because one would probably look like less of a fool imitating him. The readers placed "The Weirwoods" as first in the issue; as Bonfiglioli notes in **81**: "Mr. Swann's large and loyal following shows no sign of tiring."

At the end of **77** is another completely forgotten gem, Philip Wordley's "Goodnight, Sweet Prince," the last of his four stories for *Science Fantasy*. Time-traveling movie-makers led by a crass imitator of Samuel B. Goldwyn are shooting on location in the past, this time in Shakespeare's day. And here's Shakespeare himself, writing to his wife Anne Hathaway in bitter despair and self-loathing, confessing his adultery. Needless to say, the two plot lines come together. It's a brilliant little tour de force, made by the sections comprising Shakespeare's letter. Of course it's nothing like Shakespeare would actually have written. The archaic edges have been smoothed and the usage modernized. But it's powerful nonetheless. There's a trick at the end which diminishes it a bit, but it's still very fine: sharp, smart, economical, vivid. It is shameful that it's now totally forgotten. Readers placed this second best in the issue: he got "a number of warmly appreciative letters about this one," Bonfiglioli commented, "from people who do not usually write in." Then, in **80**: "It is only fair to Philip Wordley to state that we are still receiving letters of warm admiration for his *Goodnight Sweet Prince*. If I recalculated the ratings for No. 77 he would probably now take first place." For this relief much thanks.

Aside from "The Weirwoods" and "Goodnight, Sweet Prince," the stories in 77 are well executed but not too interesting. Pamela Adams (no other genre credits, per Miller/Contento) contributes "Ragtime," a polite and capable semighost story—vanished partiers from forty years ago reappear every year, and you can join the party if you want, though you won't be coming home soon. W. Price (also no other SF magazine appearances) has "Green Goblins Yet," which begins, "We ain't very scientific down at Kate's Grill and we don't dig this outer space lark," so of course an extraterrestrial comes into the place looking for somebody to help him find his goblin. E. C. Tubb's "State of Mind" is about a man who realizes his wife is an alien out to kill him, and a man's gotta do, etc.

Johnny Byrne's "The Foreigner" (blurbed "A thumping good yarn") is a curiosity. He has contributed several very literate and surreal pieces to the magazine, but now he seems to have decided to write SF stories and start from scratch. This reads like a contrived beginner's piece, about a man upstairs who makes a lot of noise rolling off a platform wrapped in a mattress and landing on the floor. After some bizarre back and forth with the protagonist (the tenant downstairs who has come up to find out what's making the racket), he runs into the street in front of a truck. He's just trying to get home, and impact is what it takes. Bonfiglioli puts this story into third place for the issue, saying: "J. B.'s rather crazy stories have not been too well received hitherto but this one seems to have hit the mark." Too bad on both counts.

§

78 is an improvement, starting with the cover story, Brian Aldiss's "The Day of the Doomed King," a retelling of Serbian legend (Aldiss published his Yugoslavian travel book *Cities and Stones* the previous year). In *The Twinkling of an Eye* Aldiss confirms that it's "based on the old Serbian dynasty of the

Nemanijas." It's not my cup of tea but nonetheless very good, one of the early stories in which Aldiss began to shake the dust of SF as he had known it off his boots and to head for more ambiguous territory. Bonfiglioli says in **80**: "A natural first, but there were plenty of predictable complaints like 'not true science fiction,' 'not progressive' (whatever that means) and conversely 'not like the old Aldiss touch.'"

Josephine Saxton's first story, "The Wall," is here; Bonfiglioli puts it in second place, saying it's "a strange little allegory by a newcomer which seems to have captured many people's imaginations," with some corroboration, since it was reprinted in Judith Merril's annual anthology and several times since. Ernest Hill splits the difference here between "Chemotopia" and "Joik," with "The Saga of Sid," about an extremely precocious kid ("Can we get on with the christening? I'm very uncomfortable in this absurd linen garment."), who turns out to be Baldur reincarnated, as revealed by Odin and Frigg, who drop in by flying saucer. It's actually better and funnier than the description makes it sound.

"Yesterdays' Gardens" by Johnny Byrne is a return to form, about a little girl and her uncle living underground after a nuclear war; I say *literate and surreal*, but the readers probably again said *rather crazy*. Judith Merril said let me have this for my annual anthology. Unfortunately this is Byrne's last appearance in *Science Fantasy* or any other SF magazine, and he would soon be snared by television.

"Beyond Time's Aegis," published when Brian Stableford was seventeen or so, is readable though irritating. Bonfiglioli reports: "Extravagantly praised and fiercely condemned in roughly equal proportions. Certainly rates third place by virtue of the sheer volume of comment received." It's set in a very far future where ennui has taken over, and this self-introduction by the main character will give you the flavor: "I call myself the Firefly, because I reject this world and its torpor, and cast my own light." The Firefly has heard tell of a man who walked through time (subsequently denominated The Man Who Walked

Through Time) and he is going to catch up with him so he can get sent back to the past, when things and people were livelier. In his quest he has a series of encounters with the likes of the Red Wolf Queen, the Sun, the Condor, the Lungfish, etc., each more colorful and allegorical than the one before, until he finally catches up with The Man Who Walked Through Time and learns that you can't go back, you can only go forward. I suspect that this story was heavily influenced by Brunner's "Earth Is But a Star." Stableford expanded it to novel length in *Firefly: A Novel of the Far Future* (Borgo Press, 1994).

28: *SCIENCE FANTASY*, VOLUME 24 (ISSUES 79-81)

Science Fantasy **79-81**, December 1965 through February 1966, contain Harry Harrison's serialized novel "Plague from Space," and are the last issues of the magazine under this title. The cover of **81** has "Impulse" in gray half-tone behind *Science Fantasy*, and the next issue of the magazine is just *Impulse*, albeit with a blurb line saying "The *New* Science Fantasy."

The title change is announced in the editorial of **81**, in which Bonfiglioli recounts watching a bishop buy a copy of *Science Fantasy* with interest "clinical rather than empathetic." He confesses that he only ever bought one issue of *Science Fantasy*, though he acquired others. His reluctance stemmed from the seemingly bastardized nature of the product the title advertises and because it made him self-conscious to ask for it at the bookstall. "All this is, I agree, very stuffy and pompous and cowardly of me, but I cannot help feeling that there is a large potential market for our product amongst the stuffy, pompous and cowardly—after all, they seem to make up some seventy per cent of the population."

He confesses being horrified at *Astounding*'s title change to *Analog*, but thinks this change will help reach a wider audience. He doesn't mention that the publisher had to talk him out of changing *Science Fantasy* to *Caliban*.[80] Now there's a path to

80. "Bonfiglioli liked the name Caliban, but [publisher David] Warburton did not, feeling that it suggested something deformed and malignant." Mike Ashley, *Transformations: The Story of the Science Fiction Magazines from*

a wide audience. He concludes with a plea for reader support: subscribe ("the proportion of subscribed sales to casual sales is a vitally important factor in magazine economics"). Send your copy ("or a spare") to a friend overseas who might subscribe. And promote the magazine "verbally in your own circle," which will of course be much easier now that it's not called *Science Fantasy* any more.

How fortunate we are to have escaped the shame and repression of the past and to live in this modern age where literary award-winners such as Michael Chabon openly boast of their devotion to comic books.

Otherwise the magazine is mostly unchanged in presentation, with a few cracks in the façade. J. Parkhill-Rathbone is replaced as Associate Editor by Keith Roberts, for reasons to be explained in *Impulse*. The covers of these issues are mostly abstract (though there's a recognizable bottle, beach, and human on **81**) and pretty attractive to my taste. There's no attribution for **79**, but both **80** and **81** are by Keith Roberts, though **80** is unsigned.[81] It's hard to understand Bonfiglioli's discomfiture at the image of the magazine. To me it looks both respectable and lively, and somehow I don't think it was the titles on SF magazine covers that raised the eyebrows of bishops.

Inside the magazine, story blurbs have gradually crept back in, starting an issue or two previously. Most of the stories here are blurbed, though the blurbs are *pro forma* and inconsequential, without information on the authors. Bonfiglioli makes another capitulation in these issues: an American fan, he says in his editorial in **79,** has succeeded in changing his mind about story ratings. He still thinks that they are "invidious and statistically worthless," but bows to popular demand—partly. He declines to present statistics. "On the other hand, the rating [sic] are definitely NOT made up arbitrarily: they are the result not

---

1950 to 1970 (Liverpool University Press 2005), p. 245.

81. See these covers at http://www.sfcovers.net/mainnav.htm or http://www.philsp.com/mags/sciencefantasy.html.

only of counting the times a story is praised but of weighing the kind of praise—and to some extent the praiser." So he identifies the three most popular stories, often with a characterization of the readers' response. These appear either in the editorial or (in **81**) as a separate page-filler. The concession was inconsistent and short-lived, however. The ratings for **78** and **80** are here but **79** is missing, and they disappear altogether in *Impulse*.

In **81**, the small ads are back, though three-fourths of the space is taken up with house ads—Compact SF paperbacks and the ad for *Impulse* ("a rare collection of new works by several of the greatest sf writers: Anderson, Aldiss, Ballard, Blish, Harrison, etc., assembled with Bonfiglioli's editorial flair. More pages (160), improved cover, price 3/6 monthly. Publicity and demand will be big, so order your copy of *Impulse* No. 1 now.") A separate small ad offers the Compact edition of Harness's *The Rose* or other paperback to new subscribers. On a separate page there's a filler listing authors in *Impulse* **1** and claiming "surely the most impressive line-up in a single edition of any science-fiction magazine, anywhere. You really cannot afford to miss this one." This is more commercial pizzazz than has appeared in the entire run of the Bonfiglioli *Science Fantasy* to date. Interestingly, there is still no ad for *New Worlds*.

§

The editorial in **79** notes Bonfiglioli's attendance at the Worldcon in London, and here's one of the very rare references to *New Worlds*: both Moorcock and Bonfiglioli have obtained novellas from Judith Merril, "an authoress far too rarely seen in this country." In fact, both of these ("Homecalling," to appear in *Impulse*, and "Daughters of Earth," in *New Worlds*) are reprints from the 1950s. At a subsequent gathering at Brian Aldiss's house, Bonfiglioli obtained agreement from Aldiss, Poul and Karen Anderson, Ballard, Blish, and Harry Harrison "to join in an all-star issue early next year with specially written stories round the theme of 'sacrifice.'" This of course would be the first issue of *Impulse*, and all those listed but Karen Anderson would actually appear in it.

Bonfiglioli also denies being Brian Aldiss in a false moustache and dark glasses—"they are wrong: that's Harry Harrison." And he's not an anagram, either, so stop trying to prove he doesn't exist. There is also a Books Received section of the editorial which notes the Compact paperbacks of Edward Bradbury's Mars stories, notes the style is reminiscent of Moorcock, but either doesn't know or pretends not to know that Moorcock did indeed write them. This is followed by a lukewarm squib for Moorcock's *The Fireclown*, also from Compact.

80's editorial consists of a letter from Chris Priest, partly arguing with the prior letters from Brian Stableford and Ken Slater, and eliciting (finally) a comment from Bonfiglioli concerning *New Worlds*, as well as the most explicit statement in a while about his editorial approach. Priest says: "*New Worlds* seems to go along with this literate line, but your policies regarding this seem to be a little uncertain to say the least," eliciting the following tart reply:

> Now wait a minute, Mr. Priest. Do you mean literary or literate? Or do you really mean either—or both? If what you're implying is that progressive equals literary equals literate and, conversely, that traditional equals unliterary equals illiterate, then I can only reply in Sir Winston Churchill's magnificent phrase that "the answer is in the plural—and they bounce." But I'm sure you don't. If you mean that *New Worlds* is calculated for the latitude of a progressive group of young writers and fans and attracts contributions of a more daring nature than this magazine, then I agree. If you mean that editor Moorcock has a burning determination to establish SF as a spearhead of modern writing, while I go bumbling along trying to please everybody at once, then I agree again. If you mean that I'm an old square, too pig-headed and too fat to try to fit the new with-it

round holes, then I still agree. But steady with those words like "literary" and "literate."

Priest praises Aldiss's "Man in His Time" and Pippin Graham's (Hilary Bailey's) "In Reason's Ear" but notes the persistence of "stories that went out of vogue many years ago," eliciting from Bonfiglioli:

> The point is that I am not alone in my squareness. You would be surprised how many loyal readers *like* stories which remind them, however faintly, of "the good old days when sf was sf and there weren't any messages." As for "out-of-vogue"—surely this is an almost meaningless term in literary criticism. Thomas Burnett Swann's stories were out of vogue some two thousand years ago, yet his following is very strong, and increases with every story.

All of this suggests a certain amount of resentment of *New Worlds* and Moorcock and might account for the complete absence of advertising for *New Worlds*. By contrast, *New Worlds* often advertised *Science Fantasy*. For example, here's *New Worlds* **158**, January 1966, contemporaneous with these issues of *Science Fantasy*, with a full-page equal-opportunity joint subscription ad, characterizing the magazines as follows:

> In *Michael Moorcock's New Worlds* you will find each month a selection from the best British and American writers, established and new; comprehensive news of sf published in Britain and the US. Sf activities and science developments, plus stimulating comment and letters. *New Worlds*, now widely regarded as the trend-setter in its field, is always coming up with something fresh and original. *Kyril Bonfiglioli* edits the new *Science Fantasy*, and aims to broaden its appeal with a mixture of old-style solid-fuel stories, out-of-the-way

fantasy and the occasional experimental piece. This is being achieved by including the work of many of the best-known names in mainstream sf writing, and adding that of a number of highly talented newcomers, several of whom are now contributing regularly as the result of readers' enthusiasm.

I should also mention a piece of advertising matter found in **79**. It also appears in my copy of **78**, but since no provenance was indicated, I first thought it might be somebody's bookmark. But two issues in a row is good evidence of original intent. It's a folded flier headed "? ? ? ? *A New Approach to Love And Marriage*," and touts a book called *Sex And Security*, in which you may "Read the answers to these challenging questions: * What is 'preliminary love-making'? *Is the safe period really safe? * What are the 'old wives' tales' about sex? * Are oral contraceptives harmful?" On the back, we see the real agenda: with the book, you get a free copy of *Modern Family Planning*. In fact, you can get that one free without ordering *Sex And Security*. I wonder if this is paid advertising or a public service of Bonfiglioli or Compact. Either way, bravo.

§

The most substantial piece of fiction in these issues, Harrison's "Plague from Space" ("The Plague from Space" on the cover), indicates what a middle-of-the-road magazine *Science Fantasy* mostly is these days, consistently with Bonfiglioli's editorial and contrary to later-developed image, which I suspect is mainly the product of the association with Moorcock's *New Worlds*—an association Bonfiglioli is clearly trying to keep at arms' length.

"Plague from Space" is typical of non-comedic Harrison, a robust and fast-moving adventure story. A spaceship returns from Jupiter and crash-lands, a deadly disease begins to spread, there's a problem to be solved and the characters (especially the protagonist, ex-military man now a hospital intern) roll up their sleeves to deal with it, leading up to the final highly improbable but ingenious revelation. En passant we encounter Killer Dominguez, the daredevil ambulance driver, plus a beautiful pathologist who hits it off with the protagonist but gets the deadly disease just in time to pump up the final chapters. There's the obligatory sniveling bureaucrat who actually tells the protagonist "don't rock the boat." And there is the take-no-prisoners general who flouts every order and chain of command because, by God, he has faith the protagonist is the only one who can save the world.

This is essentially *Thrilling Wonder Stories* with a college education, and a very pleasant time-passer. Again Bonfiglioli is not averse to turning over a very large proportion of the magazine to serial installments, and doesn't seem to care whether they approach even length: these installments are fifty-seven, twenty-nine, and seventy-three pages respectively in this 128-page magazine. There's a synopsis at the beginning of part 2 but not part 3, and the break between parts 2 and 3 is in the middle of a chapter.

§

Unfortunately the short fiction in these issues is mostly pretty silly or inconsequential, though it's all capably written and goes down smoothly despite its faults of substance. In **79**, Alan Burns' "Passenger" is distinguished by being the second story in the issue featuring a character called Killer. This is Cilla O'Dare, the protagonist's girlfriend, who goes with him to help his old friend Handley search out aliens to destroy. Except they get kidnapped into space by the aliens, and then Killer turns out to be an alien herself, or inhabited by one. "Does that shock you, Rankin Crayle? That you desired to mate with a mere instrument," says one of them. Crayle then contrives to get inhabited by an alien himself. He and Killer outwit the aliens, lead them back to earth, and seem to have made peace; Burns seems to be channeling van Vogt, with overtones of McIntosh's *World Out* *of Mind*, all in 16 pages, and a bit too much to swallow in one bite.

Richard A. Gordon's "A Question of Culture" (**79**) is one of the more ludicrous *Galaxy* knock-offs. Here, the world has been taken over, not by advertisers, but by the Aesthetics Council, whose minions prowl the streets and museums quizzing people on their knowledge of art, music, etc., and pack the slackers off to Cultural Realignment Centres. Gordon—Richard Alexander Steuart Gordon (1947-2009)[82]—had half a dozen stories in the Compact magazines and *Visions of Tomorrow*, 1965 through 1970, and nothing more in the SF magazines, but went on to write numerous novels as Alex Stuart, Alex R. Stuart, and finally Stuart Gordon, under which name he methodically produced *One-Eye* (1973), *Two-Eyes* (1974), and *Three-Eyes* (1975), and later the non-fiction (sort of) *The Book of Miracles*, *The Book of Hoaxes*, and *The Book of Curses* (all 1995).

"Democratic Autocracy" (**79**) by the catastrophically uneven Ernest Hill is just as heavy-handed as "A Question of Culture" but several times as crazy and therefore a bit more entertaining. It features a dictatorship run by Child Manaton on the Benthamite principle of the greatest good for the greatest number, which means putting to death the old and the useless, the latter including, e.g., a thirty-year-old ballerina who has broken her leg, and Manaton's own mistress, Lilith, who has become genito-revulsive (sic) after a radiation leak at the sterility centre (sic), and then Manaton himself, who becomes inconvenient to the Ministers in the Debating Chamber after a particularly infelicitous eradication is televised, resulting in riots.

R. W. Mackelworth's "Cleaner Than Clean" (**79**) is about an eccentric who keeps complaining to the Public Works office about the Evil Down the Drain, which proves to be life evolved from discarded detergent along the lines of Wilhelm and Thomas's *The Clone*, or a liquid "It," and it's bent on cleaning us all up. The author isn't sure if he's writing farce or horror and

---

82.   http://sfscope.com/2009/02/author-richard-gordon-aka-alex.html (visited 10/19/11).

winds up with not much of either.

§

80 has the longest piece of short fiction in these issues, John Rackham's "The God-Birds of Glentallach" (**80**), which adds to my irritation with Rackham—a capable writer who seems mostly to content himself with clichés. Here's an aviator stranded freakishly by a time-slip in savage Scotland of a millennium ago, trying to leave a record. Flash forward and the protagonist, orphaned and reared in Canada, has come to his inherited Scottish estate, intending to sell it rather than settle in as laird. But archaeologists are digging on the site, including a beautiful young local woman, and find something inexplicable. And there's a strange old legend from the savage days. Of course it all fits together, and the subtext is how fitting it is that the laird really is back on his throne, or Chesterfield, or whatever lairds sit on.[83]

Things look up slightly with Edward Mackin's "Sealed Capsule" (**80**), which is amusingly sardonic, a welcome relief from Hek Belov. Feckless astronauts on a long voyage are driving each other nuts, except maybe they haven't really gone anywhere, or have they?

But D. J. Gibbs' "The Satyrian Games" (**80**) is about as bad as the title suggests. A reporter is sent at the behest of King Kopulus of Satyria, along with a socially undesirable photographer named Randy, to report on the eponymous games, which are more like the Sex Coliseum than the Sex Olympics. They can't leave again, being conscripted to help keep the race going because of the Satyrians' declining potency. The rest is just as tiresome. This might have seemed daring in 1965—just the thing for light reading in between installments of "The *Playboy* Philosophy"—but at this late date it's merely tedious. This is Gibbs' only credit in the SF magazines.

---

83. And why can't you ever find a tumbril when you need one?

Daphne Castell contributes "For One of These" (**80**), about a baby who is orphaned by an auto accident and taken in by a young widow, and then proves to be an alien. The interesting possibilities and good build-up are truncated by a Sturgeonesque "The Sky Was Full of Ships"-style ending.

§

81 starts out on an equally unpromising note with the cover story, "Ballad from a Bottle" by Hugh Simmonds (no other SF magazine credits), an improbable and not very interesting story about a deformed and lonely beachcomber who finds a bottle on a Brazilian beach. He's summoned by a voice within to Durban, South Africa, to assist an alien pie vendor (I'm not making this up) who has been superintending the evolution of humanity but who needs to be killed so she can be replaced by a more advanced supervisor (Scanners. they're called). He obliges with the bottle.

Another silly story, but at least intentionally so, is John Brunner's "The Warp and the Woof-Woof." Martians, looking to grab at long distance an astronaut about to set off for their planet, get his dog instead, to their fatal chagrin.

Fortunately these misfires are followed by M. John Harrison's first story in the SF magazines (this one bylined just John Harrison). "Marina" is a lyrically surreal story about a girl taken away from the sea after her mother dies, and who seems to think she is going to find it in the attic. It's spookily effective and the first story in these issues that really makes me want to read more of the author's work.

Paul Jents' "Our Man in 1900" features a stage magician stalking his rival to learn the secret of his great illusion, the materialization of dozens of people. The answer is not magic, but indistinguishable from it except in an SF magazine. This one is clever and entertaining.

Special mention should be made of E. C. Tubb, who has a story in each of these issues. "As Others See Us" (**79**) is about a total failure, down at the beach nerving himself to commit suicide, who finds an ancient device that allows him to hear everyone's thoughts. The problem is that now he *really* knows what people think of him. "'In Vino Veritas'" (**80**) is about a writer who has lost it, broke and alcoholic, and who begins to muse about all the characters he has created and abandoned, and realizes that that's exactly what he is, somebody's abandoned character. "Sing Me No Sorrows" (**81**) features a spaceman who has committed a crime on an alien planet and has been locked up in a cell in total darkness for some unspecified period of time, told in the second person, nine pages of him floundering around in misery and despair before he finally hits the button that will release him or kill him. So there you have it—misanthropy, futility, anti-heroes, solipsism and preoccupation with subjectivity—I give you E. C. Tubb, doyen of the New Wave. The first two of these stories especially are sort of *noir* fairy tales, and all of them are distinguished by utter professionalism, with not a wasted or misplaced word. One has to admire them whether or not one likes them or finds them interesting (my feelings are mixed).

29: *IMPULSE*, VOLUME 1 (1-3)

Impulse, vol. 1, **1-3** (March-May 1965), is, as the cover proclaims, "The NEW Science Fantasy"—so new that the numbering starts over, which as Mike Ashley recounts in the Tymn/ Ashley volume, meant that distribution arrangements had to be renegotiated, to the detriment of circulation at least in the short run.

The magazine has gone up from 128 to 160 pages in length and from 2/6 to 3/6 in price. The format is otherwise unchanged. There is no non-fiction other than the editorials, and no advertising or fillers. There is plenty of blank space at the ends of stories. The cover of **1** is a striking design by Judith Ann Lawrence, James Blish's wife. The other two are by Keith Roberts, reasonably attractive within the limits of their arts-and-crafty presentation (or the limits of my taste), including an unusually illustrative one on **2** for "The Lady Anne," the second in the *Pavane* series.[84] Roberts resumes his dominant role in the magazine. In addition to the two covers, Roberts is listed as Associate Editor, contributes three novellas (the first three *Pavane* stories) plus an Alistair Bevan novelette, and is no doubt also responsible for the cryptic diagrammatic design that appears at the head of each *Pavane* story.

§

---

84. See these covers at http://www.sfcovers.net/mainnav.htm or http://www.philsp.com/mags/sciencefantasy.html.

Bonfiglioli says in the editorial in *Impulse* **1**, "I take leave modestly to doubt whether any first issue of a magazine has been able to boast so distinguished a contents-page." In fact, it's a pretty competitive Table of Contents for any issue, first or not: Brian Aldiss, Poul Anderson, J. G. Ballard, James Blish, Harry Harrison, Richard Wilson, Jack Vance, and Keith Roberts. Of course we now know that Vance never submitted his story, "The Secret," to the magazine and has no idea how it wound up there (see below).

Bonfiglioli further says (after noting that around him "the ghosts of long-dead editors squeak and gibber") that "We feel that jettisoning the old name enables us to broaden our frame of reference to embrace any kind of speculative and unusual fiction which is of the quality we are looking for." He says the change of price will enable him to pay writers more and the size increase will "enable us to continue to give new writers a chance in every issue without stinting the ration of professional work by established names." Further: "Non-fiction, for the present at least, is out. So are interior illustrations: the cost of art-work and engraving for a half-page drawing by a competent artist would buy ten pages of good fiction," and his policy is to provide the greatest possible value in stories and "the minimum of editorial matter and other guff." And: "Imaginative fiction of the past will figure regularly in *Impulse* and suggestions from readers on the selection of this—as well as on the rest of the contents— will be very welcome." And finally, the fate of former Assistant Editor James Parkhill-Rathbone is disclosed: he has launched his own literary magazine *The Idler*.

The next issue's editorial goes on for most of a page about how Bonfiglioli's not sure what he should write in editorials, briefly touts the contents of the issue, and then—out comes what's really bothering him. He notes the greater length of the stories in this issue and adds that "it will be noticed that there is an absence of what one reviewer calls 'typical Bonfiglioli space-fillers.'" He then quotes Chris Priest on the wide varia-tion between the best and the worst in the magazine, and attributes this to length. Most novices, he says, tend to turn out short squibs at first. He then waxes incoherent on the subject of length and merit. Clearly these jabs have gotten to him. In **3**, unfortunately, the passion is spent. Bonfiglioli merely bloviates uninterestingly about SF and the mainstream, after having eschewed precisely that kind of activity in the previous month's editorial.

§

The first five stories in the first issue are supposedly on the theme of Sacrifice, as previously negotiated among Bonfiglioli and the authors at a post-convention gathering in Oxford, though the connection to the theme is sometimes a bit tenuous. First up is a well done if tendentious story by Brian Aldiss, "The Circulation of the Blood," which melds a family (melo)drama plot with the discovery of an immortality virus, and which made me think of his "A Kind of Artistry," probably because of the near-incest motif.

Poul Anderson's "High Treason" is in his oratorical vein. A man is waiting to be executed for betraying Earth in an interstellar war, having made a sensible judgment that everybody would be better off if Earth lost, and this is his windy soliloquy. It's followed by Ballard's "You and Me and the Continuum," the first published of the iconic New Wave items that later became *The Atrocity Exhibition*, though this one appeared towards the middle of the book. In the blurb, Ballard explains the sacrifice connection:

> The theme of sacrifice led me to think of the Messiah or, more exactly, the idea of the second coming and how this might take place in the twentieth century. In my version, which I would describe as a botched second coming, the Messiah never quite managing to come to terms with the twentieth century, I have used a fragmentary and non-sequential technique...and have tried to invoke some of the images that a twentieth

century Messiah might see. You'll notice that the entries are alphabetized.

Indeed, starting with Author's Note. It's interesting enough on a sentence-by-sentence and image-by-image level but still escapes me as a whole.

In James Blish's amusingly loopy "A Hero's Life," his hero goes to a planet with a thriving treason industry in order to sell out Earth. This ridiculous premise and the convoluted plot are spun out with deadpan solemnity and the occasional rimshot that reminds one how funny Blish could be when he felt like it. ("Hedonism was the commonest of philosophies in the civilized galaxy, but it was piquant to hear a playwoman trotting out its moldy clichés with such fierce solemnity.") This is blurbed as Blish's first original story in a UK SF magazine.

Blish later published an expanded version in *Galaxy* (May 1970) as "A Style in Treason," explaining when he collected that version in *Anywhen* that the first version "was written in a vast hurry to meet Mr. Bonfiglioli's deadline, and I didn't realize until too late to start something else that I had too much material to fit comfortably inside ten thousand words." He describes the *Impulse* version as a "sketch." His rendition of the origin of this whole scheme: "The five stories and the cover were all to develop the theme of a man who sacrifices his life for a cause— or who doesn't. Except for this bare statement, which as I recall was Mr. Aldiss' suggestion, we had no other instructions except (for the writers) to stay inside ten thousand words."

Finally, we have Harry Harrison's "The Gods Themselves Throw Incense," a sort of misogynist (or a more enthusiastically misogynist) "The Cold Equations." When a spaceship blows up, two men and a woman escape in a lifeboat. There's only enough air for two to survive until rescue. After the woman tries to manipulate the two men to save herself, they finally toss her out the airlock. It reads well here, better than it did when I first encountered it among hundreds of pages of Harrison in his collection *50 X 50*.

The other contents of this first issue include Richard Wilson's "The Deserter": the war of the sexes is on, fought with nonlethal weaponry, but the protagonist can't put his wife out of his mind and winds up sneaking behind enemy lines to see her; Wilson's matter-of-fact and low-key delivery muffles the farcical aspect of the story and there's not much to it other than farce.

Vance's "The Secret" is one of the least interesting Vance stories I've read. People live idyllically on an island, because, it turns out, they're all young, and when they hit about 20 they start making boats and heading out to another island, where they learn that people get old and die. And they can't go back and give warning because of the prevailing winds. *Cosmopolis*, the Vance Integral Edition puff sheet, discussed the history of this story, and here's what it said:

> "The Secret" entered Vancean legend when *Worlds Beyond* folded before the story could be printed and the manuscript was lost. Some years later Vance rewrote the story, but this second manuscript disappeared while his agent was circulating the story to potential markets. Vance was unable to find the carbon copies of either manuscript. He decided the story was jinxed and gave up on it, but in 1976 he was startled to learn that the story had appeared in an English SF magazine, *Impulse*, in 1966 without authorization. Where the manuscript had been, and how it got to England, are mysteries.[85]

Also mysterious is why Bonfiglioli didn't call Vance's attention to the publication by paying him. I wonder if there is a similar story about "Alfred's Ark," which appeared in *New Worlds* **150** (May 1965).

The issue closes with Keith Roberts' "The Signaller," the first

---

85. David B. Williams, "Heroes and Villains: Jack Vance's Early Editors," *Cosmopolis* 57, Jan. 2005; now to be found at http://www.vancemuseum. com/vance_bio_1.htm (visited 10/19/11).

published of the stories that became *Pavane* (though it wound up second in the book). It's listed as "Pavane" on the contents page and "*Pavane*: The Signaller" on the story itself. It's an unprepossessing start. Direly wounded and bleeding in the woods, a man struggles back to his shelter, which is a sort of semaphore signaling station. After a flashback to his early life and how he became a signaller, a female apparition nurses him back to health. She's one of the Old Folk, i.e. Fairies, and he follows her away; later of course he's found dead in the hut surrounded by Fairy graffiti. And by the way, his wounds were from an ill-tempered wildcat and not the human attack one would expect. But it does introduce the reader to the Pavane world, and also to several of Roberts' preoccupations: machinery, landscape, and cold weather.

So overall this debut issue (if you want to think of it that way) doesn't quite live up to its line-up, but it's not a bad beginning at all.

§

The longest piece of fiction in these issues is Judith Merril's "Homecalling," serialized in **2** and **3**. The installments run 62 and 32 pages respectively, with no synopsis—in fact, the second installment starts in the middle of a chapter. This is one of three stories that Merril sold as reprints to the Compact magazines at a point where she had stopped writing fiction. The others were the novella "Daughters of Earth" in *New Worlds* and "The Shrine of Temptation" some months later in *SF Impulse*.

"Homecalling" first appeared in Robert Lowndes' *Science Fiction Stories* for November 1956, where it was ignominiously displaced from the cover by a meretricious Murray Leinster short story, despite running 87 pages and appearing pretty much at the peak of Merril's writing career. Also the precipice—this was the 20th piece of magazine or anthology SF under her name during the first eight years since her first SF story, and she had also published *Shadow on the Hearth* and two novels and a short story with Cyril Kornbluth under the Cyril Judd pseudonym during that time. After this, her productivity dropped sharply. She published only five more stories and *The Tomorrow People* under her own name, plus three stories as by Rose Sharon, from 1957 to 1963, and that seems to have been it except for a vignette in 1974. I suspect that having this long, careful, and substantial piece bounced from all the major markets (which must have been the case—given its theme, I'm sure she sent it to Campbell as well as to Gold and Boucher) and ultimately buried in a penny-a-word salvage market was a sort of negative turning point in Merril's writing career.

"Homecalling" is quite good, if dated. A married couple is out exploring the galaxy with their eight-year-old daughter and infant son in tow (evidently in the future, there will be no Bureau of Child Welfare). They crash-land, the adults are killed and the children survive, on a planet with breathable air that is populated by an intelligent bee-like species. The story is alien contact from the perspectives of the alien queen and an eight-year-old. By today's standards it's probably hopelessly naive. But by the standards of its time, it's a tour de force, both affecting and well worked out. (Apparently I'm not the only one who thinks so, since it is the title story of the NESFA compendium of Merril's short work.)

Interestingly, the unusually long blurb at the beginning of the first *Impulse* installment, which reads like something John Campbell might have written, is actually Lowndes' blurb from *Science Fiction Stories*. Bonfiglioli's own comment about the story in his editorial is "I don't believe I have ever read a more successful attempt to imagine an utterly alien way of thought."

§

The non-reprint contents of issues **2** and **3** vary from the sublime to the ridiculous. The former is represented by Roberts' second Pavane story (wisely, he put it first in the book), "The Lady Anne," **2**'s cover story. It was retitled "The Lady Margaret" for book publication for no reason apparent to me. In Roberts' parallel England, internal combustion is limited, there's no rail, and coal-fired steam trains run by small entrepreneurs travel the highways. A long-distance hauler, in futile love with a tavern-keeper, encounters highwaymen. It's still very fine on third or fourth reading. Keith Roberts is finally telling stories that stand up to his solemn style. And there's even more machinery, land-scape and cold weather than in "The Signaller."

The standard drops a bit in "Brother John," the next Pavane story in **3**. An artistic monk, assigned to draw the goings-on at the Inquisition, is driven crazy by them and by his own guilty enjoyment of them. He becomes a rebel and popular symbol, and his following is swelled mightily by a miracle in the heavens, which I am pretty sure Roberts meant to be a meteorological phenomenon. Unfortunately there's a lot of long-distance telling rather than showing in this story, mostly of the growing rebel-lion in the countryside. The great strength of "The Lady Anne" is its focus on the concrete details of one viewpoint character's existence and on his personal preoccupations, which are used to reveal the story's larger concerns and serve to balance Roberts' rhetorical tendencies. That balance is missing in "Brother John." It's not at all a bad story, but it suffers by comparison to its predecessor.

The ridiculous reports for duty in the cover story of issue **3**, "The Seventh Moon" ("Seventh Moon" on the Table of Contents) by John Rankine (pseudonym of Douglas R. Mason), which is more like what you'd expect to find in an old *Vargo Statten's SF Magazine* than in this self-declared outpost of literacy.

It starts off as a string of clichés, albeit smoothly rendered ones, and proceeds downhill. It seems a spaceship has disap-peared on or around Bromius, a planet with six moons. Who you gonna call but Dag Fletcher, Rankine's series character, who is dispatched on this mission by the Senior Controller, no less. He takes inventory of his crew in canonical fashion: "... Dark, short, stocky build, a very steady man... Another first class man...one of the best navigators in the fleet and veteran of many missions." They get to Bromius, and (of course) things are fishy, so Fletcher sneaks off with his assistant Tamar, who is (of course) a babe, and they find an enclosure where it appears people have been chained up and killed.

Inscriptions tell the tale: Bromius really has seven moons, but nobody has noticed the seventh because its orbit is a spiral, and it's only visible at certain times, and only from the equator, which they are on—but its spiral orbit with 40-day periodicity is also Bromius-synchronous. Not bad for a humble satellite! Celestial mechanics rocks! Dag sends his ship and crew away and stays on Bromius with Tamar. They are soon captured and chained up, the seventh moon appears, and a horde of Bromians arrives to carve them up ritually. But here's their spaceship in the nick of time, the seventh moon blows up (having been mined by the crew), and the knife-wielding mob are mowed down. Exeunt omnes, hot times in store for Fletcher and assistant. Bonfiglioli either thought so much of this hackneyed story, or thought the readers would, that in the previous issue he said: *"Impulse* 3 will contain our first John Rankine story—*Seventh Moon*, a sound and racy solid-fuel job of the best kind."

Almost as ridiculous is Keith Roberts' "The Pace that Kills" (3), under the Alistair Bevan pseudonym, which explores a theme that might have seemed pretty original when David H. Keller published "Revolt of the Pedestrians" in 1928. Here, the peds have taken over and stifled the existence of the motorists, requiring everybody to drive Safe-Ti-Peds, which don't go faster than 30 mph or so. Motorists have formed an underground. The background is set forth in a John Galtian three-page screed by their maximum leader. The plot involves rescuing a young woman driver who has committed the appalling crime of speeding and is about to be leucotomized. But she isn't what she seems to be. The author veers erratically between farce and oratory and doesn't do much of a job with either. This goes on for thirty-six overbearing pages. Robert Sheckley might have been amusing with this plot at ten pages.

In between these extremes is John Brunner's second Traveler

in Black story, "Break the Doors of Hell" (2), appearing after a lapse of six years from the first one. It's another stout and courageous blow in Brunner's propaganda campaign against magic. Here the Traveler—the man with many names but only one nature—comes across a city of people who have lost the knack of magic but haven't picked up any practical know-how either, so everything's falling apart, the harbor's silting up, etc. Their efforts to rediscover magic aren't working, and they really have a bone to pick with their ancestors for letting things get into this state. The Traveler gives them what they ask for, with the usual results. At bottom it's a slightly prissy morality/fairy tale, but well enough written not to be irritating. Bonfiglioli says, "I have read nothing so gruesome since M.R. James. Nothing so bravely fantastic since James Branch Cabell." And nothing so apocalyptic since Revelation, no doubt. With this and the blurb for the Rankine story, a whiff of pandering begins to creep into Bonfiglioli's presentation.

The best of the remaining short fiction is Chris [sic] Priest's "The Run" (3), his first appearance in the SF magazines. It's a rather pointless but well written and surreally vivid period piece about a militaristic Senator trying to get back to his office as nuclear war is breaking out. He finds himself running a gauntlet of juvenile delinquents, according to the custom of the time. It's the sort of thing the word "promising" was invented for, and also a good exhibit for the New Wave museum.

John Rackham's inconsequential "A Light Feint" (2) is a sequel to the similarly weightless "Room with a Skew." This time the backyard genius invents a system of light-operated fencing foils that, he learns only after the match has started, creates something like a laser beam that will cut through table legs. But no problem, he has too strong a battery in that one, the ones the fencers have are innocuous. These stories are so insubstantial it's hard to have any reaction at all to them. At least Hek Belov is annoying.

Last and definitely least is "Cry Martian" by Peter L. Cave (1940-), the first appearance by this Little Known Writer. He had four stories later in *Visions of Tomorrow* and two in *London Mystery*, according to Miller/Contento. A kid says he sees Martians but his parents won't listen. The kid goes back to look for more Martians but doesn't come back. The kicker is they're on Mars and the Martians were supposedly exterminated years ago. At the conclusion, again worthy of *Vargo Statten's SF Magazine*, "the two huge moons hung like melons in the dark green sky." If there's a "typical Bonfiglioli space-filler" per the anonymous critic who got under Bonfiglioli's skin, this is it.

30: *IMPULSE*, VOLUME 1 (4-5)

Impulse **4** and **5**, June and July 1966, carry on the same format, price, and general look as their predecessors, except that the title band on the cover has shrunk and the lead story title is now spread across the top of the pictorial area. The cover of **4** is a nifty scene of a futuristic city, or maybe a petroleum processing plant, against a starry background. It's by Keith Roberts, though I don't find a signature and it's unlike any of his other covers. The **5** cover by Roberts is an agreeably artsy earth-tone illustration of his *Pavane* story "Corfe Gate," castle in the background and army with horse and cannon in the foreground.[86]

The back covers of recent issues tellingly proclaim "A monthly collection of fantasy, science fiction, and strange stories edited for the connoisseur by Kyril Bonfiglioli." The late issues of *Science Fantasy* claimed only science fiction. The last of them specified fantasy and science fiction. *Impulse* **1** announced itself "enlarged and ranging far wider to take in more of the fertile field of sf, fantasy and speculation." Matters settled down to "fantasy, science fiction, and strange stories" with **2**. In fact, this magazine seems in general much less strange now than either the late Carnell *Science Fantasy* or the earlier issues under Bonfiglioli. Most of its contents are relatively straightforward SF or, if fantasy (as Roberts' *Pavane* stories may be considered), familiar varieties of it. I suspect Bonfiglioli adopted

---

86. See these covers at http://www.sfcovers.net/mainnav.htm or http://www.philsp.com/mags/sciencefantasy.html.

"strange stories" as license to publish off-trail non-genre items, like Aldiss's "The Oh in Jose" (discussed below) and deflect reader complaints.

The evidence of Bonfiglioli's waning interest in the magazine continues to accumulate. In **4**, there is no Bonfiglioli editorial, just a guest editorial by Harry Harrison, and no story blurbs at all (except some lines of poetry—from Aldous Huxley, no less—quoted at the head of "The Golden Coin of Spring," discussed below), even though they might actually be useful in places. For example, the lead story in **4** is by Mack Reynolds, who was at the time quite prolific in the US magazines, but as far as I can tell this is only his second appearance in a UK SF magazine and his first substantial one, the first being a vignette in *New Worlds* the previous year. Some comment on his stature, or at least his familiarity, in the US might have been in order.

In **5**, Bonfiglioli manages one blurb, for the *Pavane* story, noting that it is the last "for a while, at least." His editorial in **5** begins: "This is not the first time that I have complained on this page about the difficulty—and, to my mind, the futility—of trying to churn out a breezy, newsy (ugh), analytical eight hundred words each month about fiction in general and speculative fiction in particular." Yes, it's become pretty familiar. So he announces that he's had it and Harry Harrison will commence a column called "Critique" in which he will "praise the best, trounce the worst, review current science/fantasy/fiction" and maybe respond to readers' letters, all without editorial interference. And by the way, Harrison's novel *Make Room! Make Room!* will start in the next issue. And, of course, we now know that Harrison became the editor two issues after that.

Bonfiglioli does manage a drive-by statement of editorial philosophy combined with what seems to be a swipe at *New Worlds*:

> Well, *Impulse* is not particularly modernist in tone—
> although I see that our most advanced contemporary
> has recently started a sort of Old Codgers page—but

neither is it devoted to science fiction alone. We be-lieve in allowing our writers all the liberty of factual context formerly arrogated by sf writers alone but not binding them with the curiously dated rules which sf writers alone have always patiently shouldered.

So what is this Old Codgers page? *New Worlds* has run some material in recent issues by John Brunner, E. C. Tubb, and Philip E. High, but it's hard to believe that's what Bonfiglioli is exercised about. Maybe he's referring to some of the reaction-ary opinions voiced in *New Worlds*'s letter columns. But there are plenty of non-reactionary ones too. Or maybe he is referring to "Dr. Peristyle," a satirical column authored pseudonymously by Brian Aldiss purporting to answer readers' questions.[87]

Harrison's guest editorial in **4** decries the staleness of much SF, and says: "I feel that sf is best today when it is the greatest distance possible from its pulp magazine antecedents"—amus-ingly to me, since I described his novel *Plague From Space* a few issues back as "*Thrilling Wonder Stories* with a college education." Well, his beef is cardboard characters, and *Plague From Space* managed at least sheetrock. He also notes: "Adult stories are about adults—a truism that might safely be done up on samplers and hung from every sf writer's wall. Adults carry on a variety of activities. They pick their noses, eructate, shave, eat, make love, pare corns and so forth... I am not plugging for an ashcan school of sf writing—though that is not a bad idea. The field will hold at least one ashcan-novel; quick someone, write it."

He praises experimentation in SF with writing technique, but declares William Burroughs' experiments to be failures. "James Ballard has shown us that the classical pulp hero that must be identified with him [sic] can instead be done away with." Mainstream writers who want to write SF should read

87. *New Worlds* 153, 155, 157 (August, October, December 1965). The October 1965 issue includes Aldiss's celebrated coining of the term "shaggy god story."

SF; SF writers should read everything but SF for a year. In "Critique" in **5**, he complains that even intelligent reviewers of SF in the mainstream press don't know anything about it, but decries the insularity of devotees and admits that "A Martian Odyssey" is now unreadable. And then, God help us, he offers a free subscription to *Impulse* for the best definition of SF. Not a promising beginning.

The small ads are back in **5**, though it's not clear why—half the page is a subscription ad, there are ads for SF groups in London, Bristol, and Birmingham, one book dealer's ad and a Compact house ad. There must have been an otherwise irremediable blank page.

§

The best of the fiction, predictably, is the end of the *Pavane* series, "Lords and Ladies" in **4** and "Corfe Gate" in **5**. (There was one more, "The White Boat" in *New Worlds* a few months later, which did not appear in the UK edition of *Pavane*, was added to the US edition, and is now in the Gollancz UK reprint.) "Lords and Ladies" is an oddly powerful story given that it doesn't exactly have a plot. Jesse Strange, the road train hauler become magnate, is dying, and a priest is performing an exorcism. His niece slips in and out of reveries comprising her life story, which includes getting brought home for wining and dining by a loutish lord who, by the end of the story, has fallen for her. At this point in the series Roberts' world has become so compelling he almost doesn't need a story.

"Corfe Gate" is something else entirely, with story to burn: the stately and powerful account of the rebellion of Eleanor, daughter of Jesse Strange's niece and the loutish lord, and now mistress of Corfe Castle, against the exactions of the Papacy, and the beginning of the general rebellion against Papal rule. Late in the story there are flash-forwards in which parts of the story are told as ancient history by a mysterious minstrel to an impatient swell sightseeing in the ruins of the castle. It all adds up perfectly—even the recurrence of the Fairy motif that Roberts can't leave alone—and this time his portentous style, in which the pathetic fallacy is virtually a way of life, suits the material just as perfectly. This is about as good as the SF magazines ever got.

By contrast, Mack Reynolds' "Hatchetman," the cover story in **4**, has little to recommend it. The writing is as uninspired as usual for Reynolds, and the idea's pretty boring too: interstellar diaspora, planet settled by Italians who of course inadvertently bring the Mafia with them, and now the latter have just committed a political assassination on Earth and the assassin is on the run, but he's really only a nineteen-year-old kid who mainly wants his mother. This is part of the series that otherwise ran in *Analog* between 1961 and 1980, starting with "Ultima Thule" and the serial "Beehive."

§

Of the remaining short fiction, my guilty favorite is probably R. W. Mackelworth's novelette "A Visitation of Ghosts" (**4**), which is a bit longer than "Lords and Ladies." Boraston, a neurotic and obnoxious schoolmaster, is haunted by strange dreams, spells or seizures, and a vision of a girl's face. He finds himself arbitrarily in the ruins of his school, obviously in the future, confronted by people who make assumptions about him that he doesn't understand, and who threaten to kill him. He leaves with a group of children, some of them badly deformed. They are attacked by bee-like points of light, which are referred to as diabols, which may or may not have something to do with a war that has wrecked everything.

Sure enough, time travel and paradox are invoked as Boraston comes to understand his own nature and destiny—and then forgets it. This gritty and jerkily-paced van Vogtian piece, a throwback to some of the unpretentious off-trail SF stories that popped up from time to time in the Carnell *Science Fantasy*, reads as if it was drastically and not too carefully edited from something several times as long. (It might well have been. It was either the spawn or the genesis of Mackelworth's novel *The Diabols* a.k.a. *Firemantle*, published a couple of years later.) A close analysis would probably reveal that it doesn't entirely add up, but it has plenty of plot and is in a sense a welcome back-to-the-gutter relief from the generally tidy mainstream of this magazine's current contents.

In literary terms, the highest-profile of the remaining items are probably Brian W. Aldiss's "The Oh in Jose" (**5**), first published in *Cad* just a few months earlier,[88] and Peter Redgrove's "The White Monument" (**5**), which is subtitled "A Monologue" on the story's first page, and was allegedly "First published by broadcast on the Third Programme."

Aldiss's story is a pleasant diversion in which three men traveling in the mountains take turns making up stories about a big rock seemingly graffitied by one Jose, all the while ignoring the elderly woman who cooks for them and knows more than they give her credit for. This is very much in the new vein that Aldiss was working in his short fiction after about 1965—clever and well executed but to my taste much less substantial than a lot of his work from about 1958 to 1965.

"The White Monument" is the second of only two appearances by Redgrove in the SF magazines (the other being a poem in *New Worlds*), but he gets a substantial entry in the *Encyclopedia of Science Fiction* for his strange borderline novels. This story is pretty strange too, about a man whose chimney begins to emit a lot of noise, so he has concrete poured into it, but the concrete leaks into one of the other rooms of the house and entirely fills it up, entombing his wife. Peel away the house and there, sure enough, is The White Monument. It's so well done one can almost overlook how ridiculous it is.

Almost as well done is Paul Jents' "Clay" (**4**), a clever story

---

88. *Cad* was one of the many low-budget American *Playboy* knock-offs. I suppose if you draw a line from *Playboy* to *Rogue* and extend it, you arrive at *Cad*. But what next? Was there a *Bounder*? a *Blackguard*? a *Jackanapes*? But I digress.

about a teacher minding a classroom full of children with rather unusual talents, such as investing their clay models with life and building worlds for them, one of which looks a lot like ours. The sentiment is ultimately conventional but the story is lively.

Some attention must also be paid to Roger Jones' amusing "Hurry Down Sunshine" (**5**), a novelette by length, in which the march of social science has wiped out crime, but nonetheless society demands a Scapegoat, a notion that is played out in a solemnly nonsensical fashion which reads as if it were smuggled over from *New Worlds*, perhaps under John Sladek's overcoat. (Here's an excerpt, comprising an entire chapter: "*Eight(A): A Long Time Passed.* A long time passed.") This is Jones' second and last contribution to the SF magazines.

§

The agreeable middle range is represented by John Rankine's "Pattern As Set" (**5**), a mild surprise after the idiotic "The Seventh Moon." On an interstellar long-voyage, one crew member is awake at a time except that they overlap for a few days as the relief is thawed. When our hero goes to wake up his relief (the pulchritudinous Deena, over whom he has been drooling in anticipation), the system has failed and she's dead and rotted, along with everyone else. What to do? Carry on, of course. In the end, something else entirely is going on, and there's a second twist at the end which is gratuitous but goes down smoothly enough.

"The Golden Coin of Spring" (**4**) by John Hamilton (his third and last story for the SF magazines, the other two in *New Worlds* in 1964 and 1965) spins out Stock SF Plot XXIIIb: the aliens who surveil Earth with conquest in mind are scared away by something quite innocuous, in this case stage magic. George Hay has "Synopsis" (**4**), a satirical summary of What Has Gone Before in a stereotypical SF novel. It's basically a good fanzine piece.

Then there are the ones that capable writing can't save,

though it may mitigate one's irritation at silly ideas and clichéd plots. Angus McAllister contributes "The Superstition" (**4**) in which two intrepid explorers are informed by the indigenes that their comrade has been taken by the Zungribs. Sure enough, he has, and the Zungribs take them too, apparently to saw pieces off them and fry them up for dinner periodically (though the Zungribs are giants, so the implication that this is going to go on for a while seems unwarranted). This story is mainly distinguished by its scientific reasoning, as impressive as John Rankine's freestyle orbital mechanics of a few issues ago: it takes place on an asteroid so small and low-gravity that the characters swim, rather than walk, in the breathable atmosphere that has collected in cracks and crevasses. Not bloody likely. There's an Angus McAllister who some 30 years later was editor of *Mind Boggling Science Fiction* (no, really), and did one vignette and a couple of interviews for it. Unless he is the author of "The Superstition", this is the present McAllister's only SF magazine appearance.

Several others are by writers with only one credit in the SF magazines—probably just as well, too. Robert Clough's "The Beautiful Man" (**5**) is about some guys in a primitive society who find a cave with various old artifacts including a small sculpture of, yes, a beautiful man. It's revealed that he is the figure on a crucifix, and they think he's beautiful because they are all deformed, presumably after a nuclear war. "Hot Summer Day" by John Bell (**5**) is an all-dystopia-in-a-day number: it's hot, the traffic is terrible, the tubes are overrun, the streets are full of hooligans, the blacks, whites, fascist students, anarchist students, and the Simbas[89] are all at each other's throats, everybody's pissed off, and it all blows up and reduces London to rubble. Think of J. G. Ballard's *High Rise* without wit or imagination. Russell Parker's "The Report" (**5**) is a tiresome though

---

89. The Simbas were Congolese rebels against the regime of Joseph Mobutu, famous long ago for having kidnapped the CIA base chief in Stanleyville in 1964. See Tim Weiner, *Legacy of Ashes: The History of the CIA* (Doubleday, 2007), p. 281.

blessedly brief morality tale. After a nuclear war, started by an H-bomb on Norfolk, the Prime Minister of India gets the report of an expedition to Britain, which found that it wasn't an H-bomb but a huge meteorite that set it all off.

Bringing up the rear is "George" (**4**) by Scottish writer Chris Boyce, the first of his three stories for *Impulse*. There was one more in *Interzone* in 1988. His 1975 novel *Catchworld* got a lot of play, and he published two or three more books, then died at 56 in 1999. It's an extremely irritating New Wave look-at-me piece consisting of dialogue and staccato stream of consciousness—"Kick doors open. Run through infuriating empty room after empty room. Strangely bare."—in which, after some sort of disaster or invasion resulting in alien dinosaurs ruling the earth, the ineffectual protagonist is shed by his wife and kids, and serves him right.

31: *SF IMPULSE*, VOLUME 1 (6-8)

Impulse **6-8**, August-October 1966, is now redubbed *SF Impulse*, and it also looks a bit different because Keith Roberts is becoming more versatile. If you didn't know these three covers were by the same artist, you might not figure it out. These covers are lively and colorful, much better to my taste than some of Roberts' drabber recent efforts.[90]

More significantly, it's time for regime change. With **8**, Bonfiglioli is gone, Harry Harrison becomes Editor in Chief and Keith Roberts is bumped from Associate Editor to Managing Editor, whatever that means. On the back cover, Bonfiglioli's "fantasy, science fiction and strange stories" becomes "new thoughts, new ideas, the best in science fiction and fantasy." Perhaps equally significant is that the first Harrison issue contains three pages of ads—one full-page house ad for a Moorcock novel, another for the next issue of *SF Impulse*, and a page half full of small ads and the other half occupied by a subscription ad for *SF Impulse and New Worlds*. Detente!

The transition from Bonfiglioli to Harrison was not quite direct. J. G. Ballard was briefly slated to be editor, but quit in a matter of days because of conflict with Roberts. Ballard wrote to Christopher Priest: "I was very keen, & still am, to take over the magazine, and I assumed that as editor certain basic rules would be observed —however, on Saturday I found my

---

90. See these covers at http://www.sfcovers.net/mainnav.htm or http://www.philsp.com/mags/sciencefantasy.html.

so-called assistant editor discussing with the editor of another magazine the covers for my first two issues & about to send them to press, two issues of which I had been unable to see a single line of copy."[91] Roberts, who had been doing most of the work of getting the magazine out, described matters differently, stating that "the trouble flared because I hadn't brought the slushpile for the great man's delectation. In fact I hadn't been asked to, but in any case I couldn't have; we were still working on Bon's last issue, it hadn't even been put to bed." The argument concluded with Ballard declining Roberts' offer to fight.[92]

There is no editorial in **6**, only Harrison's "Critique," which first notes the formation of the Science Fiction Writers of America (SFWA) led by the "reluctant warrior, Damon Knight," and then proceeds to extravagant praise of Aldiss's "The Saliva Tree," because it is written in the diction of the Nineteenth Century. Harrison finds this profoundly revelatory and liberating. Much as I like the story, I'm not sure I'd go that far, and certainly not primarily for that reason. Bonfiglioli is back in **7** with a brusque farewell, allowing that he's left a thriving product and is putting it into good hands. He's right.

This is followed by another Harrison "Critique," which goes on about Asimov's *Fantastic Voyage*, which he allows "is not a great book, it just has great parts"—the science, as opposed to "the inane drivel of love story, spy story, crud story in which they are set." And he stakes out what one presumes will be his editorial territory, starting next month:

---

91. Letter, Ballard to Priest, June 7, 1966. See http://www.christopher-priest.co.uk/journal/746/when-j-g-ballard-met-keith-roberts/ (visited 10/19/11). As David Pringle has pointed out, Priest's transcription of the letter mistakenly refers to "contents"; the handwritten letter refers to "covers." Ballard also referred to Roberts as "an utterly 10th rate mediocrity" and slagged "his appalling covers & general crudity & lack of imagination." These opinions are not widely shared.

92. Personal communication from David Pringle, quoting an unpublished essay by Roberts.

There is grandeur and there is crud... I do not agree with the Catholic sfists (P. Schuyler Miller, Sam Moskowitz) that Lovecraft and E.R. Burroughs and such belong in the hagiography just because they wrote sf and were popular. They are bad: chuck them out. I do not agree with the Ecumenical sfists such as Judy Merril that a lot of borderline stuff is sf and should be dragged into our Church. If it's not baptized SF—chuck it out.

Right, no more of those dodgy "strange stories" Bonfiglioli used to harbor. These never made up a large proportion of the contents under Bonfiglioli, and now it appears they are being read out entirely. We'll see, in the Harrison-edited issues (all five of them), if that's the case.

After this peroration, what? Harrison's editorial in **8**, titled "Picking Up the Reins," more modestly expresses surprise at being the editor, gives thanks for Keith Roberts' presence, says there will be a monthly letter column—and asks the readers to submit definitions of science fiction. Haven't we already seen that sitcom, broadcast on a dead channel? Never mind. Here's the statement of policy: "We feel that a magazine should be liberal and print the best examples of the entire spectrum, from hard science to gentle fantasy. We feel that taboos are a limitation, not an aid, and we intend to use any story, irrespective of current taboos, that falls within the brackets of what might be called good taste." Maybe he should have asked the readers to submit definitions distinguishing taboos and good taste. Never mind that either.

There are a couple other pieces of non-fiction in these issues. E. C. Tubb has "A Comment" in **6** in which he quaintly takes up the cudgels against...sex. Authors "forget that sex is not, and will never be, science fiction." "But sex is not The Answer!" (Did anyone say it was? If so, Tubb doesn't identify the culprit.) Two issues later, the cover story is "Day Million" by Frederik Pohl. So much for that argument. Tubb previously had five stories, including a novel, in Moorcock's *New Worlds*, but no more after this. Maybe his quarrel was with Moorcock.

G. D. Doherty, recruited from Aldiss and Harrison's short-lived *SF Horizons*, contributes "Fantasy and the Nightmare" in **8**, which (tediously to my taste) argues that SF and fantasy are most powerful when they appeal to readers' subconscious needs. And, also in **8**, there is a book review, by Aldiss, of Kate Wilhelm and Theodore L. Thomas's *The Clone*, ambivalently praising it as "so reactionary as to be almost daring." Further: "This little novel never departs from the old formula by a hair's-breadth." But "It all makes a good read" and "The relentlessness of the book carried me over all the cliché characters and situations...." Increased emphasis on nonfiction is characteristic of the Harrison issues, which ran more articles and reviews than Bonfiglioli ever did.

§

The big noise among the fiction is of course Harrison's serial *Make Room! Make Room!*, which was the basis for the movie *Soylent Green*. Once more Bonfiglioli turns over a very large chunk of the magazine to it: the installments are eighty, seventy-two, and fifty-seven pages, though now that the magazine is 160 pages there's still plenty of room. In the previous issue's editorial he said "We snatched it, I may say, from the very teeth of a large national daily paper." The paper is not named and I am skeptical; it's not clear to me that any large national daily paper would have been prepared in 1966 to run a novel containing more than one John Galt-like lecture on birth control, not to mention a female lead who is a serial liver-in-sin.

This novel was a pretty big deal in 1966, and it holds up reasonably well today, albeit as rather a period piece. It's pretty clearly the novel in which Harrison had decided he would buckle down, turn it up a notch and Signify. Much good it did him. Charles Platt, who interviewed Harrison for his book *Dream Makers* volume II (Berkley, 1983), sometime in the early 1980s, says: "The job took five years, and he has not tackled anything with that degree of social relevance since then." My guess is that writing it and seeing it go nowhere in particular had a signal effect on his attitude towards his craft. Harrison himself says in Platt's book that he has tried to get out of the SF field: "Every fourth or fifth book I take a deep breath and write one that can bridge—and no one notices it. With *Make Room! Make Room!* I tried to get out, and Doubleday said, 'No, Harry, if we do it as a straight novel we'll sell three hundred copies.' They wouldn't have promoted it or anything." It looks to me as if he mostly pulled in his horns and stayed within comfortable genre boundaries after this, although his *Eden* trilogy set in a world where intelligent dinosaurs lived alongside humans was perhaps even more ambitious.

The novel is set in the grotesquely overpopulated New York City of 1999. There's no longer running water in residential buildings; you have to fill containers at a public pump. Most people survive on seaweed crackers, though of course there's a thriving black market in real food for those with money or influence. The story is told mostly from the point of view of Andy, a police detective—a good choice, since cops get around—and his quarry, a Chinese kid who lives with his refugee family on a derelict ship and has killed a big shot in panic during an amateur burglary attempt. Andy winds up living with the big shot's girlfriend Shirl, a nice young woman whom the big shot kept and treated abysmally. She was and is doing what she has to do to get by.

Andy shares an apartment with Sol, a cranky old Jewish man who serves as the John Galt/Jubal Harshaw figure for most of the book (and also memorably refers to Shirl as a "chachka." I would like to think that that is a joke and not a goyish malapropism.) When Saul dies, a family of loud low-lifes moves into the apartment, Shirl can't stand it and finds herself a higher-class arrangement, and the century turns with the population of the US at 344 million (in hindsight, 20% or so too high—but by 2011 it was 312 million and increasing steadily).

Overall the novel is quite well written and constructed. Its main fault is the opposite of most dystopias; Harrison gets a bit too enamored of his police procedural plot at the expense of a broader sense of how this world works and doesn't work and how it got this way. But for its time it's a pretty respectable show. It made the first Nebula ballot (there was a long list and a short list that year) but not the Hugo ballot.

Interestingly, Platt's above cited interview with Harrison doesn't say a word about his editorship of *SF Impulse* or his association with the New Wavicles. But the interview does say this:

> It seems odd that Harrison, who sold most of his early work to Campbell's magazine, should continue to write straightforward storytelling himself, at the same time that he advocates breaking the old storytelling rules. Of the "new wave" of the sixties, he remarks: "I could never write that kind of thing. I couldn't afford to write it, I am a slow writer, which means I have to be a commercial writer, because if I'm only doing one book a year I can't afford to have that book not sell. So as a writer I have a specifically defined area that I can work in. As a reader and as an editor I have a much larger one."

Keith Roberts is back after the *Pavane* stories without missing a beat. As Alistair Bevan he has a long novelette in **6**, "The Scarlet Lady." The blurb says Bonfiglioli asked for a "motoring fantasy" and this isn't at all what he expected. It seems a bucket of clichés to me, even though very smoothly rendered. Bill Fredericks of Turnpike Garage is a car mechanic, his brother buys a custom car that, he discovers, likes to run over things and people, but the brother is in thrall to it.

> "...Do you think it's sentient, Bill?"

I said, "Hell, Charlie, it's just a heap of iron. You know it can't be sentient."

Unfold per instructions in the box. Bah. There is one good tasteful line. The car has run off the road and hit a cow: "The cow went on for yards."

Bevan is back in **8** with another "motoring fantasy," "Breakdown," a shorter novelette also featuring Bill the mechanic. This time an elderly townsman complains that his car broke down, a funny little man helped him fix it, and now it runs too well and he needs our Bill to slow it down. Of course the funny little man is an alien who needs a mechanic to fix his space ship, and putting a funny little device in the old man's car was a way of advertising for one. Again, by the numbers. But this one runs good for its mileage.

These stories mark the last appearance of the Bevan pseudonym in this magazine, though Roberts used it once more a few years later in a *New Worlds* revival anthology for "I Lose Medea." Surprisingly more substantial is "Timothy" in **7**, under Roberts' own name, in which Anita the witch is brought back, allegedly by popular demand. Anita is bored as winter wears on, so she brings the local scarecrow to life, teaches this *tabula rasa* everything, and then puts him down, or tries to, when Spring starts to show. It's a sharp story about careless love, and unlike its predecessors, about as comical as cutting your throat.

The longest piece of fiction here is Chris Boyce's "The Rig," the cover story in **7**. It starts out like an annoying New Wave artifact. The first three pages are mostly devoted to the main character's seasickness, with a passing observation about his flatulence. However, there's actually a story here, and not a bad one, starting with the premise of Mark Clifton's "The Conqueror" and van Vogt's "The Harmonizer": a plant that suppresses human aggression. This is the Sea Lily, provenance unexplained, which is growing next to a North Sea oil rig and causing all its occupants to love each other—a pretty awful result, since the characters themselves are all grotesque figures of black comedy—until the effect spreads and the UK is drowning in love, and the rest of the world realizes what's in store and sends bombers before the seed pods explode. It's good nasty fun, and vastly better than Boyce's previous dreary and annoying story.

Also interesting is the novelette in **8**, Chris Hebron's first story, "The Experiment," very capably written and relentlessly high-minded. This new writer has actually bought all that stuff we used to tell the tourists about SF as the Literature of Ideas. After a limited nuclear war, mutants—espers—begin to appear, the object first of public alarm and then of the Esper Act, which among other things says they can only marry each other. But the espers' kids—who have been genetically manipulated by the government, without notice to their parents, to maximize their talent—prove near-autistic in behavior, though clearly intelligent and aware and esp-talented. The Race Purity League has got wind of this and is gearing up for action. It's clearly a case for Dr. Edwin Caradoc, called in much to his annoyance to figure out what is going on, which he does with the assistance of I.A. Richards' *The Meaning of Meaning*, William Empson's *Seven Types of Ambiguity*, and Arthur Koestler's *The Act of Creation*, which his desperate clients have checked out of the library for him. (So much for van Vogt and his Korzybski! And Edgar Pangborn and his Plato and Santayana!)

The answer is that the genetic tinkering has been too successful. The kids are perfect telepaths, and "human personal consciousness, in part at least, is the result of ambiguity in language." So the kids aren't really persons, and we'd better get rid of the Esper Act with its marriage restriction. (In one risible moment we learn that the mother of one of the kids is sexually frustrated because her husband won't have sex with her for fear of generating another near-autistic kid. This in 1966 in the same issue with Harrison's perorations about birth control.)

This Chris Hebron was another *Science Fantasy/Impulse* flash in the pan, with three stories including this one in the space of half a year, then nothing. A Chris Hebron is the co-author of *All In 17* from 1972, one of a series of "poetry posters," in or on which his poem "An Easter Holiday Honeymoon Eating Hornpipe (With Overtones)" appears with Anne Tibbles' "When the Folk Song Tells You." Same writer? Probably.[93]

Among the short fiction, the most notable item is Fred Pohl's celebrated "Day Million," reprinted from *Rogue* of the same year, and blazoned on the cover of **8**, though the cover itself depicts dry bones in the desert. It can't be meant to illustrate this more or less post-Singularity love story, as the covers of **6** and **7** at least nominally illustrate those issues' cover stories.

While there's nothing else nearly as good as the stories just mentioned, most of these issues' contents is at least interesting and readable. Several stories are by *Science Fantasy/Impulse/ New Worlds* usual suspects. Rob Sproat's "Wolves" (**6**), the second of his two stories, is about a man who, unlike the rest of us, can see and hear a pack of supernatural wolves. The wolves are not pleased by this development. It's short enough to work pretty well. Daphne Castell's "Martians at Dick's End" (**7**) is another one about aliens dropping in on the hillbillies, except these are UK hillbillies, and it's no worse than usual for this worn-out gimmick.

The irrepressible Ernest Hill is back in **8** with "The Inheritors," which is actually pretty good if you don't mind something like David R. Bunch on amphetamines. It opens with the Manager of a mostly automated factory ranting about how much he hates it, so the factory tranquilizes him. At quitting time he rides a capsule through a tube to his house, where his wife produces dinner through the alimentary tube. But he's still agitated and throws his dinner down the waste disposal infundibulum, and rather than joining his wife in the connubium he goes out on the Street (which is of course deserted except for the automated street cleaner that almost kills him) for the first time in a long time—they've been taking Longevitum so they

93. There is also a Chris de Winter-Hebron who in 2004 published *Dining At Speed: A Celebration of 125 Years of Railway Catering*, unlikely to be the same.

can't really remember, they must be centuries old. Of course the automated cops pick him up and take him to court, where he is the only suspect. Since he hasn't done anything, the auto-magistrate orders him taken home (he couldn't find it without help); the auto-doctor recommends Relaxatabs three times daily; and by now it's clear that he and his wife are the last humans, maintained at considerable effort by the machines. These clichés are rendered with great and entertaining enthusiasm, and I suppose in 1966 they weren't so clichéd.

Peter Tate, who has had several stories in *New Worlds*, appears in **6** for the first and only time in *Science Fantasy/Impulse* with "The First Last Martyr." Tate (b. 1940) published novels with intriguingly cryptic titles: *Moon on an Iron Meadow*, *Gardens One to Five* a.k.a. *Gardens 12345*, *Faces in the Flames*, and others. A buttoned-down type becomes obsessed with youth culture and particularly a rock band called the Saddlebums, and responds like any sensible aggrieved person: in a crowd with an automatic weapon. This one is definitely ahead of its time.

Brian Stableford is back in **8** with his first story under his own name, the brief "The Man Who Came Back," about a man who is captured by aliens and returned to humanity transformed. The point is obscure and so is the reason to care. Robert J. Tilley, who published eight stories mostly in the UK magazines from 1957 to 1960, and then eight more in scattered markets over the next 25 years, has "The Unsung Martyrdom of Abel Clough" in **8**, a labored effort about a member of an exploitative alien race who reconnoiters by impersonating the town drunk, to his disadvantage.

There are several one-shot writers (no other SF magazine credits) in these issues. The most notable is T. F. Thompson; in "Disengagement" (**6**), a young woman is killed in an auto accident, except that her brain is kept alive by one Dr. Theosophus Dog, and the story is told in alternating excerpts from Dr. Dog's hand-wringing diary ("It's wrong, you bloody mad fool, utterly wrong") and the bewildered mind of Sadie Smith. The story reads like the work of a pretty experienced writer who hasn't read much genre SF and fantasy or is pretending he hasn't. Bonfiglioli says "We are often asked for some really chilly horror. Try this." It would be easier to read it that way (i.e. with a straight face) if the male lead were named Smith or even Zilstein.

M. J. P. Moore contributes "The Writing Man" (7), about a fellow who sits every day at a desk and writes. Either he's a psychotic murderer or an alien who appears to be a psychotic murder. The story is an annoyance mitigated by brevity. Fred Wheeler's "Audition" (7) superfluously recapitulates and updates the plot of Dunsany's "Mars on the Ether." Again, brevity is its only virtue. These two would fit the epithet "typical Bonfiglioli space-fillers."

There is also a reprint in **8**, "The Boiler" by C. F. Hoffman, originally titled "Ben Blower's Story." Hoffman lived 1806-1884, and Harrison declares this the first of a series of "great fantasy stories of the past," but no more is heard of this series—the only reprints in the remaining issues of the magazine are recent items by Thomas Disch and Judith Merril. A sailor lies down in the ship's idle boiler to sleep, with obvious consequences. He does escape, and so does the point.

32: *SF IMPULSE*, VOLUME 1 (9-11)

SF Impulse **9-11**, November 1966 through January 1967, displays the hand of new editor Harrison in significant respects, though the fiction contents are mostly by familiar names. Suddenly the magazine has become less austere, more like a conversation and less like a lecture. Each issue has features in addition to the editorial: letters, book reviews, fake book reviews, an interview, an article on a film festival. Almost every story has a blurb, some of them quite chatty. There are more authors' names on the covers. There are even interior illustrations, most by Keith Roberts, but at least one by Jim Cawthorn. Two of the three covers are by Roberts, vigorous and striking to my taste. The third is a more conventional image, except that the spaceship is rocketing *down* on the page—maybe it was intended for *New Worlds*.[94] **9** has two pages of ads (the SF Book Club and the Compact SF line), but the ads disappear again in the next issues. Once more there is a flyer for *Modern Family Planning* stuck in the magazine. Bravo again.

§

The editorial in **9** is a guest editorial by Judith Merril, who makes all the obligatory obeisances to this magazine and *New Worlds*, Moorcock and Bonfiglioli:

---

94. See these covers at http://www.sfcovers.net/mainnav.htm or http://www.philsp.com/mags/sciencefantasy.html.

One might fairly say that Moorcock's *New Worlds* is generating more exciting new thinking than science fiction has known since the early years of the Campbell *Astounding*—and as fairly, that Bonfiglioli's *Science Fantasy/Impulse* sustained a level of literate imaginative writing unequalled since the peak of Boucher's tenure at *Fantasy & Science Fiction.*

As to Bonfiglioli, she mentions the £40,000 Tintoretto he picked up at auction for £40, the Victorian villa, the Rolls in the drive and the stuffed birds in the hallway.

In **10**, Harrison recounts his visit to the SF film festival in Trieste, involving a surreal interview with Arthur Clarke and him by Italian TV, etc. (There's a longer account of the festival in **9** by one Francesco Biamonti.) In **11**, Harrison bemoans the critical vacuum in which SF writers mostly work, and notes that Gordon R. Dickson has sent his latest book, *Mission To Universe*, to the entire membership of the SFWA, requesting comment. So he comments, observing that Dickson has improved upon the standard of flat characterization but only to the extent of creating one completely dominant character, and complaining about the book's pervasive violence and the assumption that violence is the only way to solve problems.

Book reviews ("Book Fare") in **9** are by publisher Tom Boardman, who has mixed feelings about Pohl's *A Plague of Pythons* but seems to like Hal Clement's "new" (actually, serialized 1958) novel *Close to Critical* a bit better. In **10** we have no "Book Fare," but instead "The Plot Sickens" by Brian Aldiss, reviews of fake books inspired by George Hay's "Synopsis" of a few issues ago. E.g., *Something In the City* by up-and-coming Stan Kenyonne—"great, like an Avram Davidson story rewritten by John W. Campbell, Jr.", and clearly a take-off on Wilhelm and Thomas's "The Clone" which Aldiss recently reviewed. And *Ingurgitators of the Infinite* by Lance Corporal E. E. Green ("Like his equally famous namesake, Graham Green, E. E. gets down to the plot straightaway.") In **11** Aldiss has "Book Fare," four pages on Disch's *The Genocides*, in which he deplores merely commercial pessimism, and writes, "Now, I believe, a genuine pessimist of a new writer has come along, to delight us with an unadulterated shot of pure bracing gloom." He hopes that "we shall be treated to many more descents into the Dischian abyss."

Disch is very much in evidence in these issues. In addition to being reviewed, he has two short stories and an interview with Kingsley Amis, "Hell Revisited" (**10**). Amis says he hasn't been keeping up with SF, which may have to do with its failure to measure up. He cites Aldiss's "The Saliva Tree" and admires its self-restraint but (contra Harrison of a few issues before) complains of its lack of finish ("the half-hearted way in which the Victoriana were employed, the quarter-hearted way in which the dialogue was written"). He expresses disappointment in the post-*Rogue Moon* Algis Budrys and also in J. G. Ballard, specifically the first few of the stories that would become *The Atrocity Exhibition*. "Let me go on record as saying that I'm too stupid to understand what they're about. I cannot make any contact with them at all." Though he enjoyed *Naked Lunch* and thought it very funny, he thinks Burroughs is a disastrous influence on Ballard.

Then he complains that run-of-the-mill SF is more so than ever and that D. F. Jones' *Colossus* is written as if there had never been SF novels before. Disch asks Amis about the writers he especially admired in *New Maps of Hell*.

> Pohl has been one of the big disappointments of my life... Bradbury's gone in the direction one might have expected him to go, and has become completely drowned in whimsicality and fantasy... Sheckley... seems unfortunately committed to repeating himself on a lower level of energy, and in a style devoid of that earlier wit.

He's not quite as hard on Clarke and Blish and, astonishingly, confesses to having enjoyed Blish's *The Night Shapes*. "Kurt Vonnegut's all right, though he seems to be getting a bit cute and impish for my taste." He hasn't equaled *Player Piano*, and *Cat's Cradle* "wasn't science fiction enough for me." And finally, unalloyed praise for someone: Anthony Burgess. Has the battle for SF's respectability been won? Externally, yes. Internally, no, in that SF writers still don't pay enough attention to style and finish.

> Carelessness, indifference, complacence, or apathy about stylistic questions is very well demonstrated by an appalling fact that I learned from an equally authoritative source recently: that when that very gallant, valuable and always interesting critical journal, *Science Fiction Horizons*, was offered to members of Science Fiction Writers of America at special rates and under a simple arrangement, out of a membership of a hundred and fifty or thereabouts *three* writers thought it was worth the trouble of sending in a dollar to find out what was being said about their craft.

§

The letter column appears in **9**, with the request for definitions of SF fortunately forgotten (for now at least). Instead, after a brief letter by Archie Potts defending short material, there is a rebuttal by Brian Stableford to E. C. Tubb's denunciation of sex in SF (Harrison replies that the truth is somewhere in between), and a defense of William Burroughs by Michael Butterworth in response to Harrison's claim that Burroughs had failed.

Most interestingly, historian Colin Pilkington takes issue with the historical premises of Roberts' *Pavane* stories, saying the assassination of Elizabeth in 1588 could not have brought about the results Roberts portrayed—to get those, you'd have to go back to 1485 and the Battle of Bosworth. Roberts is noncommittal on the historical analysis, but says:

> The origins of *Pavane* lie in the Surreal disparity between the primeval Wessex landscape and the excesses of the modern tourist trade. My butterfly cars tangling with the hooves of Henry's cavalry are no more bizarre than a girl in a bikini ogling the great barbicans of Corfe. I think it was images like this rather than an urge to warp history that led me to write the book.
>
> I recently had the pleasure of the Lady Eleanor's company on a drive across the Purbecks. As ever, she was calmly confident of previous incarnations. Corfe Gate was a green place, little harvests of moss glowing on its stones. The air was clear, scrubbed with rain. In the quiet the mutter of old guns was louder than before.

The letters return in **11**, and Tubb vs. Sex is still the topic. Langdon Jones politely suggests that restrictions in general are not a good thing. Chris Boyce responds more robustly that he has to differ with Tubb, having just sold the magazine a story in which "the man and girl jump into bed and roll around for a while," denounces those who would banish spaceships from SF, and rather diffusely seems to be condemning the state of British SF and the ascendancy of Ballard and Aldiss, concluding: "Much of what we pretend is British sf is rapidly deteriorating into a riot of babbling ballads becoming tragically blinded by the brilliance of their own imagery!"

§

The dominant piece of fiction in these issues is Michael Moorcock's *The Ice Schooner*, which appears in installments of fifty-five, sixty-eight, and seventy pages (shortened from the book version) and gets a fine cover by Roberts on **9**. Harrison notes that this novel was contracted for by Bonfiglioli before his departure.

It is, appropriately for the editor of *New Worlds* on his return (sort of) to the birthplace of Elric, a work of Barbarian Entropy, in which Konrad Arflane, accustomed to commanding a land-bound sailing ship in a glaciated world but now unemployed, winds up piloting an ice ship with a crew of etiolated aristocrats with a few screws loose in search of the legendary city of New York. They have the usual quota of adventures along the way (though some are unusually grotesque). At the end, it's clear that things are warming up again, which for Konrad represents only decay and the compromise of standards, so naturally he heads off into the North to freeze to death while there's still time. This is not my cup of tea at all, but it's entertaining enough and much more carefully written than a lot of Moorcock's earlier work in *Science Fantasy* (or for that matter some of his more recent work in *New Worlds*).

Most of the rest of the fiction is pretty short, the exception being Chris Boyce's novelette "Mantis" (**11**), which could have been appropriately prefaced "Non Compos," a bracingly loony, never-reprinted story in which a sculptor's wife (also his main subject) comes home after having left him for 18 years or so (she does this every now and then, people live a long time), only to be accused of being an alien android by a demented security agent with his own agenda. This is told in a style that might have been Robert Sheckley's annoyed reaction to someone saying "Why don't you stop being so uptight?" but that unfortunately defies excerpting.

The other outstanding item is Disch's "The Roaches" (**9**), an unacknowledged reprint from *Escapade* of a year earlier, one of his early near-perfect and entirely perverse pieces. A young woman with "a perfect horror of cockroaches" learns to appreciate them by comparison with her neighbors—obviously foreigners with disgusting habits. This is clearly a writer who read Lovecraft and guffawed. Disch's other story, "Three Points on the Demographic Curve" (**10**) reads as if it were tossed off pretty quickly, and it probably was. The blurb says, "He visited London recently and, the day before he left, we succeeded in extracting this manuscript from him." It's a time travel lampoon that hasn't much to it but cleverness.

The other big names turn in relatively lackluster performances. Brian Aldiss's "The Eyes of the Blind King" (**9**) is another of his stories of medieval Serbia, a preoccupation I can't get interested in, and after the first, "The Day of the Doomed King," the stories are not especially compelling either: they read like something Aldiss thought he ought to do and not something he really liked doing (although, many years later, Serbian tales formed a central part of the armature of his great *Helliconia* trilogy). Keith Roberts has two Anita stories, "The Simple for Love" (**9**) and "The Familiar" (**10**), which are amusing enough but a considerable letdown after the unexpectedly wrenching "Timothy" in **7**. Richard Wilson is here twice, in **10** with a short collaboration with Kenneth Bulmer, "Inside Out," a nicely turned but trivial gimmick story about a visiting alien who loses his matter duplicator to a con man who isn't as smart as he thinks he is, and in **11** with "Green Eyes," another silly story about the war of the sexes. (This and "Deserter" in **1** comprise a series.)

Judith Merril has "The Shrine of Temptation" in **11**, reprinted from a 1962 *Fantastic*, an earnest interstellar anthropology job, much more labored and less interesting than "Homecalling" in **2** and **3**. Editor Harrison has "The Voice of the CWACC" (**10**), a successor to a couple of earlier stories in *Analog* published under the name of Hank Dempsey so as not to offend Harrison's employer, a medical newspaper (or at least to offend them untraceably). CWACC is the Committee for Welfare, Administration, and Consumer Control, which sponsors medical quacks—an idea straight from one of John Campbell's editorials of a few years earlier, in which, as part of his campaign against the tyranny of Orthodox Science, he proposed allowing quacks to roam free and licensing them as long as they called themselves quacks. Quaintly enough, the daring piece of quackery in this sitcom-plotted lightweight story is acupuncture, which I guess hardly anybody outside China knew about in 1966.

There are several stories by the *Science Fantasy/Impulse* regulars (i.e., those who appeared here and hardly anywhere else). The best of them is Robert Wells' clever and creepy "Stop Seventeen" (**9**). After the Disaster and the Exodus, the subway still works, but it doesn't stop at the seemingly deserted Stop Seventeen. The protagonist wonders why and manages to contrive a stop there, where he discovers that upstairs is the Central Index of Memories and Dreams, to which everyone wanted to escape—and even with that revelation things aren't quite what they seem.

Eric C. Williams contributes "The Real Thing" (**10**), about some barnstorming spacemen in their battered ship who are hired by a rich writer to give him a Space Experience to use as background. They give him and themselves more show than was bargained for. It reads like something you might find in the back pages of an old *Planet Stories*.

Chris Hebron, the newest regular and one of the quickest to vanish (three stories and gone from the SF magazines) has "Coincidence" (**11**), in which an intercontinental experiment in telepathy has bizarre and not too well rationalized consequences for a bewildered third party. Finally, we have a Little Known (SF) Writer, Pete Hammerton, with "Grutch" (**11**), in which a not-too-well-wrapped protagonist is beset by telepathic Martian mice and ultimately has to get the Venusians to help him out. Hammerton also had seven stories in *London Mystery* from 1959 to 1970.

These issues represent a certain falling off in interest for me, though that's probably as much a matter of taste as quality, given my lack of interest in Moorcock's novel and Aldiss's Jugoslavian opus, among others. But the overall standard of competence remains high. And the end is near.

33: *SF IMPULSE*, VOLUME 1 (12)

Here we are at the final issue of *SF Impulse*.

SF Impulse **12**, February 1967, still lists Harry Harrison as Editor in Chief and Keith Roberts as Managing Editor, but it's clearly Roberts' show now. According to Mike Ashley, in Tymn/Ashley, it's really been Roberts' show all along:

> [N]o sooner had Harrison assumed control than he was called away, first to Italy, then to the United States, so that while he still rustled for stories from leading writers, the main functions of reading and selecting manuscripts and assembling and illustrating the issues fell on the capable shoulders of Managing Editor Keith Roberts.

Roberts' presence is more pervasive in this issue, though. He writes the editorial (explaining that Harrison has "made tracks for Philadelphia"), contributes an article ("Keith Roberts Rereads Lucian of Samosatos"), and as Alistair Bevan is responsible for "Book Fare." Plus he has several illustrations, though not the cover. That's by Agosta Morol, who also did the covers or *Science Fantasy* **70** and **77**. It's a pleasant enough daub, not discernibly illustrative, that does nothing much for me.[95]

There's no hint of impending demise here, except for this

_____

95. See this cover at http://www.sfcovers.net/mainnav.htm or http://www.philsp.com/mags/sciencefantasy.html.

harbinger, in a box at the end of the last page: "Life after death? College of Psychic Science (est. 1884), non-profit making, not a religious body, offers opportunities for personal private investigation. Research, meditation, healing, séances, lectures, library. Write or call 16, Queensberry Place, London S.W.7 [etc.]" But there wasn't any life after death for this magazine, unlike *New Worlds*, which enjoyed a lively career as revenant.

§

Roberts' editorial is a run-through of the issue's contents. He says he has "put together a group of stories that seemed to me to present a coherent whole," i.e., each one "illustrates, in its own special way, an odd aspect of the human psyche." Well, sort of. "Book Fare" first touts a couple of science books, Dole and Asimov's *Planets For Man* and C. Maxwell Cade's *Other Worlds Than Ours,* then proceeds to the current list of Rupert Hart-Davis, praising D.F. Jones' *Colossus* in terms obviously responsive to Amis's trashing of it in his interview a couple of issues previously. Roberts concedes that it is "wholly derivative" with "no shatteringly original ideas," but suggests that this is a "snide form of attack I find particularly distasteful" and "can't help feeling the current obsession with originality is largely a device of critics who just have to kick something... It's the *manner* in which the job is done that counts."

He mildly praises a Douglas Hill anthology and a Tubb collection and then launches a paean of praise for Bradbury's *The Machineries of Joy*: "Read Bradbury and you read the work of a major artist, a man I wouldn't hesitate to place alongside Dylan Thomas as one of the great innovators of our time." And that's not the half of it. (But—innovator?) Roberts as Bevan then coyly acknowledges that Hart-Davis "have also published Keith Roberts' *The Furies.*"

Roberts' article on Lucian's *True History* mainly just recounts the plot and displays long excerpts, amusingly enough, though there is also (speaking of coy) a footnote to one of Lucian's plot devices: "I must confess there was something horribly familiar about the notion of large spiders spinning webs through inter-planetary space. It almost reminded me of a book I read once. But perhaps I'm mistaken."[96]

The letter column starts out with Michael Butterworth tediously and not too coherently continuing his defense of William Burroughs, and finally the long (but not long enough) awaited results of the competition for a definition of science fiction, an enterprise ably discredited by Tony Sudbery ("Worse than futile, the search for a definition of science fiction could well prove pernicious in leading to interminable acrimonious arguments of the type that once disfigured jazz criticism.") The prize is divided between Malcolm E. Wright, whose entry is not worth repeating, and Peter Redgrove, who submits a long and not entirely boring letter on the affinity between SF and poetry. The prize is a subscription to the magazine, which is defunct as of this issue—apt commentary.

§

The fiction is a pretty good collection, representative of what the magazine has been for the last several years: a good mix of big names, burgeoning names, and going-out-of-business names—the last genre stories of Paul Jents and Chris Hebron are here. The outstanding item (and the biggest name) is Brian Aldiss's "Just Passing Through," the first of the Acid-Head War stories that became *Barefoot In the Head.* This piece might seem less impressive outside the context of the book, since it's mostly stage-setting rather than story. Charteris is in France about to reach England and also about to realize that he's been affected by the military psychochemicals that have doused Europe. But we immediately know something's afoot:

Outside Milano, where the triple autostrada made of the

---

96. The allusion is, of course, to Brian Aldiss's *Hothouse,* a.k.a. *The Long Afternoon of Earth,* a Hugo-winning quasi-fantasy.

Lombardy plain a geometrical diagram, he had narrowly avoided a multiple crash. They were all multiple crashes these days. The image continued to multiply itself over and over in his mind, like a series of cultures in their dishes: a wheel still madly spinning, crushed barriers, buckled metal, sunlight worn like thick make-up over the impossibly abandoned attitudes of death. Charteris had seen it happen, the fantastic speeds suddenly swallowed by car and human frames with the sloth of the super-quick, when anything too fast for retina register could spend forever spreading through the labyrinths of consciousness. By now, the bodies would all be packed neatly in hospital or mortuary, the autostrada gleaming in perfect action again, the death squads lolling at their wheels in the nearest rastplatz, reading paperbacks. But Charteris's little clicker-shutter mechanisms were still busy re-running the actual blossoming moment of impact.

One wonders what J. G. Ballard made of this, six years or so before the publication of *Crash!* It's sharp and vivid and whets the appetite for more—definitely much livelier than the mini-epics of King Vukasan a few issues earlier. A quick check of the book version, by the way, shows that overall it's pretty much the same as this one, but it received a line-by-line sharpening, tightening, and polishing to pervasively good effect before book publication.

The runner-up in this issue is Jents' novelette "The Pursuit of Happiness," which all by itself makes me regret this Little Known Writer's disappearance. An extraterrestrial near-human raised on Earth has to evacuate and head home when Earth is faced with destruction. Home, which he's never known, proves to be surprisingly primitive. And the people in charge start talking to him about when he's going to want his operation. This society has avoided disaster by avoiding most high technology, but people manage to withstand lives of repetitive menial labor by means of a brain implant bringing dreams of adventure and wish-fulfillment while they're at their labors. No need to whistle while you work here. Our hero is shocked and rebels. And how much support do you think he gets? This one is sharp enough to cut yourself on, a reinvention from a different direction of John D. MacDonald's "Spectator Sport."

The other long-established name is Richard Wilson, who is here with "See No Evil," about a man who wakes up invisible one day. As usual with Wilson's work, it is skillfully done and agreeable to read if you don't have anything else to do, but has no edge. It's insipid as comedy and flaccid as suspense or problem story, and gives the impression of a writer on autopilot. I know there are exceptions in his work, but this isn't one of them.

The rising names are led by Thomas Disch (by 1967 he was probably more than rising—better-known than Wilson, I suspect) with "The Number You Have Reached." World War III was conveniently fought with neutron bombs, so all the people are dead but the buildings are still standing. The phones still work too, and a survivor is being telephonically stalked by a woman (maybe the only other survivor) whom he's never managed to see and who can't quite bring herself to drop over, and who may be a figment of his imagination anyway. This is one of the incisively cruel short stories that made Disch's name before *Camp Concentration* made his name much bigger, one of his best early stories.

Brian Stableford is here with "Inconstancy," a portentous and no doubt allegorical piece about some people who find themselves living in and around a deserted town on a beach, isolated by a cliff, with no memory of how they got there; it's forgivable because it's so well written. Also present is Chris Priest with "Impasse," about a Denebian spy captured on Earth, and his captors' reaction to his threats. While the blurb claims "mordant and satirical," it reads to me like a rock thrown at some of John Campbell's contributors. Then there is D. G. Compton, with his only SF magazine appearance, "It's Smart to Have an English Address," about an elderly pianist rebelling against the pressure to allow his personality to be recorded. It's a worthy story but might have been a great one at half the length. Unalloyed high-mindedness wears thin quickly.

The last item—actually, the lead story—is "The Bad Bush of Uzoro," Chris Hebron's final SF magazine appearance, about a supposedly haunted religious mission in Nigeria. Roberts' blurb says it's "almost in the form of a classic ghost yarn." Actually it's entirely in that form: weird stuff happens, it gets weirder and more threatening, here's the climax and of course there's a prosaic explanation, but wait! here's the telling detail that *can't be explained by rational means*. A bit hackneyed to my taste, but undeniably well written, and the local color is convincing.

§

So there you have it: *Science-Fantasy/Science Fantasy/ Impulse/SF Impulse* (and almost *Caliban*), 1950-1967. On, finally, to the post-game show and funeral oration.

34: FINALE

One could put together at least as good an anthology from the twenty-nine post-Carnell issues as from the sixty-four Gillings and Carnell issues. The anchor tenants would be, of course, the big names: Aldiss's "Man in His Time" and maybe "The Circulation of the Blood," Roberts' "The Lady Anne [Margaret]" or "Corfe Gate" or both, maybe Ballard's "You and Me and the Continuum," and Swann's "Vashti." And then as many as could be fit in of the following, most of which are completely forgotten and many never reprinted at all.

Thom Keyes, Period of Gestation (**67**)
Johnny Byrne, Love Feast (**67**)
Douglas Davis, Present from the Past (**69**)
Johnny Byrne, Harvest (**69**)
Robert Wells, Song of the Syren (**70**)
John Rackham, Bring Back a Life (**70**)
Ernest Hill, Chemotopia (**75**)
A. K. Jorgensson, Coming-of-Age Day (**76**)
Robert Cheetham, Omega and Alpha (**76**)
Philip Wordley, Goodnight, Sweet Prince (**77**)
Johnny Byrne, Yesterday's Gardens (**78**)
M. John Harrison, Marina (**81**)
Paul Jents, Our Man in 1900 (**81**)
Chris Priest, The Run (**3**)
R. W. Mackelworth, A Visitation of Ghosts (**4**)
Keith Roberts, Timothy (**7**)

Chris Boyce, The Rig (**7**)
Rob Sproat, Wolves (**6**)
Ernest Hill, The Inheritors (**8**)
Chris Boyce, Mantis (**11**)
Robert Wells, Stop Seventeen (**9**)
Aldiss, Just Passing Through (**12**)
Paul Jents, The Pursuit of Happiness (**12**)

But, of course, while Damien Broderick and I, and readers of this book, would buy that anthology, we'll probably never see anything like it, alas.

§

In its slightly less than three years, these post-Carnell issues published an impressive list of high- or upper-medium-profile serials, all of them attaining book publication in short order: Swann's "The Blue Monkeys" and "The Weirwoods," Harrison's "Plague from Space" and " Make Room! Make Room!", Roberts' "The Furies," and Moorcock's "The Ice Schooner"— not to mention the *de facto* serial that became the best book to come out of the magazine, Roberts' *Pavane.*

This is all quite competitive with the longer fiction appearing in the US magazines at the time (*Analog* falling into senility or at least crankishness! And all that drab Mack Reynolds!) The shorter fiction was more of a mixed bag. About the only recognized classic the magazine printed, excepting the *Pavane* stories, and reprints like "Day Million," is Aldiss's "Man in His Time." Actually some fairly weak material appeared from big names—some pretty bad Aldiss and Bulmer, some hackneyed Harrison, washed-out Wilson, extremely minor Vance and Anderson, etc. At the bottom, there was a steady though not large layer of dregs, stories that were bloody awful or, more often, just abjectly inconsequential—Bonfiglioli space-fillers, as they were named at the time.

The post-Carnell magazine's strength was in the middle

range: strong, well-written, unpretentious stories by writers who for the most part were just passing through and did not have substantial SF careers outside this magazine or after its demise, in some cases were never heard from again, and have mostly been forgotten. (Though there were a few exceptions: the magazine did launch Christopher Priest and Brian Stableford and nurtured Keith Roberts.) These Little Known Writers were a big part of what made this a magazine worth reading as a whole, rather than just a platform from which a few classics were launched.

Despite its association with the Moorcock *New Worlds*, *Science Fantasy/Impulse* was New Wavish only tangentially and in its spare time. Recall Bonfiglioli's editorial in **80** virtually boasting of his squareness and responding to a charge of publishing material that is "out of vogue": "Thomas Burnett Swann's stories were out of vogue some two thousand years ago, yet his following is very strong, and increases with every story." Most of what went on in the magazine was literate storytelling on standard models—mostly SF models, since the magazine published less outright fantasy than under Carnell.

There was little formal innovation and what there was tended to be superficial, like Aldiss's section headings in "Man in His Time," otherwise a conventionally told story. Ballard's "You and Me and the Continuum" (his only appearance in the post-Carnell magazine) was conspicuous by its lack of company. There were a modest number of stylistically splashy stories— Chris Boyce's and a couple of Ernest Hill's come to mind— and a few that pushed the attitude envelope, like Thom Keyes' "Period of Gestation," Pohl's reprinted "Day Million," and in a very different way Disch's "The Number You Have Reached" and Cheetham's "Omega and Alpha." There were also a few impressionistic and/or abstract items that might well be booked for suspicion of allegory, like some of Johnny Byrne's, or Stableford's "Inconstancy." But these were scattered and no overall agenda is apparent from them. "Science fiction for adults" and "literacy" were the agendas Bonfiglioli proclaimed, and it is telling that his first choice in reprints was Kipling's "Easy as A.B.C."

§

My executive summary of the first few issues of *Science Fantasy* was: Pretty bad start. But Carnell's magazine picked up over the years, as post-War desolation brightened into the Sixties, and became an enjoyable and important venue for fantasy, SF and even, occasionally, science fantasy. And my postmortem judgment on the post-Carnell *Science Fantasy/Impulse/SF Impulse* is, all things considered, and like its predecessor at its best: Good show.

ABOUT THE AUTHORS

JOHN BOSTON is Director of the Prisoners' Rights Project of the New York City Legal Aid Society, where he has worked for many years, and is co-author of the *Prisoners' Self-Help Litigation Manual*.

DAMIEN BRODERICK is an Australian science fiction writer, editor and critical theorist, with a Ph.D. from Deakin University. Formerly a senior fellow in the School of Culture and Communication at the University of Melbourne, he currently lives in San Antonio, Texas. He has written or edited some 60 books, including *Reading by Starlight, x, y, z, t: Dimensions of Science Fiction*, and *Unleashing the Strange. The Spike* was the first full-length treatment of the technological Singularity, and *Outside the Gates of Science* is a study of parapsychology. His 1980 novel *The Dreaming Dragons* (revised in 2009 as *The Dreaming*) is listed in David Pringle's *Science Fiction: The 100 Best Novels*—and with Paul Di Filippo, he has written a sequel to Pringle's book, *Science Fiction: The 101 Best Novels, 1985-2010*. His recent short story collections are *Uncle Bones, The Qualia Engine*, and *Adrift in the Noösphere*.

INDEX OF NAMES

Bester, Alfred, 53
Bevan, Alistair (Keith Roberts), 238-39, 247, 256, 262, 270, 290, 298, 329
Bixby, Jerome, 70
Blish, James, 46, 63, 157-58, 281, 290-91, 293, 324
Boardman, Tom, 205, 322
Bok, Hannes, 26
Boland, John, 92, 95, 106, 111
Bond, Nelson, 19
Bonfiglioli, Kyril, 13, 92, 225-27, 229, 231-33, 235-36, 238, 240, 244-45, 248-51, 253-54, 256-58, 262-85, 291-94, 296, 298-303, 310-13, 320-22, 326, 336-37
Boston, John, 11-12, 35
Bounds, Sydney J., 32, 51, 93, 220
Boyce, Chris, 309, 316, 325-26, 336-37
Brackett, Leigh, 190
Bradbury, Ray, 186, 282, 323, 330
Bradley, Marion Zimmer, 81
Bradley, Peter, 231
Brandon, Frank (Kenneth Bulmer), 182, 189
Broderick, Damien, 35, 47, 55, 71, 77, 80, 113, 130, 132, 225, 247, 336
Brody, John, 111
Bronowski, Jacob, 20
Brown, Fredric, 111, 185
Brundage, Margaret, 26
Brunner, John, 10, 14, 60-61, 65, 70, 73-74, 76, 82-85, 89, 107-08, 115-16, 120-24, 129-31, 149, 152-53, 159-60, 173-74, 184, 186-87, 197-98, 221-22, 224-25, 278, 288, 298-99, 303
Budrys, Algis, 28, 323
Bull, Reina, 26, 33, 157
Bulmer, Kenneth, 10, 65, 94, 107-08, 118, 121-22, 134-36, 149, 157-58, 161-62, 182, 189-90, 221, 223, 230, 232, 238, 327, 336
Bunch, David R., 203, 318
Burgess, Anthony, 324
Burke, Jonathan F., 36, 40-41, 62-63, 65-68, 100, 118, 223
Burns, Alan, 256, 260, 285
Burroughs, Edgar Rice, 148
Burroughs, William S., 213, 219, 303, 323-24, 331

Butterworth, Michael, 324, 331
Byrne, Johnny, 240, 245, 254, 271, 276-77, 335, 337
Campbell, E.D., 99
Campbell, H.J., 30, 33
Campbell, John W., Jr., 9, 33, 42, 67, 81, 208, 296, 322, 327, 333
Capek, Karel, 169
Carnell, Edward John (Ted, or John), 11-13, 18, 24-25, 30-33, 36-37,
    40, 43, 47, 49, 51, 66, 72-73, 75, 77-78, 80, 86-87, 90, 92, 101-02,
    109, 114, 118-19, 126, 128, 133, 135, 140-41, 143, 148, 157, 164, 167,
    177, 179, 186, 194-95, 202, 204-06, 211-12, 215, 219, 226-27, 233,
    236, 237-38, 246, 251-54, 260, 270, 273, 275, 301, 305, 335-38
Cartier, Edd, 35
Castell, Daphne, 233, 288, 318
Cave, Peter L., 299
Cawthorn, Jim, 194, 211, 321
Chandler, A. Bertram, 26, 32, 42, 49, 51, 61, 89, 101, 106, 110-11, 125,
    131, 223-24
Chapman, G. Ken, 30
Cheetham, Robert, 272, 335
Christopher, Hugh, 210
Christopher, John, 31, 35, 42
Clarke, Arthur C., 20, 22, 24-25, 49-50, 129, 131, 133, 225, 271, 322,
    324
Cleator, P.E., 20
Clement, Hal, 68, 322
Clifton, Mark, 316
Clingerman, Mildred, 89
Clothier, 29, 33
Clough, Robert, 308
Clute, John, 17
Cockcroft, W.P., 44, 211
Cogswell, Theodore R., 193
Cole, Les, 50
Collins, Les, 50
Colvin, James (Michael Moorcock), 215, 218
Compton, D.G., 333
Conan Doyle, Arthur, 133
Conklin, Groff, 120
Cook, Stephen, 203

Coster, Arthur, 41
Cracken, Jael (Brian W. Aldiss), 229-30, 255-56, 258
Craig, Brian (Brian Stableford and Craig MacKintosh), 274
Cross, John Keir, 148
Cutler, P.W., 43
Dali, Salvador, 163, 167-68
Davidson, Avram, 177
Davis, Douglas, 245, 335
de Camp, L. Sprague, 9
del Rey, Lester, 114, 118, 120, 125, 140, 141
deMille, Richard, 41
Denbigh, Colin, 193, 223
Dewey, G. Gordon, 50
Dick, Philip K., 62, 95, 126, 132, 176-77, 200
Dickson, Gordon R., 322
Disch, Thomas M., 320, 323, 326, 333, 337
Doherty, G.D., 313
Dudley, Geoffrey A., 169
Elders, Joycelyn, 268
Ellison, Harlan, 92, 205
Fearn, John Russell, 20, 21, 22
Finlay, Virgil, 33
Flood, Leslie, 37, 148
Forster, E.M., 60, 127
Freas, Frank Kelly, 120
Frey, Julian (John Hynam), 79, 118, 223
Fritch, Charles E., 65
Gardener, Wanless, 51
Gernsback, Hugo, 21, 99, 179, 259
Gibbs, D.J., 287
Giles, Geoffrey (Walter Gillings), 19
Gillings, Walter, 12-13, 18-19, 21-24, 99, 335
Goddard, James, 233
Goldsmith, Cele, 179, 183
Gordon, Richard A., 286
Graham, Pippin (Hilary Bailey), 261, 283
Griffith, George (Walter Gillings), 34
Guthrie, Alan (E.C. Tubb), 61, 90
Hall, Adam, 252

Hall, Steve, 193, 201, 203-04, 210, 221-23, 254
Hamilton, John, 307
Hammerton, Pete, 328
Harbottle, Philip, 17
Harding, Lee, 176-77, 210, 221
Harness, Charles L., 281
Haro, 227
Harris, Roger, 227
Harrison, Harry, 14, 114, 120, 125, 221, 236-38, 241, 248, 250, 264, 270, 272, 279, 281-82, 284, 288, 291, 293, 302-03, 310-15, 317, 320-25, 327, 329, 336
Harrison, M. John, 288, 335
Hawkins, Peter, 32, 34, 43, 90, 95, 97, 100, 116, 223
Hay, George, 252, 307, 322
Hebron, Chris, 317, 328, 331, 334
Heinlein, Robert A., 19, 95, 259
Hemming, Norma K., 28, 29, 31
Heywood, D.R., 250
Hickey, H.B., 65
High, Philip E., 200-02, 223, 254, 303
Hildebrand, Leonard, 112
Hill, D.W.R. (E.C. Tubb), 91
Hill, Ernest, 241, 254, 269, 277, 286, 318, 335-37
Hocknell, Patricia, 246, 256, 263
Hoffman, C.F., 320
Howard, Robert, 213
Hubbard, L. Ron, 19
Hughes, Herbert (Walter Gillings), 19, 20
Hume, Colin, 240
Hunter, 29, 33, 35, 185
Huxley, Aldous, 302
Hynam, John, 51, 79, 118
Jackson, Kevin, 13
Jackson, Shirley, 164
James, E.R., 20, 28, 31, 34, 64, 93, 99
Jarr, 94, 134, 156, 157
Jents, Paul, 234, 256, 263, 288, 306, 331-32, 335-36
Johns, Kenneth (John Newman and Kenneth Bulmer), 10, 94, 157
Jones, D.F., 323, 330

Parnell, Frank H., 43
Partridge, 47
Peake, Mervyn, 204-06, 209, 220, 224
Penn-Bull, Gweneth, 221
Phillifent, John T., 111, 209
Phillips, Peter, 49, 79
Pilkington, Colin, 324
Platt, Charles, 244, 259, 313-15
Poe, 212
Pohl, Frederik, 70, 78, 89, 139, 312, 318, 322-23, 337
Porter, Dr. J.G., 148
Potts, Archie, 231, 324
Powell, 18
Powers, Richard, 103, 106, 113, 120, 178
Pratchett, Terry, 205, 210, 225
Pratt, Fletcher, 9
Presslie, Robert, 98, 106, 108-09, 118, 126, 224
Price, W., 276
Priest, Christopher, 282, 291, 299, 310, 333, 335, 337
Pringle, David, 104, 142, 233, 311
Pritchett, Ron, 262
Quinn, Gerard, 29, 33, 35, 37, 47, 53, 55, 58, 69, 71, 80, 94-95, 169,
    178, 185, 194, 204
Rackham, John (John T. Phillifent), 107, 111, 131, 139, 160, 173, 176,
    183, 198-99, 207-08, 222-23, 232, 236, 238, 241, 251, 270, 287,
    299, 335
Radcliffe, Anne, 212-13
Rand, Ayn, 170
Rankine, John (Douglas R. Mason), 307
Rathbone, James (James Parkhill-Rathbone), 232-33
Rayer, Francis G., 20-21, 27, 31-32, 35, 37-38, 43, 50-51, 119
Redgrove, Peter, 306, 331
Reed, Clifford C., 118, 126, 140, 223, 270
Reynolds, Mack, 302, 305, 336
Richardson, Dikk, 271
Richardson, Francis (Lawrence Edward Bartle and Frank H. Parnell),
    43
Rigg, George, 240
Roach, Robert W.A., 269

207, 215, 219-20, 222, 224, 235, 236-38, 248, 254, 256, 258, 260, 273-75, 283, 335-37
Tate, Peter, 319
Temple, William F., 27, 31, 52, 71, 101, 136, 141
Tenn, William, 68, 107, 110
Terry (F.J. Terence Maloney), 75, 94
Thompson, T.F., 319
Tilley, Robert J., 319
Tomerlin, J.E., 93
Trevor, Elleston, 252
Tsiolkovsky, Konstantin, 156
Tubb, E.C., 28, 31, 35, 38, 41, 50-51, 61, 64-65, 67, 69, 82, 90, 101, 117, 125, 131, 136, 139, 154, 157, 205, 223-24, 270, 272, 276, 289, 303, 312, 324-25
Tucker, Wilson, 45, 65
Turner, 18
Tymn, Marshall B., 17, 24, 47, 52, 215, 228-29, 290, 329
Urban, Helen M., 62, 68
van Vogt, A.E., 46, 97, 102, 200, 202, 229, 262, 286, 316-17
Vance, Jack, 115, 191, 291, 294, 336
Varne, Richard, 56, 64
Verne, Jules, 156
Vonnegut, Kurt, 324
Walsh, J.M., 20-21, 33
Warburton, David, 279
Webb, W.T., 139, 176, 184, 221
Weinbaum, Stanley G., 169
Weiner, Tim, 308
Weir, D.Sc., Arthur R., 133
Wells, H.G., 22, 34, 134, 236, 266
Wells, Robert, 236, 250-51, 328, 335-36
West, Douglas, 62
West, Wallace, 178, 183, 223
Wheeler, Fred, 320
White, James, 64, 180
Whitley, George, 41, 49, 106-07, 111, 131
Wilde, Niall (E.F. Russell), 70
Williams, Eric C., 271, 328
Williamson, Jack, 78, 81

INDEX OF TITLES